HUMANISM AND LETTERS
IN THE AGE OF FRANÇOIS Ier

HUMANISM AND LETTERS
IN THE AGE OF FRANÇOIS Ier

PROCEEDINGS OF THE FOURTH
CAMBRIDGE FRENCH RENAISSANCE COLLOQUIUM
19–21 SEPTEMBER 1994

edited by

Philip Ford and Gillian Jondorf

CAMBRIDGE FRENCH COLLOQUIA
CAMBRIDGE · 1996

Contents

Illustrations

Acknowledgements

We should like to express our gratitude to the following institutions, whose generosity made the Colloquium possible: The British Academy; Cambridge University Department of French; Clare College, Cambridge; Downing College, Cambridge; Girton College, Cambridge; Gonville and Caius College, Cambridge; Jesus College, Cambridge; Pembroke College, Cambridge; Robinson College, Cambridge; Schlumberger Cambridge Research Ltd; Trinity College, Cambridge; and Trinity Hall, Cambridge. We are also grateful to Liz Guild and Hugo Tucker for their help as members of the Steering Committee of the Colloquium, and to Peter Bayley, the head of the French Department, for his continued encouragement and support. Finally, our thanks go to King's College, and in particular to the College Librarian, Peter Jones, for the exhibition in King's College Library of 'Printing in the Age of François Ier'.

PJF
GJ

Introduction

Few French kings left such an enduring legacy in their nation's cultural heritage as François Ier. The building programme he initiated, which led to the development of the palace of Fontainebleau, with its innovative mannerist decoration, as well as to many of the châteaux of the Loire, was matched only by his patronage of literature and humanism, with institutions such as the Bibliothèque Nationale and the Collège de France tracing back their origins to his reign. His birth, on 12 September 1494, therefore seemed a suitable occasion to commemorate.

In deciding to devote the fourth of the Cambridge French Renaissance Colloquia to marking this event, the organisers particularly had in mind the King's patronage of humanism in the early years of the sixteenth century, and its contribution to the literary climate of the times. Papers were invited on François's fostering of the arts and learning, on the image of the King which emerged during his reign, and on the literary works which the intellectual climate of the early decades of the sixteenth century helped to produce. An exhibition of books printed during François's reign was kindly arranged in the library of King's College by Peter Jones, the College Librarian, presenting members of the Colloquium with tangible evidence of the development of printing in the period.

A number of the papers given at the Colloquium provided examples of how the King was presented to his people. David Cowling explored the way in which *rhétoriqueur* language could shape political ideology and help form an image of François, before his accession to the throne, which relied considerably for its effect on religious allegory and allegoresis. Stephen Bamforth's paper, on the other hand, considered the Italian dimension of the King's reign, demonstrating how humanists from across the Alps might exhibit all the patriotism and loyalty to the French crown associated with native-born writers, as well as bearing witness to François's wide-ranging humanist interests, which took in cabbalistic texts as well as more mainstream works. Michael Heath presented us with a contrasting view of the King in his paper on the thorny question of the education of the prince. Could his early devotion to knightly skills and territorial conquest be reconciled with his championing of humanism and literature? Finally, Frank Lestringant explored the way in which the reign of François Ier was considered with nostalgia at the end of the century as a golden age, after the country had been torn apart by decades of religious civil war. Here too, it was the King's ability to reconcile arms and letters which impressed writers such as André Thevet.

Of the various writers who flourished during François's reign, Helisenne de Crenne might be seen as one of the more original in her presentation of feminine sensibilities, aimed at a specifically female audience. Liz Guild chose to consider the first book of *Les Angoisses douloureuses qui procedent d'amours* from the point of view of the body as a site of representation, demonstrating the differences between its treatment in male-authored and female-authored texts. Jean Dupèbe, on the other hand, looked at the contribution of François Olivier, an enlightened humanist, working for the benefit of the state, and helping to propagate an atmosphere of religious tolerance which was not destined to endure.

The last four papers all took Clément Marot as their starting point, a poet whose outstanding contribution to the literary life of François's reign was very effectively eclipsed by the arrival of the Pléiade. Nevertheless, it is clear from comments by members of his wide circle of friends and acquaintances that he was much admired for his learning as well as his poetry, and this was reflected in the papers given by Gillian Jondorf and Pauline Smith. The first of these two papers investigated Marot's version of Virgil's first eclogue, and showed that many of Marot's more surprising translations could be explained in artistic or scholarly terms, including the use of Servius' commentary on the text. Pauline Smith's contribution to the debate looked at a wider range of texts demonstrating Marot's interest and involvement in classical literature, in particular Ovid, and concluded that he was a highly successful vulgariser who managed, through his reading, to enhance and enrich French poetry. Jeanne Veyrin-Forrer, for her part, returned to the controversial issue of the printing of the 1538 edition of Marot's works, dealt with by Gérard Defaux in the previous colloquium. She rejected his conclusion that they were printed by Jean Barbou, instead pointing to François Juste as the printer of the first collective edition, under the direction first of Étienne Dolet and subsequently of Sebastian Gryphius. Finally, Hugo Tucker turned to Marot's exile in Ferrara to consider the whole question of humanist exile, and the paradoxes which this involves, concentrating in particular on Ortensio Landi's consideration of the subject.

When François died in 1547, many of the fruits of his reign remained to come to maturity, and if his successor, Henri II, continued his father's building programme, notably at the Palace of Fontainebleau, even those who sought the new king's patronage could make no claims for his encouragement of the arts and humanities. Yet the period from 1547 to 1562 saw the rise of the Pléiade, the introduction of humanist drama, the spread of enlightened humanist education in the colleges both of Paris and the provinces, and a level of culture which was the envy of Europe. It is hardly surprising that the myth of François Ier should have become so firmly rooted.

'Saint' François and his Temple in 1508: BN MS français 1680

David Cowling

François faictiz, francz, fortz, fermes au fait,
Fins, frecz, de fer, feroces, sans frayeur,
Telz sont voz noms concordans à l'effect.[1]

Chacun Françoys desire son Françoys.
Ce qu'il doit estre pour parler c'est tout ung;
Il fault enfin que l'on se renge au run
Et demonstrer que naturel franc soys.[2]

It is my aim in this paper to explore the impact of the use of language on the formation and expression of political ideology in early sixteenth-century France. Punning on national adjectives, as practised in the above examples by both Jean Lemaire de Belges and the anonymous author of Bibliothèque Nationale manuscrit français 1680, represents more than simple word-play in the taste traditionally associated with the *rhétoriqueurs*. Such adjectives permit the discovery and expression in language of essential characteristics of the nation; the *rhétoriqueurs*, a group of writers with considerable linguistic sensitivity, tapped into the semantic resources of words and, in so doing, contributed to the creation of a distinctive ideology of the kingdom of France at a formative period in its development from feudal state to increasingly centralised monarchy.

---

[1] Jean Lemaire de Belges, *La Concorde des deux langages*, edited by Jean Frappier (Paris, Droz, 1947), 'Le Temple de Venus', ll. 583–5).
[2] Paris, Bibliothèque Nationale, fonds français, 1680, f. 13^v. In this, as in all subsequent quotations from this source, I have silently expanded abbreviations, distinguished between <i> and <j> and <u> and <v> according to modern conventions, marked elisions with an apostrophe and added acute accents to final stressed <e>. The initial letters of names of personifications have been capitalised. Punctuation is mine.

I wish to exemplify this exploitation of the resources of language in a single *rhétoriqueur* political text, the anonymous *Livre de la dédicace du temple Saint Françoys* contained in BN MS français 1680. This text, although unedited, has of course received the recent attention of Anne-Marie Lecoq, who has studied it in the context of her *François Ier imaginaire*.[3] My focus will, however, be different from that of Lecoq, and is intended to complement her work. Instead of concentrating, as she has done, on the iconographical and historical interest of the manuscript, I shall study the text's literary technique, especially its use of metaphor and allegory, and consider its presentation of the narrator figure (*acteur*) and his own interests and aspirations. By replacing the text in its literary context, both in terms of the techniques it uses and the tradition of writing to which it belongs, I hope to demonstrate that *rhétoriqueur* use of allegory and the political significance of their works are inextricably linked. One reason for this is that language, for the *rhétoriqueurs*, is a fundamental political tool.

Before I do this, however, it will be necessary to go over some ground already covered by Lecoq in order to place the work in its historical context. The manuscript, although lacking an explicit dedicatee, appears to have been produced for presentation to a wealthy, possibly royal, patron (Delisle classifies it among the manuscripts of Louis XII and Anne of Brittany,[4] although, given the work's subject-matter, it is more likely to have been produced for the circle of Louise de Savoie). Written on thirty-four parchment leaves, the text is illustrated with six fine full-page miniatures (five of which are reproduced by Lecoq), numerous historiated initials, and coloured baguettes blocking out the space left at the end of each line of verse. The financial investment involved in the production of the manuscript would seem to indicate either that the piece had already found favour at court, or that its author had financial backing in his bid to gain court patronage. Lecoq notes that the only indication of ownership occurs on the final page, which is blank but for the name 'Loys de Lautier'.[5] In fact, it is just as likely that the mysterious Loys was author of the *Livre de la dédicace*, since the final two stanzas of the text present the name as an acrostic:

---

[3]   *François Ier imaginaire: Symbolique et politique à l'aube de la Renaissance française* (Paris, Macula, 1987), pp. 56–65.

[4]   Léopold Delisle, *Le Cabinet des manuscrits de la Bibliothèque impériale*, 4 vols (Paris, Imprimerie impériale, 1868–81; reprinted Amsterdam, van Heusden, 1969), I, 123.

[5]   *François Ier imaginaire*, p. 58, n. 14.

Lors bien souldain me delaissa Somnus.
Ouvry mon oueil et seullet me treuvé,
Ymaginant les songes advenuz;
Sur ce propos, qui vault fait appreuvé,
Desir me tint jusque a tant que eusse ouvré,
Et que eusse mis par escript ceste ystoire:
La chose vault qu'il soit d'elle memoire.

A tant je pry ung chacun m'excuser,
Veue la matiere en laquelle me harpe;
Trop plus sçavant s'i pourroit abuser:
Juxte coupper ne peult petite serpe,
En petiz ditz petit ouvrier s'adonne,
Remplir ne peult petit vaissel grant tonne.[6]

These stanzas, which relate the end of the narrator's dream and his composition of the text, and ask readers to excuse the author's mistakes, contain no reference to any dedicatee for the work. Acrostic signatures at the end of a work are of course a common *rhétoriqueur* device. 'Loys de Lautier' may itself be a pun; the word 'l'autier' occurs in the text as a synonym of 'l'autel' (f. 26^v), making of the signatory of the piece an acolyte of the altar of Saint François. There are similar problems surrounding the text's date. Lecoq suggests as a *terminus post quem* the repression of the revolt at Genoa in 1507, to which a clear allusion is made in a speech by Louis XII (f. 4^v). Yet the work's prologue makes reference to the year in which 'la paix par femmes fut comprise' (f. 2^r), suggesting that composition took place in 1508, the year of the Peace of Cambrai brokered by Margaret of Austria.

The poem's theme is suitably royal: it celebrates the nomination of François d'Angoulême as official heir of Louis XII after ratification of the decision taken by the États généraux of Tours on 14 May 1506, and François's engagement to Claude de France later the same month. The *Livre de la dédicace du temple Saint Françoys*, while choosing to ignore the engagement, transposes the first of these events into a complex allegory which narrates the dedication of an altar to 'Saint' François within the Temple of France. The frame narrative of the work's prologue takes the form of a conventional trigger for *rhétoriqueur* allegory: the narrator (or *acteur*), pensive and preoccupied by 'mainte matiere', lies down to sleep and, in a dream, is visited by the personified 'Messire Desir', who leads him to the court of Louis XII to witness the dedication

---

6   BN MS français 1680, f. 33^v. Further references will be incorporated into the text.

3

of 'le grant temple / De Dame France' (f. 2^{r-v}). First, the reigning monarch is given the opportunity to praise his own achievements. He concentrates on his unification of the kingdom, his popularity with the common people and the success of his military campaigns. Throughout the text, peaceful aspirations are expressed side-by-side with assurances of the military power required to enforce peace; Louis's metaphorical epithet of 'le grant pasteur', which is used consistently to refer to him within the text, serves to reinforce this notion of a kingship combining the maintenance of civic harmony with vigorous defensive capabilities.[7] The King incorporates this metaphor into his self-panegyric ('Priser l'on doit pasteur qui tousjours veille', f. 5^{r}). He also expresses succinctly his conception of the duties of the monarch: 'De militer ce n'est que œuvre royalle' (f. 4^{v}). There follows an address to the King by the personified Dame France, who lauds both Louis's military accomplishments and the historical prerogatives of the French crown.[8] Among such unique honours as the title of 'treschrestien', the possession of relics of the Passion, and the carrying of the oriflamme, the king of France has the ability to perform 'miracles' just like 'les saints gysans en tabernacles' (f. 6^{v}). This second metaphorical equation, this time between king and saint, appears to be based here on the shared gift of healing (the allusion is probably to the royal healing of scrofula). The metaphor prepares the subsequent allegory of the Temple of France, within which members of the royal family occupy 'tabernacles' and are worshipped as saints. Dame France introduces the metaphor of the temple explicitly in the peroration of her speech as follows:

> ...Je concluds et tiens
> Que sur tous roys et princes terriens,
> Ce que dit est bien veu et memoiré,
> Que vostre terre, vostre lieu et voz biens
> Ung temple sont ou il ne deffault riens,
> Fors dedicace au hault dieu honoré.

(f. 7^{v})

---

[7] For the history of the metaphor of the ruler as shepherd, see Dietmar Peil, *Untersuchungen zur Staats- und Herrschaftsmetaphorik in literarischen Zeugnissen von der Antike bis zur Gegenwart* (Munich, Fink, 1983), pp. 29–165.

[8] See Colette Beaune, *The Birth of an Ideology: Myths and Symbols of Nation in Late-Medieval France* (Berkeley, University of California Press, 1991); (translation of *Naissance de la nation France* (Paris, Gallimard, 1985), by Susan Ross Huston, edited by Frederic L. Cheyette).

Louis's immediate response is to reject the image:

> Comment cela comparés vous a temple,
> Bien si ample, triumphant, magnifique?
> Et me semble, comme bien le contemple,
> Que l'exemple n'est assés antentique [*sic*],
> Et si dis que ce ne peult militer;
> Souvent l'on fault par trop peu meriter.

(ibidem)

This hostile attitude can be explained by the fact that the analogy between kingdom and temple is not immediately obvious to the king. His explicitly-stated reason to doubt its appropriateness is that a building (and an ecclesiastical one at that) is not sufficiently bellicose an image; it is, on the face of it, dissonant with the ideology of 'militer' as the privileged royal activity. A further reason for the unfamiliarity, or even un-popularity, of this image may be sought through consideration of the dominant metaphors for the kingdom of France in the early Renaissance period. From about 1450 onwards, the standard image for the territory of France was that of the garden;[9] works of political theory, like those of Louis XII's panegyrist Claude de Seyssel, preferred the image of the body politic, which permitted exploration of the relationships between different social groups within the polity.[10] The image of the royal dynasty as a building, a 'house', was not popular in France, perhaps because of its possible connotations of collapse. Already in Lucretius, the end of the world is figured as the collapse of a building; in Horace, this catastrophe figures the end of the Empire. Strong individuals are required to prop up the potentially ruinous edifice of state.[11] These negative con-notations had already been developed in the vernacular by Alain Chartier in his *Quadrilogue invectif* of 1422, in which the personified France struggles to prevent the demolition of the tottering palace of the French

---

9 Beaune, pp. 292–7.

10 *La Monarchie de France et deux autres fragments politiques*, edited by Jacques Poujol (Paris, Librairie d'Argences, 1961), pp. 108, 110, 114, 124, 160, 161.

11 Lucretius, *De rerum natura*, II. 1131–74; Horace, *Odes*, III. 3. 7–8. See Heinz Berthold, 'Die Metaphern und Allegorien vom Staatsschiff, Staatskörper und Staatsgebäude in der römischen Literatur der ausgehenden Republik und frühen Kaiserzeit', in *Antiquitas græco-romana ac tempora nostra*, edited by Jan Burian and Ladislav Vidman (Prague, Ceskoslovenská Akademie Ved, 1968), 95–105 (pp. 103–4).

monarchy during the darkest days of the Hundred Years War.[12] Chartier was still widely read at the start of the sixteenth century, and the *rhétoriqueurs* acknowledge him as their master in literary composition.[13] Claude de Seyssel is still using the metaphor of the ruin of the monarchy alongside that of the body politic in his *Monarchie de France* of 1515.[14] The metaphor of the state or its royal dynasty as a building is, however, commonly used in positive contexts by the Burgundian historiographers Georges Chastelain and Jean Molinet in the second half of the fifteenth century. Molinet in particular shows a fondness for the image and the allegorical developments it permits, most notably in the prologue to his *Chroniques*.[15]

In order to justify her use of a metaphor associated with both past political disasters and the rival ideology of Burgundy, Dame France demonstrates the temple in plastic form to the king, courtiers, and narrator Desir. She unlocks the door to 'ung lieu fructueulx / Et vertueulx, / Qui se nommoit largesse ou habondance' (f. 8r). The abundant fertility of the place recalls late medieval celebrations of the fertility of the Garden of France; indeed, the site of the temple is bounded on one side by the sea and on the other by mountains, and is crisscrossed by rivers, whose names (Yonne, Marne, Loir, Loiret, etc.) are listed at length.[16] In order to reproduce linguistically the abundance of the kingdom, the narrator even lists its bishoprics and duchies, and enumerates the different classes of society, who are all present in the place. Thus the temple, whose detailed description follows, is situated

---

12 *Le Quadrilogue invectif*, edited by E. Droz, 2nd edition (Paris, Champion, 1950), pp. 6–10. See also François Rouy, *L'Esthétique du traité moral d'après les œuvres d'Alain Chartier* (Geneva, Droz, 1980), pp. 139–49.

13 See for instance Jean Lemaire de Belges, *Le Temple d'Honneur et de Vertus*, edited by Henri Hornik (Geneva, Droz, 1957), p. 89, and the article by Suzanne Bagoly, '"De mainctz aucteurs une progression": un siècle à la recherche du Parnasse français', *Le Moyen Français*, XVII (1985), 83–123.

14 *La Monarchie*, p. 96.

15 Chastelain, addressing Charles le Téméraire, likens the duke to Atlas supporting the 'ancien édifice que tes nobles pères…ont fondé' (*Œuvres*, edited by Kervyn de Lettenhove, 8 vols (Brussels, Heussner, 1863–6; reprinted Geneva, Slatkine, 1971, in 4 vols), VII, 294). Molinet celebrates the allegorical 'maison de Bourgogne' at length in the *Chroniques* (edited by Georges Doutrepont and Omer Jodogne, 3 vols (Brussels, Palais des Académies, 1935–7), I, 25–8).

16 Jean Lemaire's *Temple d'Honneur et de Vertus*, written to celebrate the Bourbon dynasty, has a shepherd-duke within a garden-duchy bounded by rivers.

within the conventional metaphorical garden, which acts as a convenient vehicle for its introduction.

The presentation of the temple within this garden betrays careful manipulation of the metaphor of the kingdom as building to make it acceptable to Dame France's audience:

> Et en ce lieu en la circonference,
> Sans doubtance,
> Estoit assis ediffice moult chier,
> Et ferme estoit sans povoir trebucher;
> Et en chercher
> De mieulx fait il seroit impossible;
> Et si m'estoit presque incomprehensible,
> Inentendible,
> Pour la haulteur, l'espesseur, la beaulté,
> Le circuit et grant rotondité,
> Formosité.

(f. 8ʳ⁻ᵛ)

In order to create an effective political metaphor, Dame France develops the affective potential of the image of the building. She does this by selecting qualities of the temple that are to be shared by an idealised monarchy. First, and most importantly, the edifice is solidly constructed and safe from collapse. Secondly, its inexpressible beauty and fabulous dimensions articulate praise of the dynasty that inhabits it by expressing their perfection in plastic terms. Thus the negative potential of the metaphor is neutralised, and its suitability as a vehicle of panegyric established.

There follows a more detailed description of the temple and the rites that are performed within it. Dame France offers Desir, who has taken over the function of narrator within the *acteur*'s dream, 'la congnoissance / D'une chose de magnificence' (f. 11ʳ). First, however, there is a second *entrée en songe*. In the absence of any explanatory rubric to indicate the speaker, it appears that the dreamer is now Desir, himself a participant in the main dream-allegory. Thus the action of this section takes place at two removes from the historical context so painstakingly fixed by the *acteur* in the prologue. A possible reason for this curious feature of the text is the desire to reinforce the allegorical nature of the temple description by introducing it with a formal marker that conventionally triggers a certain type of interpretative reading, and recalls other allegories of the building. The tone of this *entrée en songe* is highly self-conscious and oratorical. The theatricality of its language doubles the material

7

disposition of the manuscript, in which it is preceded by a blank page and
an elaborate full-page miniature (reproduced by Lecoq, fig. 16) depicting
Dame France kneeling on a river bank in front of a gothic temple:

> Tresagité ou val de souvenir,
> Pensant de loing ce qu'il peult advenir,
> Voyant mon chief plain de dueil et douleur,
> Pensif, pensant, sans sçavoir revenir,
> Comme pasmé par ung esvanoyr,
> Voyant Saturne ja changier sa couleur,
> En obviant a ma ramentevance
> Le perilleux dart mortel a oultrance,
> Lequel a tous Dame Atropos pourchasse;
> Grant vent souvent m'a fait baisser la face.
>
> Baissant la face je veiz ung lieu moult ample,
> Qui bien sembloit le fondement d'un temple...

(f. 13ʳ)

Unlike the *acteur*, whose negative feelings in the preface are unfocused
(he is merely 'pensif'), Desir is a prey to real anxiety. His thoughts of
death take the form of a reference to Saturn, normally a hostile divinity
for the *rhétoriqueurs* associated with the destructive passage of time, and
to Atropos, commonly used as a personification of arbitrary, but in-
evitable, death.[17] The source of this anxiety is not explicitly stated, but it
may easily be inferred from the reference to the infertile water of the
building's moat, which contains no fish apart from 'une seulle femelle'
(ibidem). It is of course Louis XII's lack of a male heir, and the threat of
political turmoil after his death, that motivate François d'Angoulême's
nomination. The dangers of anarchy are figured within the allegory by
'ung lieu bien dur a reciter...: noir, trouble, mal plaisant' (f. 13ᵛ) which
adjoins the temple, and which the narrator side-steps before entering.

The allegorical technique used in the temple description reveals its link
with contemporary religious allegories of the building. Each element of
the temple's construction is immediately glossed by the narrator to fix its
meaning and establish its relationship with political reality. Glossing
takes its simplest and most economical form, in which a name is applied

---

17 See Jean Lemaire, *Le Temple d'Honneur*, pp. 64–5 (Saturn) and idem, *La
Couronne margaritique (Œuvres*, edited by J. Stecher, 4 vols (Louvain, Lefever,
1882–5; reprinted Geneva, Slatkine, 1969), IV, 10–167), p. 20.

to each element without the need for any explanatory formulae.[18] Thus
the temple is 'assis sur paix, fondé sur pierres vives' (f. 13r). Both these
glosses permit at once a religious and a political reading. Peace typically
provides the foundations of allegorical structures such as the *Chastel
périlleux* of the Carthusian monk Frère Robert. In this devotional text of
the 1360s, a nun is advised on how to construct a defensive bulwark
against the assaults of the devil. The initial premise is that, to be strong
and durable, this castle must be founded 'en terre de paix'.[19] The
edification of the individual, then, requires that the nun seek peace with
God, her superiors in religion, her neighbour, and herself, without which
her castle will have little chance of resisting attack. 'Pierres vives' is a
clear allusion to I Peter 2. 5, where it figures men. Yet the political
relevance of these two glosses is also discernible: peace is the necessary
prerequisite for political stability, as Louis has already emphasised in his
speech to the court, and the temple's foundation is clearly dependent on
the inhabitants of the kingdom of France, whose cities and bishoprics
have just been enumerated at length. Throughout the text, images from
the spheres of religion and politics are mixed in a way disconcerting to
the modern reader but perfectly familiar to a contemporary reader of
rhétoriqueur allegories. Political discourse, by borrowing metaphors
from the language of religious devotion, gains authority and exploits the
affective potential of well-established and powerful images. At the same
time, the author of the *Livre de la dédicace* adopts the technique of
systematic glossing used by religious allegorists in order to control the
meaning of the images he describes, thus preventing readerly conjectures
about their status and sense. The result is a text that, unlike other
rhétoriqueur allegories such as those of Jean Lemaire de Belges, strictly
limits the semantic potential of the image of the building by cutting down
its range of possible metaphorical reference.[20] The order of this glossing

---

[18] For the use of this technique in religious allegories of the period, see my article
'Interpretation in Action: Jean Lemaire de Belges and the Allegorical Temple',
Interpréter le seizième siècle, Michigan Romance Studies, XV (1995), edited by
John O'Brien (forthcoming).

[19] *Le Chastel périlleux*, edited by Sister Marie Brisson, 2 vols (Salzburg, Institut für
englische Sprache und Literatur der Universität Salzburg, 1974), II, 238.

[20] See David Cowling, 'Text and Building: Architectural Fictions in the Work of the
Rhétoriqueurs', in *Literary Aspects of Courtly Culture: Selected Papers from the
Seventh Triennial Congress of the International Courtly Literature Society,
University of Massachusetts, Amherst, USA, 27 July–1 August 1992*, edited by

process follows the narrator as he enters the temple. Political glosses occur side by side with the lavish construction materials common in contemporary descriptions of imaginary buildings, which reinforce the plastic beauty of the building, required to promote the glory of the dynasty it houses. Thus the golden porch is enamelled with 'puissance', the doors are of 'congnoissance', clear like cristal, the locks are made of coral, and the key is of 'lignee et naissance'. Again, the presentation of the dynasty as a building is made attractive and compelling to a contemporary readership by ensuring that the description conforms to accepted canons of taste in allegory.

Whereas from outside the building's permanence and extraordinary beauty are consistently foregrounded, the description of the interior exploits the connection of the image of the temple with religious rites. First, the narrator reveals that the alternative title of the building is 'Archepantheon'. As this name with its classical flavour suggests, it contains a number of shrines, or 'oratoires', to the gods who are worshipped within it ('illec faisoient mains dieux leur residence', f. 13ᵛ), notably that of Saint François, which is a centre of attention:

> L'on y prioit Saint Françoys a toute heure;
> Pour Saint Françoys la ung chacun labeure,
> A le servir ung chacun le desire.
> Eureux est cil qui peult servir tel sire.

(f. 14ᵛ)

This second metaphor activated by the text (which has already been introduced in Louis's speech) appears somewhat bizarre in the context of political discourse, and is hardly to modern taste. Its use is not, however, confined to this work. Claude de Seyssel, in an autograph rondeau appended to Anne of Brittany's copy of his *Louenges du roy Louis XIIᵉ*, has the King as a saint worshipped by his adoring wife.[21] Of course, the normative potential of the metaphor was considerable: presentation of the monarch as 'Saint Louis' exploited the King's name to make a flattering historical comparison. In the case of François d'Angoulême, use of the metaphor establishes a kind of apostolic succession which places the

---

Donald Maddox and Sara Sturm-Maddox (Cambridge, D. S. Brewer, 1994), 123–32, and idem, 'Text and Building: Uses of Architectural Metaphors in the Works of the Rhétoriqueurs (1460–1540)' (unpublished doctoral thesis, University of Oxford, 1995).

21 See *La Monarchie de France*, p. 28.

young François in the illustrious company of both Saint Francis of Assisi and, perhaps even more directly in the contemporary mind, with Saint Francis of Paola, the Calabrian hermit summoned to Tours, then Amboise, by the dying Louis XI. According to one eyewitness account, at least 6,000 mourners had attended the funeral of the 'Bon Homme d'Amboise' on Easter Monday, 1507.[22] François d'Angoulême was living with his mother at the château of Amboise during this period. The devotion of Louise de Savoie for Francis is well attested; it was probably linked to the saint's intercession on her behalf to help her overcome infertility, just as the intercession of Saint Francis of Assisi had played a role in the birth of Francis of Paola. It was thanks to Louise's personal intervention that the saint's body was exhumed and placed in a stone coffin to protect it from flooding. A source of (unfortunately) doubtful authenticity attributes to the saint a prophecy that Louise's son would become king of France; François in his turn pushed for the hermit's canonisation.[23]

The insistence on the benefits of the service of Saint François, which is figured allegorically by worship at the oratory, prepares the narrator's own later attempt to gain access. First, however, the position of the oratory of Saint François is noted and the 'ymage' (statue) of the saint that it contains is described. Made 'vers Angolesme' by the same work-man who has produced the statue on the high altar (that of Louis XII), François's effigy resembles that of Louis so much that they appear to be 'd'ung mesme arbre...deux branches sorties': it is thus through a pun on the image of the dynastic tree of France, from whose wood the statues have both been fashioned, that the narrator asserts François's claim to the succession (f. 14^v).[24] In addition, his oratory already occupies a position in the temple next to the altar where kings are crowned, suggesting in spatial terms that François is dynastically the obvious choice as successor to Louis.

Seeing a crowd of worshippers at the oratory, the narrator, too, wishes to bring an oblation. First he must pass three doors guarded by 'aliance', 'force', and 'richesse', which can only be reached by climbing the four

---

[22] See Bernard Chevalier, 'Saint François de Paule à Tours d'après le procès de canonisation', *S. Francesco di Paola: chiesa e società del suo tempo. Atti del convegno internazionale di studio, Paola, 20–24 maggio 1983* (Rome, Curia generalizia dell'Ordine dei Minimi, 1984), 184–208 (p. 196).

[23] See Lecoq, pp. 436–8; also Mgr Fiot, *Saint François de Paule à Amboise* (Chambray-lès-Tours, Club Gutenberg, 1975), pp. 35–7.

[24] For the tree of France, see Beaune, pp. 297 sqq.

steps of 'fidelité', 'credit', 'savoir', and 'bonté' (ff. 16ᵛ–17ʳ). While this activity is understandable within the economy of the narrative (all desire to serve and worship Saint François, f. 14ᵛ), the attempt to gain access to the oratory may figure a real — or merely desired — entry into François d'Angoulême's entourage. It is significant that the narrator's approach is problematised. Discouraged by the sight of the crowd grovelling at the feet of the statue, he immediately recoils:

> Je, desirant de ce lieu approuchier,
> Tost reculay doubtant le reprouchier,
> En me sentant de l'approuchier indigne;
> Car j'en veoye par la terre couchier
> Eulx ingerans l'oratoire touchier,
> Et leur chasti moy retirer feist signe.

(f. 17ᵛ)

This gesture of humility on the part of the narrator recalls the actions of other *rhétoriqueur* narrators who hesitate before entering buildings, or are ejected from them. In Jean Lemaire's *Concorde des deux langages*, for instance, the *acteur*'s offering of an illuminated manuscript of one of his works is rejected by the mercenary priests of Venus, and he is forced to leave her temple.[25] In the specific context of the *Livre de la dédicace*, however, the narrator's attempt to gain access to the saint's shrine probably constitutes a veiled request for closer access to François. The writer hints that he desires to join François's entourage by attempting to dedicate his text to the saint even before the temple he describes is dedicated to François, but dissociates himself from the base flatterers who crowd the oratory. The suggestion is that, without actually dictating terms to his prospective patron, the author of the *Livre de la dédicace* is, again like Lemaire, conscious of his power as panegyrist and publicist, using his text to articulate, in veiled form, his own claims for attention.[26]

The final section of the text describes the dedication of the temple to François. Again there is a clear debt to contemporary religious allegories, which urge believers to dedicate the building of their heart or conscience

---

25 *La Concorde des deux langages*, pp. 35–6.
26 See Cynthia J. Brown, 'The Rise of Literary Consciousness in Late Medieval France: Jean Lemaire de Belges and the Rhétoriqueur Tradition', *Journal of Medieval and Renaissance Studies*, XIII (1983), 51–74, and eadem, *The Shaping of History and Poetry in Late Medieval France: Propaganda and Artistic Expression in the Works of the Rhétoriqueurs* (Birmingham, Alabama, Summa Publications, 1985), passim.

to God so that the Holy Spirit may come and live in it. The necessary prerequisite for dedication is cleansing, which is achieved through the sacrament of confession.[27] The *Livre de la dédicace* transposes this notion of purification to the secular political sphere. The temple, which has been presented as an 'Archepantheon' in which all living members of the royal dynasty have a place, is cleared of all saints apart from François and the 'grant pasteur'. This exclusive process, which aims to suppress diversity within the structure and thus to replicate, inside, the monolithic beauty of the temple's exterior, represents a reversal of normal *rhétoriqueur* practice. In Lemaire's *Temple d'Honneur*, for instance, the feudal lord Pierre de Bourbon is admitted after his death to a temple that contains both members of his own dynasty and illustrious biblical and classical rulers. Lemaire's temple is open to all those 'haulx hommes qui ont entre les humains merité tiltres d'excellence', subject to ratification by its existing inhabitants, and can thus be extended over time.[28] The Temple de France, on the other hand, because of its unambiguous metaphorical status as figure for the French royal dynasty, potentially under threat from destabilising influences, seeks to curtail the influence of the feudal lords and concentrate attention on Louis's successor. Throughout the text, royal prerogatives are emphasised, both in Louis's own speech and in the choice and manipulation of the central image, which privileges the monarch and his successor within a politically unified kingdom of France. Indeed it is the twelve peers of the realm, under the leadership of Philip the Fair, King of Castile and Count of Flanders, who suggest the nomination of François.[29] Philip, won over by the plastic beauty of François's effigy, which he judges to be a 'chief d'œuvre paragon d'exellence' (f. 22r), echoes Louis's insistence on peace through military strength. Celebrating François's qualities in a *ballade*, he emphasises François's ability to resist the enemies of France:

> François sera paisible en suffisance,
> Tresassouvy du fleuve d'abondance,
> Qui habonde sur tout pays et voye;
> Et sera dit le roy plain de puissance,
> Prince de paix, empereur de vaillance,
> Et de tous biens l'exellente montjoye.

(f. 22r–v)

---

[27] See *Le Chastel périlleux*, II, 239.

[28] *Le Temple d'Honneur*, pp. 83–92.

[29] Philip died in September 1506, four months after the États généraux of Tours.

It is tempting to see the writer alluding to the imperial pretensions of the French kings in the reference to François as future 'empereur de vaillance'. Earlier in the text (f. 18^r), the narrator has described François as 'nostre futur roy sire / Qui n'empire, car il tiendra l'empire / S'il vit son aage sans intermission'. In both cases, however, the metaphorical nature of the assertion makes certainty impossible (the 'empereur de vaillance' could merely be an honorific title, especially in the mouth of a scion of the Hapsburg dynasty, and 'tenir l'empire' could refer to holding power within the kingdom).

The centralising political ideology of the text expresses itself in the process of selection of François in the form of unanimous decisions. First, the decision is taken to clear the temple of all other saints and their altars:

> Soudainement, et en ung mouvement,
> Ensemblement ung chacun sursurroit:
> L'on murmuroit, les ungs publiquement,
> Couvertement l'autre son dit serroit;
> Mais a la fin et *d'ung accord ensemble,*
> L'on feist vuider tout le monde du temple.
>
> (f. 25^r; my italics)

Then François is explicitly nominated:

> Le grant pasteur et *toute l'assemblee,*
> *D'une volee, par une oppinion,*
> Si ont leur voix et sentence donnee
> Et prononcee, *par une election,*
> Qu'il demourroit de Saint Françoys l'autel.
> Jamais il n'eut rencontre de loz tel.
>
> Sur ce y eut aucun petit parler,
> Mais tout par l'air passa comme fumee.
>
> (f. 25^v; my italics)

In both these passages, the insistence that the opinion of those present, despite a healthy debate, remains single and indivisible serves the notion that the monarchy is itself a stable entity whose succession is un-problematic. The stability of the institution under François is expressed in a final plastic image, that of the new altar supported by two pillars glossed as 'le bien publique' and 'les troys estats' (f. 26^v). This image depends for its effectiveness on the metaphor of men or political institutions as pillars supporting the state, commonly found in the work

14

of the Burgundian historiographers Chastelain and Molinet.[30] Philip the Fair has already referred to François as 'ferme pillier et nostre soustenance' (f. 22^r). This image, which feeds back into the architectural conception of the dynasty, defines François's position as future basis for the stability of France and present guardian against collapse. The narrator concludes:

> Doncques ce lieu de la France a Françoys
> Fut desdié et, comme je conçoys,
> Ce luy est deu a tresjuste querelle:
> C'est le plus pres du noble sang françoys,
> Il est vierge, doulx, bon, sage, courtoys,
> Aussy begnin comme la tourterelle;
> En luy n'y a pensement de malice:
> C'est nostre sainct par raison et justice.

(f. 28^v)

Again, the qualities that mark out the young François as a future king are, ironically, those of a peacemaker.

Anne-Marie Lecoq is without doubt right in seeing in the *Livre de la dédicace* a text of interest primarily to those wishing to form a picture of 'François Ier imaginaire'. The narrator pays little or no attention to the personality of the real François d'Angoulême, who remains a passive object of deliberation and veneration throughout. The text does, however, bear eloquent witness to the use of metaphor and allegory in the formation and publication of royal political ideology in the early years of the sixteenth century. The *Livre de la dédicace*, although close in technique to both sacred and secular allegories of the building, uses the resources of both modes in order to articulate a consistently monarchist line. Systematic glossing of elements of the temple, common in religious allegory, establishes clear relationships between access to the building, and to the oratory of Saint François, and political status. The metaphor of the political leader as saint establishes a close parallel between François and a man whose cult attained extraordinary proportions in contemporary Touraine. Dedication of the temple to François alone, which entails the exclusion of his dynastic rivals, reverses the accumulative nature of *rhétoriqueur* buildings designed to house the famous men and women of the past; the *Livre de la dédicace*, instead of reflecting on past glories, looks forward to a new age of peace and continuity. The image of the

---

[30] Chastelain, *Œuvres*, VII, 218, 285, 291; Molinet, *Chroniques*, I, 207. See also Peil, pp. 598–605.

15

temple assures that continuity by providing the stable and unchanging setting for the exchange of the metaphor of the 'grant pasteur' for that of the king as saint, peacemaker, and object of adoration.

2

A Forgotten Humanist Tribute to François Ier: The *Geographia* of Paolo Pietrasanta

Stephen Bamforth

This article is concerned with one aspect in particular of the subject of François Ier and humanism.[1] The interest of François Ier in humanist learning in general is of course well known, as is his cultivation of men of letters.[2] What has been less well explored is the specifically Italian dimension to the humanist ambiance at François Ier's court. François was a highly proficient speaker of Italian,[3] and his knowledge of and enthusiasm for Italian culture is well documented.[4] Through his grand-mother, Valentina Visconti, François had at least some Italian blood in his veins, and he inherited from his father, Charles d'Angoulême, an

---

[1] This article is a substantially reworked version of a paper given at the Cambridge conference. My thanks to Philip Ford for allowing me the time to develop the arguments which I put forward in draft form in the original version.

[2] For a graphic illustration, cf. the Chantilly miniature of François Ier surrounded by his courtiers listening to Antoine Macault's translation of Diodorus Siculus being read to him by the author (reproduced in R. J. Knecht, *Renaissance Warrior and Patron: The Reign of Francis I* (Cambridge, CUP, 1994), cover illustration and plate 92). François was in the habit of having learned men eat at his table, and liked to engage in conversation with them; Guillaume Budé relates an occasion when he was disconcerted by the alertness of one of the King's questions (cf. *La Philologie*, texte original traduit, présenté et annoté par Maurice Lebel (Éditions de l'Université de Sherbrooke, 1989), p. 99).

[3] Italian ambassadors to the court make frequent mention of François's skill as a speaker of Italian; cf. for example BN MS ital. 1714, f. 202, MS ital. 1715, f.16ᵛ, and MS ital. 1998, pp. 233–4. (My thanks to Marc Hamilton Smith for pointing out these references to me.)

[4] cf. Guillaume du Bellay's praise of the intellectual qualities of his monarch in his *Ogdoade*, with its particular mention of the King's prowess in Italian, and of his skills as a translator; '...usque adeo litterarum et litteratorum amantissimus semper fuit. Nam et ipse vernaculo sermone disertissime scribit et loquitur, latine scriptos libros libenter legit; Etruscae linguae perinde ac patriae studiosus, ex eo sermone quosdam libros franciscos fecit, tanta lectorum gratia, ut caeteris ejus linguae interpretibus haud dubie palmam eripuerit' (V.-L. Bourrilly, *Fragments de la première Ogdoade de Guillaume du Bellay* (Paris, 1904), p. 4).

interest in books and a love for the arts.[5] In the opening years of François's reign, however, an interest in things Italian also has a very clear political dimension. From the reign of Louis XI onwards Italy had represented the great prize for French monarchs, and in 1494 Charles VIII had mounted the first French invasion of the Italian peninsula; French involvement in Italy was not to cease before 1558. The most tangible gain of this period of Italian adventure was the temporary possession by France of Milan and the Piedmont. This happened twice, in 1499 and 1515. In 1499 Louis XII had gained control of Milan and Genoa, only to lose it again within ten years. In 1515, with the victory of Marignano, François is able to reassert French dominion over the duchy, and is able once more to style himself, as Louis XII had done before, 'Mediolani Dux & Genuae Dominus'. For François, however, the status of Italian ruler takes on a particular importance in that he is preparing his candidacy to the impending Imperial election, which took place in 1519. In short, the Franco-Italian axis is essentially a Franco-Milanese one, and it has a clear political as well as a cultural aspect. Milan becomes once more a 'Cisalpine Gaul', but conversely France itself became the focus for many Milanese. A significant example of this Franco-Milanese cooperation is the Bastille festival of 1518 in honour of the alliance between France and England, and the betrothal of Princess Mary, daughter of Henry VIII, and the infant Dauphin François. This festival was organised by Galeazzo Visconti and chronicled by Bernardino Rincio, and the Milanese component in it is important at both a cultural and a political level.[6] In the article that follows I propose to look at a second specific example of the Franco-Milanese connection, one that is more individual than public in nature, but one that is even closer to the person of the king himself. It has also, as I hope to show, more than one level of interest.

My concern is with two manuscripts preserved in the Bibliothèque Nationale, MS lat. 4811 and 8135.[7] These two manuscripts represent two versions, in prose and verse respectively, of the same text, a treatise in seven books on geography by the Milanese writer Paolo Pietrasanta. The

---

5   cf. Knecht, p. 3.
6   cf. Stephen Bamforth and Jean Dupèbe, 'The *Silva* of Bernardino Rincio (1518)', *Renaissance Studies*, VIII (1994), 256–315.
7   It is a pleasure to be able to record here my grateful thanks to Jean Dupèbe, who first drew my attention to the existence of these two manuscripts. I should also like to thank Marie-Pierre Laffitte of the department of manuscripts at the Bibliothèque Nationale, who kindly allowed me to consult her unpublished notes on the two Pietrasanta manuscripts. Mme Laffitte is currently preparing a publication on the manuscripts owned by François Ier.

work is dedicated to François Ier, and appears only to exist in this manuscript version. From the bibliographical point of view the two manuscripts represent a rarity. BN MS lat. 8135, the verse version, has conserved its original binding of blue morocco with a sober decoration of a double frame of gilded and blind-stamped lines, and on the inside of the back cover there survives a manuscript note signed by Jean de La Barre, keeper of the library at the château of Blois from 1531, recording the transfer of the volume in 1538 from the King's personal collection to the royal library.[8] Its companion volume, MS lat. 4811, has lost its binding, which was replaced during the period of Louis-Philippe, but we know thanks to the memoirs of the curator of manuscripts in the Bibliothèque royale in the eighteenth century, Jean Boivin, that the original contained an identical inscription.[9]

It follows that our two manuscripts have a quite special status. Not only are we dealing with an example of humanist writing dedicated to the King, but with two works, or rather two versions of the same work, which formed part of his personal library.[10] Both manuscripts are the original dedication copies, as is shown by their appearance, over which considerable care has been taken. The object is not ostentation, for there is neither illustration nor illumination, and ruled paper rather than parchment has been used. However, both have been written in a precise humanist italic script, albeit in a variety of hands, and the overall effect is harmonious and attractive. The text of the verse version ends with a colophon addressed directly to the monarch, in which Pietrasanta hopes that the pleasure the work may bring to its royal reader will serve as a reminder of its author's devotion to the monarch and to his glory.[11]

---

8 'En lan m.d. xxxviii le Roy a remis ce present liure pour mettre en sa Librairie dont je baille mon récépissé au Libraire de sa chambre [signed] de la barre.' Other than the two manuscripts we discuss, MS lat. 6823 and *imprimés* Rés. Vélins 515 have or had similar inscriptions; that of Rés. Vélins 515 is reproduced in Ursula Baurmeister and Marie-Pierre Laffitte, *Des livres et des rois* (Paris, 1992), p. 233.

9 cf. MS fr. 22571, p. 193.

10 cf. the discussion of the significance of the de La Barre inscriptions in *Des livres et des rois*, p. 233; 'elles confirment la provenance royale de ces volumes et attestent l'existence d'une bibliothèque personnelle de François Ier assez importante pour que le roi y affectât un bibliothécaire. Il s'agit du "libraire ordinaire du roi" qui avait en charge les livres que le roi emportait dans ses coffres lors des déplacements de la cour...Dans un cas (latin 6823) Jean de La Barre précise d'ailleurs que le volume se trouvait auparavant dans les "coffres" du roi.'

11 MS lat. 8135, f. 151r: 'Colophonem operi huic nostro Eudoxe Rex tandem addidimus, utinam eo tu animo qualecunque id fuerit suscipias, eoque tibi oblectamento sit, quo nos imprimis desyderamus, & tibi, & gloriae tuae satisfaciendi studio enixe admodum invigilavimus. Vale.'

Who is this dedicated courtier of François Ier? In the dedication to MS lat. 4811 Pietrasanta appears (mis-spelt) as 'Paulus Petrancta vir mediolanensis', and in that to MS lat. 8135 as 'Paulus Petrasancta Iureconsultus mediolanensis'. Two of the many gaps in our knowledge about him are that we know neither when he was born, nor when he arrived at the French court. We do know, however, that he returned to Milan not later than 1550, since he died there in that year.[12] It seems clear that our two manuscripts represent an attempt by him to make his fortune at the French court, an attempt that was not destined to succeed. This would appear to be confirmed by the existence of a third manuscript written by Pietrasanta and dedicated to the King, but this one in his native language. This is Bibliothèque Nationale MS italien 1043, a poem in two books and sixty eight-line stanzas in praise of the palace and gardens of Fontainebleau. Leaving aside the question of the literary merits of the work, its value for us is that it shows the lengths to which Pietrasanta was prepared to go in order to cultivate his monarch. The poem is undated, but it seems reasonable to assume that it was composed in the second half of the 1530s, or perhaps even later, when the building programme at Fontainebleau was reasonably far advanced. The tone of the dedication is that of the practised courtier, in which the note of familiarity is not absent — 'la tua FONTANABLEO luogo non manco leggiadro, che lieto, e felice, per tuo tal hora diporto scielto ti sei, di cui tant'ho visto dilettartene' — along with the customary obsequiousness: 'che non havendo io cosa che piu de'l tuo piacer mi piaccia, Deliberai con queste mie rime celebrarlo'.[13] However, in whatever sense Pietrasanta might have succeeded in ingratiating himself, he is still requesting employment:

> Resta che alcuna volta da tuoi eccelsi, e soleciti affari divertendo, ti piaccia leggerle. E cura con vari de l'animo tuo restori...et a me tuo servo sovenire possi, E tra tanto in gratia di tua maestà inchinevolmente mi Raccomando.[14]

A second document is even more explicit. This is a notarial act dated 3 November 1539, by which Pietrasanta grants to Jérôme de Beaquis, Milanese, and to Jean Bernard, of Pavia, but living in Ferrara, power of attorney 'pour demander, requerir et supplier au Roy nostredit sire tel ou telz offices qu'il plaira au Roy donner audit constituant pour recompense

---

12 See below, note 29.
13 MS ital. 1043, f. 1^v.
14 Ibidem.

des services et merites dudit seigneur constituant'.[15] The same text informs us that at this time he has his lodgings in the University quarter, in the 'rue du Plâtre, à l'enseigne de la Pie'. His profession is named as that of 'docteur en droit', confirming the information of MS lat. 8135, but he is additionally given the title of 'counsellor and senator of Milan'. The Jérôme de Beaquis named here re-appears elsewhere as an important creditor to the King,[16] and while 'Jean Bernard' is a little more elusive, it may be that he is to be identified with a 'Jean-Baptiste Bernard' whose name figures in a list of Italian creditors to the King drawn up in February 1538.[17] In other words, the milieu is financial, Italian, and linked to the court. A second document dated 21 November 1539 reveals that Beaquis lodged at the same address as Pietrasanta,[18] and we learn from a third that Beaquis was treasurer to the cardinal de Lorraine.[19] What we do not know is the nature of the 'services' that according to his *procuration* Pietrasanta had rendered the King; but since the reference post-dates the transfer of the two volumes of the *Geographia* to the royal library, it is at least possible that the reference is to that work. If so, the *Geographia* did not produce the patronage that Pietrasanta was hoping for.

This somewhat meagre harvest is supplemented by one further source of information. The name of Pietrasanta recurs several times in the correspondence of Pietro Aretino.[20] On 23 July 1537 Pietrasanta sends from Milan a letter to Aretino which he signs 'Fratel Paolo Petrasanta', and in a postscript to which he refers to the bishop of Lodi — at that time the recently nominated Giovanni Simonetta[21] — as his employer.[22] Aretino's correspondence makes it clear that Pietrasanta had a reputation as a theologian; as we shall see, this has a direct relevance to the *Geographia*. On 11 May 1537 Aretino writes to Pietrasanta as to his

---

[15] Ernest Coyecque, *Recueil d'actes notariés relatifs à l'histoire de Paris et de ses environs au XVIe siècle*, Vol. I (Paris, 1905), no. 1261.

[16] *Catalogue des actes de François Ier*, vol. IV, no. 14519: 'Mandement au trésorier de l'épargne de rembourser à Jérôme "Beaquis" une somme de 12,332 livres 17 sous 11 deniers tournois qu'il avait prêtée au roi. Jumièges, 31 juillet 1545.'

[17] *Catalogue des actes de François Ier*, vol. VIII, no. 29730.

[18] Coyecque, vol. I, no. 1289.

[19] Coyecque, vol. II (Paris, 1924) no. 3820; dated 23 April 1545.

[20] The references to Pietrasanta in the Aretino correspondence were first noticed, in a different context, by Émile Picot; see further note 27 below.

[21] Schmitz-Kallenberg (ed.), *Hierarchia Catholica medii et recentioris aevi*, vol. III (Regensberg, 1923), p. 220.

[22] T. Landoni (ed.), *Lettere scritte a Pietro Aretino*, 2 vols in 4 pts (Bologna, 1873–5), I.i, p. 321.

mentor: 'Egli aviene a la mia ignoranza, saputo uomo, vantata da la vostra dottrina come a un vile lodato per coraggioso....'[23] Even allowing for Aretino's customary irony, Pietrasanta emerges as a man of learning, 'felice interprete de gli inchiostri sacri'.[24] A letter written just over a month later, on 23 June 1537, is even more fulsome in its praise: 'il sole non è sì chiaro a noi, come le Scritture sacre son chiare a voi: i sensi ebraici e gli spirti de le lor profezie son sì bene intesi da le acutezze de le vostre scienze che non accade che altro interprete ci apra a i secreti de la verità de l'eterna vita.' [25] Furthermore, it emerges that Pietrasanta had a son, Giulio Cesare: Aretino calls him 'mio non meno che vostro figliuolo'.[26] We also learn that some time before 1539 Pietrasanta was in Lyon; the information comes from a letter written to Aretino on 20 February 1539 by Jean de Vauzelles, the translator of Aretino's religious works. Vauzelles claims to have been Pietrasanta's friend in Lyon — 'la familiarite duquel ma este fort agreable icy a Lyon, tant pour les valeurs dicelluy, que aussi pour la celebrite de son nom, canonisè par deux de voz espistres' — and he states that Pietrasanta had written 'certain works' during his stay in the city: 'Il a compose icy certains opuscules desquelz vous feray participant se il les faict imprimer'. [27] Pietrasanta was still in Lyon on 17 February 1540, when he addresses a further letter to Aretino from there, praising in his turn Vauzelles: 'il mio non bastevolmente lodato Monsegnore de Montrottiero.' [28] Finally, it is thanks to the same correspondence from and to Aretino that we know the date of Pietrasanta's death, which occurred, as we have said, in Milan in 1550, and in circumstances that suggest he was still a prominent member of society.[29]

The main difficulty is that with the single exception of the one relating to the year of Pietrasanta's death, all these references belong to the years

---

23 F. Flora (ed.), *Tutte le opere di Pietro Aretino*, 2 vols (Florence, 1960), I, p. 152.

24 Loc. cit., p. 153.

25 Loc. cit., p. 189.

26 Loc. cit., p. 153. In 1535 Giulio Cesare had attempted in vain to enlist Aretino's aid in avoiding a prison term imposed by the Venetian authorities for a crime of blasphemy (*Lettere scritte...*, I.ii, pp. 74, 76).

27 *Lettere scritte...*, II.i, p. 100. On Vauzelles's translations of Aretino's works, cf. É. Picot, *Les Français italianisants au XVIe siècle*, 2 vols (Paris, 1906), I, pp. 134–59, and on Vauzelles's letter, pp. 145–6; on Pietrasanta, p. 145, n. 5. See also Picot, loc. cit., for a discussion of the context of the Vauzelles-Aretino-Pietrasanta correspondence, which need not concern us here.

28 *Lettere scritte...*, I.ii, p. 324.

29 *Lettere scritte...*, II.ii, p. 266; letter to Aretino from 'V.S. figliuolo e servitore Il Betussi', dated 25 September 1550 from Turin: '...Il Pietra Santa morì in Milano in casa del gran cancelliere, di morte subita.'

1537–40. About the rest of Pietrasanta's career we know nothing, and in particular we have no precise information about the dates of composition of the *Geographia* itself. The evidence we have cited thus far can be summarised as follows:

(i) the Jean de La Barre inscription gives us a *terminus ad quem* for the manuscript of 1538;

(ii) we know that Pietrasanta was in Paris in November 1539;

(iii) we know that he was still in Milan, and in the employment of the bishop of Lodi, on 23 July 1537;

(iv) that at this same time (May/June 1537) Pietrasanta enjoys a considerable and well-established reputation as a theologian;

(v) that on or shortly before (Vauzelles speaks of him in the past tense) 20 February 1539 Pietrasanta was in Lyon, and had been resident for a sufficiently long time to make the acquaintance of Vauzelles;

(vi) that he was still in, or had returned to Lyon one year later, on 17 February 1540.

The dates appear to make it very unlikely that the *Geographia* was one of the 'opuscules' referred to by Vauzelles in 1539, for by that time the work had already been transferred to the royal library. It seems to us that the *Geographia*, particularly given its length, can only have been written in Milan over a period of time before 1537/8; this would correspond to the content of the work, for the nature of Pietrasanta's reputation at that time is that of a theologian, and as we shall see, the *Geographia*, despite its title, is a work that is theologically inspired.

Let us now turn to an analysis of the work itself. Not the least of its claims on our interest is the fact that Pietrasanta wrote it twice. Pietrasanta draws attention to the effort that this cost him in his dedication to the King of the prose version of his treatise:

> iteratus mehercle, & diutinus fuit labor opus arduum magis altero, & altero modo eandem rem scribere...[30]

However, Pietrasanta claims at the same time to have been sustained in his effort, and to have resisted sleeplessness, thanks to the memory of François Ier ever present to his mind, and to the knowledge that his labours would bring pleasure to his King. Without this he would have been crushed by the magnitude of the task:

> ...& succubuissem profecto ponderi, nisi assidua tui memoria Magnanime Rex, cui utrunque dicamus opus in scribendo acriorem, & fortiorem

---

[30] MS lat. 4811, first leaf (unsigned) verso.

urgentibus autem & opprimentibus vigiliis me facile renitentem in ictumque praestitisset, quicquid vero perpessus sum laboris, summum animo nostro erit solatium ubi cum haec legeris in gratiam tuam suscepisse cognovero.[31]

In fact, the prose version of the work came second. The origins of the work are as a poem, and its inspiration is religious. In the corresponding dedication to François I er of the verse version of his treatise, Pietrasanta makes it clear that the *Geographia* forms a prolegomenon to an unwritten life of Christ. His starting-point was surprise that the life of Christ had never been celebrated by the poets,[32] and frustration coupled with anger that the resources of style and elegance of expression should be wasted on false gods.[33] The ancients at least had the excuse that they lived in an age of darkness, but what excuse can those modern poets provide who fill their poems with the same nonsense?[34] Having grieved for some time over this state of affairs, it had occurred to him that he might himself set an example to be followed by others of greater eloquence, and begin a poem on the life of Christ that would at least be holy, if not inspired;[35] whereupon he felt inspiration come upon him, and even now as he recounts this to François he feels a religious ecstasy to be at hand.[36]

---

[31] Ibidem.

[32] MS lat. 8135, f. 1ᵛ: 'Admiratus sum saepe Francisce Rex, quod cum nobis per filium suum se ostenderit Deus errataque nostra suomet effuso sanguine innocentissimus Christus diluerit, nemo etiam excultor musarum Vates de Deo ipso, & servatore nostro quidpiam hactenus concinnuerit...'

[33] Ibidem: 'Ex hoc succensui saepe religioni nostrae Christianae, & mihi frequenter iratus sum, praesertim cum animo veteres plerosque evolverem Poetas praeclaros, qui à fide vera & recta aberrabant, mortales utpote pro Diis adorantes, horum tamen plerosque sciebam extitisse qui carmine, stiloque alioqui consummato inanes Deos illos religiose admodum, nedum elleganter celebraverint.'

[34] Ibidem: 'At e nostris etiam Christicolis non deffuisse, qui priscos sequentes, ineptiis illis poemata sua repleverint. Excusantur mehercule prisci, obductis enim caligine quadam oculis prodibant; deum ignorabant ipsum, quonam ergo modo illum celebrare poterant, quem nesciebant? Nos vero qua possumus nos excusatione tueri?'

[35] Loc. cit., f. 2ʳ: 'Haec cum mecum ipse diu dolens admodum perpendissem; elementiaeque hominum compaterer, venit quandoque in mentem, ut tametsi vir imbecillis ingenii sim, ad aliorum tamen magnae elloquentiae virorum excitationem, aliquid in Christi memoriam, si non ellucubrato, pio saltem edere inciperem carmine...'

[36] Ibidem: 'Perstiti demum in sententia, tumque divino veluti adflatus spiritu, ad passionem eius & mortem, mortalium vero vitam, statim adplicus animum furoreque illico eo percitus, quo ferri solent Poetae Epodos hac in re (uti materia exposcit) suspiriis plenos effundere coepi, materiam quippe gravem & Christiano dignam aggressus sum, dabit Maximus Deus in cuius dextera omnia sunt, & carmini (ut spero) facundiam, & menti quantum par fuerit ingenium; utinam

While we know little of the 'Fratel Paolo Petrasanta' who signs his letter to Aretino the tone of this dedication is unmistakably that of the mystic and the visionary. Moreover, the evidence of this dedication helps us a little further in our attempt to date the work. Pietrasanta goes on to say that he has heard that Girolamo Vida has written his own poem on the life of Christ; when taken together with his own as yet unwritten work, the aim of a poetic celebration of the life and death of Jesus will have been achieved.[37] Since Vida's *Christiados libri sex* was first published in 1535,[38] it seems reasonable to assume that Pietrasanta presents his work to the King at or about that date; the prose version will follow 'as soon as it is finished'.[39]

Pietrasanta initially seeks to justify the importance of the discipline of geography in itself. Despite the complexity and asperity of the subject — 'Porro materiam habes tametsi barbaris saepe nominibus asperisque plenam, & ex sui natura satis implicitam' — its importance is not to be doubted; however ill-suited the harsh names of peoples and regions might be as the material of a poem, as he has found to his cost, knowledge of them is both pleasurable and useful, and especially to kings: 'horrent quippe populorum & regionum strepitantia quaedam nomina adeo ut (praesertim carmine) vix illa superare potuerim, cognitu tamen mirum in modum iucunda sunt, & mortalium vitae, Regum maxime & Ducum utilia....' Pietrasanta's claim is to be the first to have reduced to a clear order what before him had been confused: 'Gaudeo vero quod primus ego omnium quos unquam Graecos, aut Latinos viderim, materiam hanc concinnata serie explicaverim.' What lies behind this is an essentially philological concern; Pietrasanta is preoccupied with the imprecision or harshness of words ('Accedit autem quod an hesantia illa, & stridentia verba quantum potuimus, lenire ellaboravimus...'). Indeed, it is of some importance to note that, in what is a typically humanist perspective, Pietrasanta's proposed reform of geography bears essentially upon the art of proper naming, and that to him the restoration of order is

---

piissime Rex dum haec mihi reminisci contingat, dissolvar totus & sim cum Christo.'

[37] Ibidem: 'Audio M. Hieronymum Vidam poetam hodie facundissimum, vitam Christi lucubratissimo carmine tradidisse, laudo sane hominem, qui sacro & religioso viro (uti initiatus ipse est) rem omnino dignam fecerit, at si ille vitam nos utique Servatoris mortem effabimur, ut totum habeamus & viventem & mortuum Iesum...'

[38] The first edition was published at Cremona by Lodovico Britannico in that year; the first French edition appeared in 1536 (Lyon, Sebastian Gryphius).

[39] MS lat. 8135, f. 2^r: 'opus autem utrunque numini tuo consecravimus, alterum quod modo exhibeo, alterum vero cum absolutum fuerit dabimus.'

to be equated with the restoration of nomenclature.[40] Pietrasanta's dedication of his work to François has therefore both a cultural and a political aptness, since it is addressed via one and the same person to the most powerful of kings and to the unique protector of men of letters ('Cui ergo opportunius quam tibi qui Regum es primus, inventum hoc primum devovere potui, tibi maxime unico litteratorum præsidio?').[41] Not least, everything is set out for the convenience of the royal dedicatee; copious indexes will save François the trouble of having to read the whole work, and even the use of the index is something that he could ask someone else to do for him....[42] It is in the same context of pleasing his royal reader that he has gone to the trouble of preparing the second prose version. The intention, he is careful to explain, is that the King should be able to consult the two side by side, turning to the prose as he wishes in order to see material more fully developed, but, Pietrasanta hopes, finding as others habitually find that subjects propounded in verse remain more firmly in the mind.[43] Furthermore, if he feels that his work pleases the King, he will be all the more encouraged — and he asks for nothing more — to complete his own unfinished work on the passion.[44]

---

[40] cf. the dedication to the King of the prose version of the treatise (MS lat. 4811, first leaf (unsigned) r°): 'Geographiam plerique tum Graeci, tum Latini summo admodum studio, exquisita nedum eruditione tradidere, verum (ut ingenue, non autem arroganter dixerim) perplexam satis, & implicitam posuere, in causa fuisse arbitror, quod impeditum omnino ex se opus est, & nominibus locorum, gentiumque constat, quae persequi inconcinna magis, quam elegans est materia. Accedit quod & locorum, & eorum nominum varia saepe facta est mutatio; Quare & authores in tradenda huiusmodi doctrina varii admodum esse videntur, & perplexi, id quod lectionem hanc minime benignam facit, licet alioqui cognosci sit dignissima; Nos igitur ad materiam hanc explicandam adcincti neminem horum imitati, omnes vero admirati sumus, modo in huius, modo illius parteis transeuntes, uti nobis gratior lucidiorque visa est pertractatio....'

[41] MS lat. 8135, f. 2ᵛ.

[42] Loc. cit., f. 3 ʳ: 'Ne vero quae hic legeris fortasse tibi fastidium adducant, cum ea sint quae interiectis frequentioribus rerum nominibus, & his quidem saepe barbaris & iniucundis constent, quid toto contineatur opere per indices rerum praeposui, ne integrum opus legeres; Verum si quid forte aliquando desyderas, id quæras tantum, sciasque quo loco invenias, ita & tu praestabis aliis ut idem faciant....'

[43] Loc. cit., ff. 2ᵛ–3ʳ: 'At tu (ubi velis) ad commentarios quoque prosaicos nostros divertere interdum poteris, ubi diffusius quam numeris ipsis elloquimur; succedet autem tibi ex lectione carminis quod caeteris etiam accidere solet, ut scilicet delicatiori quadam recordatione quae legeris memoriae promptius occurrent, herebuntque tenacius, ex pedestri vero oratione explicatiorem rerum seriem consequeris. Igitur tibi in lucro erit duos pro uno habuisse commentarios....'

[44] Loc. cit., f. 3 ʳ: 'Haec vero si numini tuo oblectamento fuisse sensero, nihil est quod mihi desyderioque meo magis gratulari queam, tumque ad passionis carmen perficiendum, superadditus mihi longe acrior erit stimulus.'

To the modern reader the *Geographia* appears as a curiously hybrid work. In the address to the King 'studioso cuique lectori' which follows the dedication of the first, verse version, Pietrasanta is at pains to explain how the *Geographia* came to be written.[45] His intention had been to commemorate and deplore in verse the passion of Christ ('Christi infandam illam omnium quae sint fuerintque passionem atrocissimam Epicidio veluti quodam carmine iamdiu deflere animo est nobis'), but when he had reached the end of his first book, several years before ('At cum libri huius volumen primum superioribus aliquando annis absolverimus'), and had come to God's creation of the world and of man, for in that event Christ's suffering had its beginning, he had started to make a separate description of the naming of the different peoples and regions of the world ('sumpta itaque ab his materia in novam hanc incurrimus descriptionem'). That description was to become the seven books of his geography. The result is an eloquent example of the expanding book of the Renaissance, or perhaps more accurately a monstrous birth, since the child rapidly outgrew the parent. Pietrasanta confesses that his 'digression' grew much longer than he originally envisaged, and that his description of the earth has detained him for six full years, such was the difficulty and complexity of his material, and what he had first thought to deal with in no more than two hundred lines had grown into over six thousand:

> Fateor digressionem hanc multo quam putaram prolixiorem fuisse, sextus namque iam agitur annus, quod hac in descriptione terrae commoratus invigilo, crevit plane & traxit me longius quam volebam difficilis haec & confusa materia, ut quod ducentis tantum carminibus elucubrare primum cogitaveram, millia super sex me etiam invitum traxerit....[46]

Here, too, he speaks as the poet inspired ('ita enim sacer ille Phoebaeus furor concitat, rapitque ut nollentem etiam trahat'). Where, then, his original intention had been that the two works should appear side by side, he has now decided to present his *Geographia* to the King as a separate

---

[45] Loc. cit., f. 3ᵛ, 'Paulus Petrasancta iureconsultus mediolanensis Francisco Francorum Regi et studioso cuique lectori S.': 'Geographiae huius nostrae invicte Rex, aliusve quisquis es lector, quae nobis (si forte efflagitas) pertractandae fuerit occasio, cum praesertim materia satis implicata sit, totque illam eruditi, & celebratissimi viri varijs temporibus variaque, & multiplici discordia exaraverint nollo omnino ut nescias....'

[46] Loc. cit., f. 4ʳ.

and self-contained work, that the main work on the passion be no longer delayed.[47]

It is the religious nature of the work that is the most clearly emphasised; it is not only in his capacity as guardian of learning but also as 'roi très chrétien' that François receives the dedication of the work: 'Nemini enim de Christo concinnus eloqui arbitror quam tibi qui titulo reque ipsa Christianissimus es.' The nature of Pietrasanta's religious inspiration, on the other hand, is anything but orthodox. The creation referred to in MS lat. 8135 is not the creation as described in Genesis, but rather a gnostic version in which God commands other 'ethereal gods' to fly down to earth to create man from the 'Damascene dust' ('ex pulvere Damasceno'); these gods or demons, as they fly through the air, admire God's work, the empty world about to be filled through His power with men and the towns in which they are to live, the mountains, rivers and woods and their population of animals — and the peoples and cities which God Himself establishes, they mark out for themselves in turn:

> …Deus ibi maximus optimus (ex hoc enim passio Domini exorta est) Aethereis Dis ut è caelo in terras ad primum ex pulvere Damasceno hominem omnium parentem faciendum devolarent mandaverit, idque (ut par fuerat) Dii exequerentur, dum inter volandum vacuam, inanemque terram ex alto undique omnem prospectant, Dei protinus magni admirantur potentiam, pietatemque laudant, qui hominibus, oppidis, montibus, fluvijs, sylvis, brutisque animantibus terrarum penitus orbem sit expleturus, ex aereque universum huius situm, futurosque quosque populos, urbeisque omnipotens uti ipse constituet, sibi invicem designant…

It is direct from these divinities that Pietrasanta will take his own inspiration. He will follow the same order as the gods, and retain the same method that they used.[48] More to the point, he will borrow from

---

[47] Loc. cit., f. 4r–v: 'Ideo geographiam hanc ab ipso passionis volumine, quam à principio decreveramus eodem cum opere legi excerpere statuimus, ne diutius quam par sit, illam immorari contingeret; volumus tamen quod primum decrevimus adhuc perficere, orbem videlicet terrarum in passione ipsa sed brevi compendio summatimque veluti congerere, tibique demum Magnanime Rex opus hoc (ut statuimus) integrum nuncupare....'

[48] Loc. cit., ff. 3v–4r: 'itaque in ea enarranda Divorum ipsorum ordinem adamusim persequemur nudis utemur verbis, carptim omnia haec Europam primum mox Africam, denique Asiam septem libris explicantes, servabimus vero hunc ubique quem Dii etiam ipsi servavere modum, situm primo provintiarum, regionumque, & unde hae nomen sumpserint, deinde populos nationesque, & hos quidem prius qui in ora sunt, demum qui intus; Oppida deinceps eodem ordine, praeterea sub quibus populis sint demonstrabimus; post haec autem promontoria, & monteis,

them the gift of prophecy, and declare the future destiny of nations; all
this he sets before the King, and with the King's permission, before his
'studious reader':

> Cum autem Dii ipsi futura haec quaecunque vaticinentur, utique nos ex futuro
> eorum quoque dicta referemus praeter tamen maria, flumina & monteis
> namque haec fere omnia cum terra ipsa exorta sunt, & quantum par fuerit, &
> huiusmodi feret materia, singula quaeque seriatim enuntiabimus; Quae omnia
> tibi Inclyte Rex nuncupatim consecramus, legenda vero studioso cuique
> lectori (te potissimum permittente) concedimus...

The description of the world is then for Pietrasanta a subject which
cannot be considered other than in a religious context, and in religious
terms ('Cum vero Geographia haec a deplorando per nos Christi obitu,
sermoneque omni religione enixe venerando dependeat...'). It follows
that it is one which must be stripped bare of any poetic or pagan
discourse. Pietrasanta consciously and deliberately distances himself
from the traditional language of poetry, and adopts *avant la lettre* a
Calvinist aesthetic:

> Iccirco à superstitiosa illa Poetarum invocatione discedendum prorsus esse
> arbitratus sum, ne divina terrenis immisceantur, Deorumque ratiocinia iocis &
> mortalium lusibus foedari contingat, Igitur in evolvendis his, nomen ullo
> modo cantatissimum illud Iovis, pro Deo usurpare, summa mihi & penitus
> effugienda visa est impietas, Apollinem quoque & musas in summo Parnasi
> bicipitique iugo seorsum à nobis omnino fecimus...

However, the frame of reference for what follows is not so much
Calvinism as the Cabbala. Pagan divinities are to be replaced by angelic
powers in Pietrasanta's poem, to be invoked in quasi-magical fashion as
presences in the world around us, with a particular emphasis on those
who have been made the governors of the different parts of the world:

> Deos autem ipsos caelicolas (cum ipsi orbem hunc universum penetraverint)
> carmini huic nostro invocare proposuimus, & hos quidem imprimis qui ab
> omnipotenti Deo nostri orbis divisores instituti à principio fuere....

What follows is an exposition of a well-known Cabbalist doctrine: the
Cabbalists contend that in each single order of angels eight stand out over
the others ('Porro Cabalistae illi omnium eminentissimi singulo cuique
Angelorum ordini octo inter reliquos esse contendunt...'). Multiplied by

---

flumina quoque postremo insulas cuique regioni adiacentes, recitabimusque multa
quae in singulis quibusque cognitu digna evenere....'

the nine orders of angels themselves, this gives the mystical number of seventy-two, corresponding to the seventy-two nations of the world, over each of which an angel governor reigns ('...quos si per novem ipsorum choros hoc ubique octonario numero adiecto computabis, duos supra septuaginta fore comperies; hi sunt qui terram universam in duas totidem & septuaginta provincias...diuisere...vocant'). These angelic powers are for Pietrasanta at one with the 'Angel of God' who at Exodus XIV. 19–20 protects the children of Israel from Pharaoh's pursuing armies by causing a pillar of cloud to come between them, the pillar of cloud which together with the pillar of fire God set before his chosen people on their journey[49] ('quive maris undas sellecto populo, Pharaone illum perse-quente diuisere quos inter duo sunt quos columnares vocant, quare in sacra pagina legitur duas tum columnas alteram igneam, nubiferam alteram populum illum effugientem praeisse...'). They are the direct agents of God's power: 'magni profecto hi Dii sunt & nomine & potentia.' More than this, however, it is clear that Pietrasanta thinks of them as powers which may be directly invoked. Their names are derived in mystic cabbalistic fashion from the infinitely mysterious Tetragram-maton, the name of God; these names are like the unutterable elements of the Tetragrammaton itself, as indeed are the names of other angels ('deducunt namque modo quodam cabalistico singuli nomen ab ineffabili illo Dei tetragrammato; suntque itidem ut Tetragrammaton ineffabilia, uti aliorum etiam sunt Angelorum...'). The difference is that these have a power, and inspire the minds of men more and more to prayer ('caetero-rum vero aliter & aliter posita Cabalei autem ut hominum mentem ad Deorum imprecationem verbo quod proferri posset superaddito, magis atque magis accenderent...').[50] The mystery then lies in the name itself, and although an association might be made between a name and a virtue or a science, that mystery is denied to mortals: 'dicunt, hos praeterea omneis quos Graeci Angelos, Hebraei Malachim, Latini Deos vocant, ab operibus tantum datum est nobis cognoscere ideo pro cuiusque virtutum usibus pronuntiamus eorum nomina, ut à fortitudine Michael, a virilitate Gabriel, à medecina Raphael; Propria autem horum nomina quoniam es-

---

49 Exodus XIII. 21–2.
50 Pietrasanta goes on to give the following examples: '...Itaque singulis divisorum horum nominibus, aut El addidere ut Iezalel, Haziel, Cahetel, Mizrael, Aliorum vero Michael, Gabriel, Raphael, quod quidem el unum est ex nominibus Dei, nomenque potentiae, ut illud est numeri sexto decimo, El Deus spirituum omnis carnis, num uno peccante, contra omneis ira tua desæviet? aut Iach quod aliud quoque Dei nomen est sed clementiae ut Haaiach, Laviach, Hakamiach, Pahaliach, unde Cabalistae super David Regis sermone cum ait si iniquitates observaveris Iache Domine quis sustinebit?...' (loc. cit., f. 5r).

30

sentiam ignoramus, mortalis imbecilitas non reperit nec reperire potest'. Hebrew can express in one word an attribute that in Latin needs several: 'Igitur Hebraei Eliach uno exprimunt, quod pluribus verbis Romani Deum Optimum Maximum vocant. Potentiam enim & clementiam mixtum hoc unum nomen complectitur.' It is for these reasons that when it comes to the naming of the regions of the earth, Pietrasanta can do no other than invoke those 'Angeli divisores' in whom that knowledge is vested, together with those who first fashioned man upon the creator's orders:

> Hos ergo Angelos divisores nuncupatos, terrarum veluti omnium scientis-
> simos primum, mox illos omneis quos ad effingendum hominem creator
> Deus miserat exorandos censuimus.

These are the angels who will be the direct source of Pietrasanta's inspiration, and the source of his knowledge:

> Convenit quidem, ut qui universum orbem peragraverint, & futuros cuique
> regioni posuerint terminos urbeisque, & reliqua omnia praedixerint me
> quoque haec enarraturum edocerent.[51]

In this way Pietrasanta claims to have written a religiously-inspired and infallible work, in which the point of reference is not other writers but a mystically-inspired revelation ('Mallui equidem cum Diis esse Dei veritate adflatis atque omnia haec, una tantum omnium sententia dictantibus quam cum diversis tot hominum discrepantibus & (uti humanae est naturae) allucinantibus ingeniis').

What we have at one level in Pietrasanta's *Geographia*, therefore, is a previously unknown Cabbalist-inspired treatise dedicated to the King, testifying further to François Ier's known interest in the occult sciences, and to which the two obvious parallels would be the two manuscript treatises on the Cabbala dedicated to the King by the Franciscan Jean Thenaud.[52] This is a parallel to which I shall return in a moment, but the obvious difference is that in Pietrasanta's case the Cabbala is a starting-point rather than an end in itself, and, hardly surprisingly, the work itself does not quite live up to the claims which Pietrasanta makes for it. The bulk of the treatise is marked not so much by the influence of the angels as by the influence of Strabo,[53] and there is another respect also in which

---

[51] Loc. cit., f. 5ᵛ.

[52] cf. Anne-Marie Lecoq, *François Ier imaginaire* (Paris, 1987), pp. 301–2.

[53] Although there are some variations, there are obvious broad similarities between the order in which countries are discussed in Pietrasanta's work and the sequence

Pietrasanta could be said to have his feet firmly on the ground. Prominent within the context of Pietrasanta's flattery of his royal master is the theme of *imperium*. François Ier's is a universal presence within the work since, as its future ruler, he is to be associated with every part of the world which Pietrasanta might set out to describe:

> At tu demum Regum Rex gloriose occurristi, a quo in pertractanda hac materia opem maxime peterem, cum enim orbis huius universi (sicuti cum de Gallia dicemus intelliges) moderator sis futurus, Quid est quod in describendo orbe hoc tuo tota mente non imprecer? libelloque meo veluti in re tua uti praesens adsis non invocem?[54]

The words are from the dedication to the original verse version of the treatise, and the theme returns elsewhere of a dedication to a monarch 'qui mundi dominator futurus es'.[55] In one sense the *Geographia* is a cabbalist work, but in another it is a nationalist and imperial one. The description is of the world, but the tribute, as Pietrasanta's words make clear, is to Gaul and its rulers. This is already very clear from the verse version of the treatise. In his description of the Gallic nation Pietrasanta presents to the King a mythologised account of the descent of French kings from Francus, son of Hector, but in which the lion's share is allotted to his dedicatee. The passage is representative of the standard pattern of humanist eulogy of François, but in praising François's embrace of the Muses and of wisdom, and his promotion of those who support them, we may suppose that Pietrasanta is permitting himself a personal note. The learned flock to François from every side, and Gaul becomes the seat of the Muses itself:

> Cedite tandem omnes, satis est vixisse Tropaeis
> Innumeris, me aliunde trahunt præconia magni
> Postrema hac ex gente Viri, cui maximus almas
> Corporis, atque animi vires Deus afferet omneis,
> Francisco cui nomen erit, latum cui sidera spondent
> Terrarum Imperium, celebris quem Celtica gignet
> Gallia, Vasco suis cui proximus ibit ab oris,
> Relligione Deum summa venerabitur, ipsos
> Lance gubernabit populos Iustissimus Aequa,

---

adopted by Strabo. Both start, for instance, with the Iberian peninsula, before passing on to Gaul and Britain. For Pietrasanta as for Strabo Britain is no more than a triangle lying off the northern coast of Europe: 'Forma Triquetra illi est' (MS lat. 8135, f. 25r).

[54] MS lat. 8135, f. 5v.

[55] Loc. cit., f. 3r.

> Et Musas Sophiamque animo amplexabitur omni,
> Illarumque adeo cultores evehet altos,
> Huius ut in patris complexus undique doctae
> Concurrent gentes, Musaeum Gallia fiet....[56]

The 'prophecy' that follows is one of world dominion, an expansion of the theme of 'terrarum imperium'. In the manuscript this prophecy extends over a full three pages, and ends with a dithyramb in praise of François the great pacifier, ruler of the universal orb, and the founder of a dynasty without end:

> Sceptra tenens animos hominum mulcebit et iras,
> Regna quoque adjiciet regnis tranquillaque reddet
> Omnia, Caesareos titulosque acquiret in orbe,
> Tum Maria, et Terras omni dicione tenebit,
> Imperioque suo metas, nec tempora ponet
> Omnipotens, stabilesque illi dabit orbis habenas,
> Prognatisque suis cunctos regnare per annos....[57]

In themselves the imperial allusions are not surprising. They are equally prominent in the *Cabale métrifiée* of Jean Thenaud, presented to the King in late 1519, in which the soul of the King's father, Charles d'Angoulême, delivers a similar 'vaticination au roy'.[58] However, the context of Thenaud's work is that of the imperial election; what is more curious about Pietrasanta's own 'prophecy', with its equal stress on the imperial theme, is that it is written at least some fifteen or so years later, at some point in the 1530s. By this time François has not only seen his candidacy to the imperial throne defeated, but he has also suffered the defeat of Pavia. In this way Pietrasanta's treatise becomes a striking commentary on the relationship between historical realities and the needs of royal propaganda. In the prose version which follows, the theme is yet further developed.

This is all the more worthy of note in that while there is no explicit reference to its having been a commissioned work, it is in the context of dedicating his work to the King, as we have seen, that Pietrasanta refers to his writing of the prose version. Again, and as we have already noted, it is with the writing of the prose version that the inspiration of François

---

[56] MS lat. 8135, ff. 16v–17r.

[57] Loc. cit., f. 18v.

[58] cf. Lecoq, *François Ier imaginaire*, p. 454.

is explicitly associated.[59] Could it be that the evolution of Pietrasanta's treatise followed a pattern similar to that of Thenaud's treatises on the cabbala dedicated to François Ier: a first version in verse (*La saincte et tres chretienne Cabale metrifiée*),[60] followed by a second in prose written to royal orders (*La Cabale et l'estat du monde angélic ou spirituel*)?[61] We might note further in passing that Thenaud, like Pietrasanta, complains of the difficulty he has had in matching his subject to the demands of verse, and refers to the extent to which prose permits both greater detail and greater accessibility.[62]

Whether speculatively or on the orders of the monarch, then, six pages are devoted in MS lat. 4811 to the chapter 'Galliae uniuersae situs cur dicta Francia et Deorum de Francisco Rege vaticinium'.[63] The title, and the note of patriotic fervour, are as in the earlier verse account, but Pietrasanta takes the opportunity of being considerably more expansive. His text joins a whole current of neo-Latin humanist writing produced in the wake of the Italian campaigns of Charles VIII and Louis XII, the aim of which is to glorify both the Franks as a nation and French kings as suitably epic heroes.[64] François Ier in particular is the focus of this heroicising literature,[65] and with Pietrasanta's treatise we have a further striking example of the genre. The 'historical guarantee' for this

---

[59] cf. the passage quoted at p. XX above: 'succubuissem profecto ponderi, nisi assidua tua memoria Magnanime Rex....'

[60] Bibliothèque Nationale MS fr. 882.

[61] Bibliothèque de l'Arsenal, MS 5061.

[62]   Mais par autant que d'icelle matiere
       L'arduyté et le profond mistère
       Qui requiert grand élévation d'esprit
       Estoit un peu en contraincte descript
       Pour la rigueur du stile qui est en mètre
       Votre plaisir fut me commander mettre
       Ceste matiere en prose et amplement
       La déchiffrer plus familièrement...
(Quoted by F. Secret, 'Jean Thénaud, voyageur et kabbaliste de la Renaissance', *Bibliothèque d'Humanisme et Renaissance*, XV (1954), 139–44 (p. 142); cf. MS lat. 4811, first leaf (unsigned), recto: '...quae heroico carmine, compendiariis primi omnium commentariis scribere aggressi sumus, eadem quoque hisce solutae orationis longius aperire nitimur, minime enim visum est maiestati carminis convenire, singula quaeque prolixiori oratione persequi, sed signare tantum quae diffusius pedestri hac traditione describimus....'

[63] MS lat. 4811, ff. 10ᵛ–13ʳ; cf. MS lat. 8135, ff. 15ʳ–18ᵛ.

[64] cf. Stephen Bamforth and Jean Dupèbe (eds), *Jacobus Sylvius Francisci francorum regis et Henrici anglorum colloquium, Renaissance Studies*, V (1991), pp. 11–15.

[65] cf. loc. cit., p. 12, note 68.

mythologising of the French race and its kings is provided by the *Compendium super Francorum gestis* of Robert Gaguin.[66] Pietrasanta first recounts the origins of the name of the Gauls, retracing in the process the myth of the 'Hercule gaulois':

> veteres vero Graeci Gallos, & Germanos omneis uno vocabulo Celtas appellabant, Romani vero Gallos, postquam vero Germani Rhenum transiere ab inita quasi adfinitate, Latini Germanos vocavere Gallos, Graeci autem Gallatas ab Herculis filio Gallate, Hercules enim devicto Geryone in Galliam veniens Alesiam condidit civitatem, ubi è Virginis complexu Galatem genuit, qui regnum obtinens incolis nomen dedit....[67]

Following this, there is a detailed account of the expansion and conquest of the 'Galli', until the subject becomes that of the origins of the 'Franci'. These are to be found either in a process of *translatio imperii* from Francus, son of Hector, to the foundation of German Franconia, and the conquest of the Gauls by the Frankish nation ('Horum originem, Gallorum annales iam inde a Franco Hectoris filio repetunt, qui post Troiae occasum profugus in Germaniam primum adplicuit, ubi regio nunc ab ipso, Franconia appellatur, gentèque ex eo paulatim propagata in Galliam traiecit eaque potitus de sui nomine Franciam ferunt appellasse'); or else there are those who see the origins of the name in the German tribe rather than in the Trojan hero ('Sunt qui non à Franco Troiano, sed à Franconibus Germanis qui trans Rhenum sunt Gallos esse cognominatos volunt'). Pietrasanta lays stress, as had Gaguin, on the antiquity and the piety of the 'Franci', and emphasises in particular the right of French kings to the title of 'christianissimi':

> Franconum enim gens vetustissima est...Gothis, & Aquitanis, postremo Normandis, ac Longobardis varia successione ac magna virtute superatis, tota demum Gallia potiti sunt, & in hunc usque diem inclytum inter Christianos regnum constituere Francorum, semperque barbaris nationibus pro Christi religione summo studio invictisque armis restitere, unde & soli Gallorum reges Christianissimi nomen sumpsere....[68]

Three dynasties of French monarchs have followed, respectively from Pharamond to Childéric III, from Pépin to Louis V, and from Hugues

---

[66] cf. loc. cit., p. 13.

[67] MS lat. 4811, f. 10 v.

[68] MS lat. 4811, ff. 11v–12r; cf. Gaguin, *Compendium super Francorum gestis* (Paris, Badius, 1511), ff. 6r, 55r.

Capet to the present.[69] The true founder of the sanctity of French monarchs, however, is Clovis, in a tradition consecrated by Gaguin, and here faithfully recorded by Pietrasanta. The legend is that of Clovis' vow to become Christian, and of his miraculous conversion and baptism; the sudden deficiency of baptismal oil, and the dove sent from heaven with the Holy Chrism, ever since preserved at Reims and used for the anointing of French kings:

> Clodoveius quintus Rex successit, is coniugem habuit Sanctam nomine Clotildem, quae virum ad Christi religionem adhortabatur, quam cum Rex audire nollet, bellumque cum Romanis gereret vovit se facturum Christianum, ubi victor evaderet, parta igitur victoria primus Gallorum Regum una cum tribus millibus è populo sacro perluitur fonte; eo tempore divinitus per columbam è coelo ampulsa oleo indeficiente plena, demissa est, quo ipse veluti Chrismate, tempora sibi inunxit, servataque est in Remigii sancti coenobio ad idem postea offitium futuris Regibus exhibendum.[70]

Pietrasanta like other humanists, then, believes in the divine origin of the 'regalia', the apparatus involved in the coronation of French kings.[71] Likewise linked to the humanist tradition of the heroicising of the French monarchy is the emphasis he accords to Charlemagne as the perfect monarch; he is the embodiment not just of empire, but of an equal devotion to both learning and religion. Where Gaguin presents Charlemagne as a man of culture, the founder of the University of Paris,[72] Pietrasanta too emphasises learning and religiosity as much as feats of arms:

> ...non minore etiam dignitate otium quam bellum gessit, arteis liberales coluit, Parrhisiique florentissimam omnium Academiam instituit, loca sacra

---

69 MS lat. 4811, f. 12r.

70 MS lat. 4811, f. 12r; cf. Gaguin's account of Clovis' baptism (*Compendium super Francorum gestis*, ed. cit., f. 9r) [text cited in Bamforth and Dupèbe, *Francisci Francorum regis et Henrici anglorum colloquium*, p. 134]: 'Dies abluendo regi indicitur: parato ingenti ornatu lavacro, cum sacro sanctum oleum quo liniri ritu Christiano qui abluuntur solent, sive ministrorum incuria, sive hoc agente deo, allatum non esset, ecce de superis delapsa columba phialam, quam ampullam vocant, odoratissimi liquoris oppletam ad manus Remigii detulit. Creditum est spiritus dei ministerio id perpetratum esse. Eo liquore Clodoveus primum, posteri deinceps francorum reges hactenus regnum administraturi sacrantur.'

71 cf. Bamforth and Dupèbe, *Francisci francorum regis et Henrici anglorum colloquium*, p. 14 and note.

72 cf. loc. cit., p. 14, note 76. Gaguin's portrait of Charlemagne is to be found in Book IV of his *Compendium* (ed. cit., ff. 48 sqq.).

vir religiosissimus multa aedificavit, interquae coenobia viginti & quatuor, tum nobile illud templum sancti Martini Aquisgrani....[73]

No less important, however, is the model of Charlemagne, inheritor of the mantle of Augustus, both conqueror and peace-maker, and not least the leader of military campaigns in Italy.[74] For Pietrasanta, as for other humanists of his generation, the clear parallel is to François Ier himself.[75] The third dynasty of French monarchs, beginning with Hugues Capet, has in François its most illustrious representative:

> Postremo ab Ugone Chiapeta marchione Parrhisiensi tertia incipit Regum progenies in hanc usque aetatem perdurans, haec plurimos habuit potentes & religiosissimos; At nunc Franciscum habet invictissimum....

It is in this humanist and historical perspective then that Pietrasanta will introduce a panegyric of his monarch, as others had done before. However, two elements give his 'prophecy' its distinctiveness. The first is that, in conformity with his declared intention, his will take the form of an angelic prophecy: '...At nunc Franciscum habet invictissimum qui in hanc usque diem multa egit gloriose, agetque maiora admodum in futurum, Angelorum veluti vaticinio describere iussus sum....' The second is that Pietrasanta's 'prophecy', written when it is, has to take account of past events as well as of the future. 'Invictissimus' remains the coinage, but Pietrasanta's angels have also to explain the reverse which was Pavia. Hence their declaration that François will sweep all before him in Italy, only to lose all 'through a contrary blow of Fortune':

---

[73] MS lat. 4811, f. 12ᵛ.

[74] Loc. cit., f.12ʳ⁻ᵛ: (after discussion of Pépin) '...Carolus huius filius cognomine magnus de Christiana religione bene meritus, inter caetera quater in Pontificis auxilium Alpeis traiecit, & in Italiam profectus est, obque eius merita à Leone Pontifice Imperator (adclamante populo, Carolo Magno à Deo dato Imperatori Augusto salus, & gloria) inter missarum solemnia consalutatus est, imperiumque quod annos fere trecentos cessaverat occidenti restituit, Aquitanos in deditionem accepit, Longobardos cum desyderio eorum rege per obsidionem Papiae in deditionem accepto, ex Italia annos fere ducentos et quatuor possessa eiecit, Saxones subiugavit, Aigolandum Sarracenorum Regem, Hispanosque de fide Christiana male sentientes domuit & fudit, Unnos qui diu Pannoniam occupaverant tandem repressit, & multa clade affecit....'

[75] François Ier's predecessors equally had seen themselves as the successors of Charlemagne; after Charles VIII's invasion of Italy in 1495 the humanist Ugolino Verino presented to him in Florence the manuscript of his epic poem the *Carliades*, a celebration of the exploits of Charlemagne, with which Charles was invited to compare his own (cf. Baurmeister and Laffitte, *Des livres et des rois*, p. 129).

> ...hi enim aiunt, primum Alpeis ille traiciet, Lygures, Insubresque, &
> Aemiliae partem, Parmam scilicet & Placentiam subiget amittet vero omnia
> haec Fortunae primum adverso impetu....

After this Pietrasanta is on the somewhat firmer ground of prophecy
proper: a prophecy of the recovery of Italy, followed by a lightning
campaign of universal conquest, conversion of the heathen, crusade
against the infidel, and acclamation as emperor of the whole known
world, a title in which François and his descendants will be confirmed for
ever, by decree of God Himself:

> ...deinde rediens recuperabit, tumque tenebit perpetuo, atque ulterius progre-
> diens universam subiugabit Italiam, partaque Italia ad Illyricos, Liburnosque
> & Graecos, ac Thracas vertet, hosque omneis debellatis Turcis, Christianis
> restituet Maria demum traiciens Hierosolymam penetrabit, ibique hostibus
> devictis Dominicum recuperabit monumentum, populosque illos omneis
> Syros, Asyrios, Caldaeos Iudeosque ad Christi fidem perducet, sacroque
> perlui baptismate curabit, adclamatione demum gentium & nationum om-
> nium, universi terrarum orbis Imperator efflagitabitur; Imperium illi, posteris-
> que suis Deus Optimus Maximus statuet perpetuum....

We might, in one sense, be listening to the *conseillers de Pichrocole*
— in a passage which perhaps had been published only a short time
before.[76] But here there is no hint of Lucianesque satire. The motif of
crusade against the infidel and the recapture of Jerusalem from the Turk
had been a commonplace of royal propaganda from the time of Charles
VIII, and had been used as a justification for the invasion of Italy; it had
been officially consecrated by the Treaty of London of 1518.[77] What is
more tantalising to consider is that François might have been able to read
virtually at the same time both parody and literal version side by side —
and that both should have been intended for his eyes.

Pietrasanta, for his part, remains faithful to his claim of speaking with
the voice of the angels, and his prophecy to François ends on a note of
religious transport and ecstasy. He has transcribed what the angels have
told him, and the image of François is translated in a final passage into
another dimension, as the 'prophecy' becomes a series of inspired
visions:

---

[76] *Gargantua*, chapter XXXI: 'Comment certains gouverneurs de Picrochole, par
conseil précipité, le mirent on dernier peril.'

[77] cf. Stephen Bamforth and Jean Dupèbe, 'The *Silva* of Bernardino Rincio (1518)',
Renaissance Studies, VIII (1994), 256–61; and Baurmeister and Laffitte, *Des
livres et des rois*, p. 129.

...Haec inclyte Rex illa sunt quae divi ipsi Coelites vaticinio mihi divino & certissimo renuntiarunt, volvereque cuncta haec uti tibi scriberem, scribo equidem, at tu vaticinium cape, age Gloriose Rex, invictum illum quo praeditus es Herois animum explica modo, operi te accinge, omnia vinces adsequeris omnia, fidem iam iam Christi te duce in culmen evehi video, unamque fidem unumque te Imperatore Deum demonstrari, iam iam verbum illud Domini tua potissimum opera, egregioque facto in lucem exire conspicio, unus videlicet Pastor, & unum fiat tantum ovile instimula igitur, excita te ipsum Rex, opportuna ecce tibi modo sese offert gloria....[78]

François's greatness, in a word, lies in the title of 'Christianissimus' itself:

Quid desyderas amplius? Deum ipsum habes, auxilio tibi omnia erunt, cedent populi, cedent reges nationesque omnes: renuntiavit haec Deus...Christum tandem audi, qui regum Christianissimus es — si enim Christus pro te, quis tibi adversari poterit?

What is perhaps even more remarkable than the fervour with which these words are written is that they are intended directly for the eyes of the King, and that they come to form part of the monarch's personal library. When some 180 folios later Pietrasanta comes finally to conclude the prose version of his work, it is once more the note of inspiration which is uppermost. However, angelic inspiration here gives way to the inspiration furnished directly by the monarch, as Pietrasanta returns, insistently, to the theme which he had already sketched in his dedication. The difficulty of the subject would more than once have made him give up — and he refers once more to his own foolhardiness in having translated it into epic verse — but the memory of of the person for whom he was compiling his work returned to give him, like Antaeus, new strength. He follows therefore 'at the heel of his monarch's greatness'; whatever is of worth in what he writes, can have come only from François:

Pervenimus tandem ad metam Rex Gloriose, laboriosum quidem opus, & profusum exaravimus, numeris insuave omnino, et (ut plane fateor) inconcinnum; quare minime admiratus sum, quod arduam hanc omnino provinciam nemo hactenus carmine unquam aggressus fuerit. Ego enim quam saepissime in scabris illis, praeruptisque nominibus concinnandis (quae alioqui creberrime occurrebant) animo adeo perterritus sum, ut pedem retrahere, herbamque (ut aiunt) asperitati illi tradere, multoties cogitaverim, verum cum me tui gratia Magnanime Rex ista haec congerere, et tua omnino

---

[78] MS lat. 4811, f. 13[r].

esse animo occurrebat: tum repente quasi Anteus qui Terram labore defficiens contingeret, vires mihi, animique fortitudinem sola tui recordatione interpollabam, ita ut ad calcem te tantum duce demum pervenerim. Inde est, ut si quid boni, quod perexiguum esse scio, his lucubrationibus nostris comperies, id omne tibi, et sacratissimo numini tuo, non autem imbecillitati nostrae adscribere possis.[79]

* * *

Pietrasanta's *Geographia*, then, begins and ends with praise of François Ier. As a work it is now forgotten, and yet as a witness of the milieu in which it was produced it remains a valuable document. In the first place, it underscores the reality of the Franco-Milanese axis of the early years of the century. Pietrasanta writes as a Milanese who clearly considers himself as much a subject of the French King as an inhabitant of his native city. Secondly, it shows something of the continued operation of the conventions of neo-Latin humanist panegyric well into the 1530s, and a striking example of retrospective prophecy — in which again the Italian does not demur from fostering the French King's Italian territorial ambitions. There is nothing, it appears, which prevents a Milanese showing the patriotic enthusiasm of a Rabelais. Thirdly, its cabbalistic element testifies to the continuing interest of François Ier in the occult sciences some fifteen years after the better-known treatises of Jean Thenaud. Fourthly, and not least, it shows us that the reading tastes of the monarch who was at once 'père des lettres' and 'roi très chrétien' could indeed be eclectic. However, 'habent sua fata libelli'; there is no evidence that after its transfer to the royal library at Blois François ever looked at Pietrasanta's treatise again. Nor, since that time, does it seem to have attracted the interest of anybody else either. Nonetheless, for anybody who is prepared to take such an interest, its existence serves as a silent reminder of the time when Milan was both culturally and politically 'la Gaule cisalpine', and the evidence of its text furnishes one more addition to the theme of 'François Ier imaginaire'.

---

[79] MS lat. 4811, f. 192r.

3

The Education of a Christian Prince:
Erasmus, Budé, Rabelais — and Ogier le Danois

Michael Heath

When Lemuel Gulliver visited the island of Laputa, he was shown the scientific Academy and observed the usual mad scientists, who were attempting to extract sunbeams from cucumbers. Less well known is Gulliver's subsequent visit to the school of political projectors, where he found a whole department of even madder professors:

> These unhappy people were proposing schemes for persuading monarchs to choose favourites upon the score of their wisdom, capacity and virtue; of teaching ministers to consult the public good; of rewarding merit, great abilities, and eminent services; of instructing princes to know their true interest by placing it on the same foundation with that of their people; of choosing for employments persons qualified to exercise them; with many other wild, impossible chimeras, that never before entered into the heart of man to conceive.[1]

Experience has taught us that their dreams were indeed as insubstantial as those of the sunbeam-seekers, but for the purposes of this paper the passage's main interest lies in the suggestion that the political projectors were going into unknown territory.

Swift is pointing out, with heavy irony, that giving advice to princes, however unreceptive the audience, has always been one of the favourite occupations of the chattering classes; the list of would-be counsellors stretches from Homer to *The Sun*.[2] But our concern here is with a few

---

[1] Jonathan Swift, *Gulliver's Travels*, III, chapter 6.

[2] Some of the more serious and relevant manuals, from antiquity to the sixteenth century, are enumerated by L. K. Born, in the introduction to his translation of Erasmus, *The Education of a Christian Prince* (New York, 1936), pp. 44–130, and in the article 'Political Philosophy' in C. B. Schmitt and Q. Skinner (eds), *The Cambridge History of Renaissance Philosophy* (Cambridge, 1988), pp. 389–452.

famous and fairly representative works dating from the early years of François Ier's reign,[3] some of which were actually addressed to the King. That in itself might seem curious, since François was already twenty-one when he came to the throne and so presumably beyond the reach of schoolmasters and schoolbooks. But in fact the genre *Teach Yourself Kingship* tended to be more political than pedagogic. The books were often called something like *The Mirror of Princes*, wherein a portrait of the ideal prince and his opposite, the tyrant, was provided for the real prince to reflect on.

This actually sounds rather subversive, and it might be, were it not that it is often difficult to disentangle the Mirror of the Prince from the genre of the panegyric. Any criticism is muted by being wholly unspecific, and the dedication usually disclaims any intention to give lessons to the dedicatee, who has no need of advice from anyone.[4] Some of these manuals seem little more than exercises in princely public relations; the important thing, as in some medieval illustrations,[5] was that the monarch should be seen publicly accepting the counsel of the *philosophe de service*. Perhaps it was just part of a time-honoured ritual, a game whose rules everyone understood. We may wonder whether Rabelais, for example, is simply playing Establishment games in *Gargantua* and, perhaps, mocking them in the famous chapter 8 of *Pantagruel*. I have some sympathy for the revisionist view that that sonorous and sententious chapter is a spoof.[6]

Or take Guillaume Budé's *Institution du prince chrestien*, presented to François Ier in manuscript in 1519. There is some argument as to whether it was commissioned by the King on Budé's appointment as royal librarian, or whether it was the book itself that obtained the post for

---

3   On the background, see E. Sciacca, 'Institutio principis: vicende di un genere di letteratura politica nella Francia del Cinquecento', *Studi politici in onore di Luigi Firpo*, edited by S. Ghibaudi and F. Barcia (Milan, 1990), 227–56, and for German analogues A. E. Baldini, 'Uno scritto di Johann Eberlin', ibidem, 431–79. The bibliography is immense: particularly useful on the 'political' advice-books are J. H. Hexter, *The Vision of Politics on the Eve of the Reformation: More, Machiavelli and Seyssel* (New York, 1973), and B. Copenhaver and C. B. Schmitt, *Renaissance Philosophy* (Oxford and New York, 1992), pp. 269–84.

4   Erasmus uses this *topos* twice over, in dedicating his *Institutio* to Prince Charles (*The Collected Works of Erasmus* [CWE], 27 [Toronto, 1986], p. 204), and in sending a copy to Henry VIII (Ep. 657, CWE, 5, p. 112). Budé uses it in both the dedication and the conclusion of his *Institution du prince*.

5   For example Froissart presenting his book to Richard II, the frontispiece to *The Hundred Years War*, edited by P. E. Thompson (London, 1966).

6   A view first propounded by Gerald J. Brault, 'Ung abysme de science...', *Bibliothèque d'Humanisme et Renaissance*, XXVIII (1968), 615–32.

Budé. If it was a job application by a humanist out to demonstrate his worth, it is appropriately stuffed with classical erudition, and rarely ventures into the modern world, except to praise François and the French monarchy. For example, Budé likens the sovereign power of the Dictator (not then a pejorative term) at Rome to that of the French king (p. 173), and embellishes a passage on the self-discipline of the Spartans with the gratuitous remark that 'les Roys de France sont aimés et obeiz [like the Spartan magistrates], plus qu'en nul autre païs, par unicque prerogative et singuliere grace de Dieu' (p. 178). The preface of the *Institution* is particularly obsequious, and it is amusing to see that in the margin of a British Library copy a spidery contemporary hand has written, sniffily: 'Flatterie trop ouverte.'[7] The book also contains a good deal of shameless self-promotion, as Budé devotes a whole chapter (XLV, pp. 185–7) to publicising his book *De Asse*; he also exploits his expertise in ancient economics to muse pointedly over the enormous salaries paid to scholars in days gone by (pp. 28 and 48–9).

Oddly, Budé's *Institution* was not printed until 1547, in the first weeks of Henri II's reign, long after Budé's death and much too late to instruct Henri. Suddenly there were three editions within a few months.[8] One untenable theory is that publication was not attempted earlier because the book merely resumes in French the material of Erasmus's *Institutio principis christiani* — which is far from an accurate assessment.[9] It also seems unlikely that the publishers were trying to ingratiate themselves with the new régime by praising its predecessor. Perhaps they were reminding the public — and Henri — of the way in which François had championed the cause of good letters. There may, on the other hand, have been official encouragement to publish, since one of the few specific political passages in Budé's work asserts the king's rights against the Parlement, a question that was to trouble Henri II just as much as his father.[10]

---

[7] *De L'Institution du prince*, l'Arrivour, Nicole Paris, 1547, BL 8006 f. 11, A, 6^r; other references are also to this edition.

[8] For details, see D. O. McNeil, *Guillaume Budé and Humanism in the Reign of Francis I* (Geneva, 1975), p. 37, n. 1; on the work generally, ibidem, pp. 37–45. A number of manuscripts survive, of which the best has been published by C. Bontems et al., *Le Prince dans la France des XVIe et XVIIe siècles* (Paris, 1965), pp. 77–139.

[9] This theory is advanced by Born (n. 2 above), p. 28, n. 16, quoting Geldner and Delaruelle in support; but the superficial general resemblances are far outweighed by the differences in detail.

[10] cf. McNeil (n. 8 above), p. 42.

But if Budé's advice to the prince was coloured by patriotism and self-interest, what of Erasmus, the loftily disinterested internationalist and the foremost educational theorist of the day? He provides, apparently quite deliberately, another example of the overlap between the manual of state-craft and the panegyric. One of his earliest publications was a *Pane-gyricus* addressed to his temporal lord, Philip the Fair of Burgundy, con-taining an implausible portrait of the Archduke, but also claiming an educational purpose:

> Yet the thing is not so much praise as precept; and there is surely no more effective method of reforming princes than to present them with a pattern of the good prince under the guise of praising them, so long as you credit them with virtues, and absolve them from vices, in such a way as to be evidently exhorting them to the former and warning them away from the latter.[11]

This strategy demands a discerning audience, to say the least! Whatever Erasmus's intentions, the piece won him a cash reward and an offer of employment which he did not take up. A dozen years later, when he was actually appointed a councillor to Philip's son Charles (later Emperor Charles V; note the similarity to Budé's position), Erasmus recycled much of the *Panegyricus* in his magisterial *Institutio principis christiani* (1516). It seems unlikely that the new book had much influence on the future Emperor; even so good a friend as John Colet admired Erasmus's initiative but doubted its prospects of success.[12] The book suffers from the usual drawback of being prudently unspecific, to the extent that it could be reworked for presentation to Charles's brother Ferdinand within a few years.[13] Even when Erasmus is deploring political marriages, for which the Hapsburgs were notorious, he refuses to name the guilty dynasty. It comes as a small shock when Erasmus does make a specific charge, as for example at the end of his chapter on treaties; but the rebuke is a mild one, and it is not even addressed to Charles:

> The kingdom of France is by far and in every way the most prosperous of all; but she would have been still more prosperous had she refrained from invading Italy.[14]

---

[11] Part of the prefatory letter to Nicolas Ruistre, Ep. 179, CWE, 2, p. 79; the whole work appears in CWE, 27, pp. 6–75. Erasmus actually read it before the Burgundian court on 6 January 1504.

[12] Ep. 423, CWE, 3, p. 311. On the *fortuna* of the *Institutio*, and its rather limited practical influence, see Born (n. 2 above), pp. 28–9.

[13] Ep. 853, CWE, 6, p. 56.

[14] CWE, 27, p. 277.

It is equally surprising when Rabelais, for example, steps out of his fiction to reproach François Ier for his 'stupidité' in allowing the Parisians to run riot — and, as we know, he toned the advice down in subsequent editions of *Gargantua*.

> Toute la ville feut esmeue en sedition, comme vous sçavez que à ce ilz sont tant faciles que les nations estranges s'esbahissent de la patience — ou (pour mieulx dire) de la stupidité — des Roys de France, lesquelz autrement par bonne justice ne les refrenent, veuz les inconveniens qui en sortent de jour en jour.[15]

It was obviously more prudent as well as more *distingué* to take refuge in generalisation — or in the past. Apart from the shameless Machiavelli, these writers nearly always illustrate their principles with historical examples — Budé is the obvious case here — or even, when historical precedent is lacking, with fictional examples. Rabelais's fruitless search for an example of a magnanimous conqueror forced him to invent the implausibly generous Grandgousier and the impossibly impressionable King Alpharbal.[16]

At least Rabelais is not dull, whereas most products of this undistinguished genre are neither pleasing nor instructive, neither *doux* nor *utile* — except perhaps to an author seeking employment. Gérard Defaux has recently identified a contemporary poetic example of the genre, Marot's *Jugement de Minos* (1514), but even that is ploddingly pedestrian in style, as well as utterly commonplace in its sentiments.[17] Erasmus, master of stylistic appropriateness, deems it necessary in the *Institutio principis christiani* to adopt a dogmatic, hyperbolic diction that all but defies translation into readable English.[18] In particular, his abuse of the superlative adjective encapsulates both the repetitious earnestness and the idealistic impracticality of the genre. No doubt the only place where Erasmus's relentless educational regime was successfully practised was in Thomas More's Utopia.[19]

---

[15] *Gargantua*, edited by R. Calder and M. A. Screech (Geneva, 1970), pp. 111–12; the parenthesis was omitted from the second edition onwards.

[16] Ibidem, pp. 273–5; though Rabelais does make clear allusions here to the shabby conduct of Charles V after the capture of François Ier at Pavia.

[17] Clément Marot, *Œuvres poétiques*, tome I, edited by G. Defaux (Paris, 1990), pp. 433–8.

[18] My own effort in CWE, 27, pp. 205–88, is accurate enough but is hardly a fluent piece of English prose.

[19] See the list of parallels in Born (n. 2 above), p. 129.

* * *

One interesting thing that we may do with these well-meaning but tedious manuals is to contrast their humanist principles with the values of chivalry, on which the aristocracy had traditionally been raised. One of the great Renaissance debates was over the apparent incompatibility between the careers of Arms and Letters[20] or, to put it in my terms, between Chivalry and Humanism. Were the two as incompatible as the rhetoricians suggested? It is a particularly pertinent question to ask at a colloquium devoted to a man who liked to be called both *Le Père des Lettres* and *Le Roi Chevalier*.

It is worth summarising what we know of François's actual up-bringing.[21] Louise de Savoie had intellectual ambitions for him (though they were more fully realised in his sister), commissioned books for him, and taught him Italian and Spanish herself. His academic tutor was François Desmoulins, later Grand Aumônier, who was an important Evangelical as well as humanist influence at François's little court at Amboise, though he was not above courtly flattery, either, as witness his eulogy of the victory of Marignano, *Commentaires de la guerre gallique*.[22] Nonetheless, François's Latin and history were weak and some contemporary evidence suggests that the new learning played a less important part in his education than his mother and tutor would have wished. Interesting, if unreliable, are the *Mémoires* of that *preux chevalier* and future Marshal, Robert de La Marck, sieur de Fleurange, dit *Le Jeune Aventureux*.[23] He was François's classmate, alongside a future Constable of France (Montmorency) and a future Admiral (Chabot); his book describes their restless pursuit of the nobility of arms, through hawking, hunting, jousting, tilting, archery, mock battles, royal tennis, and even something which may have been cricket (*l'escaigne*). François's successive governors Rohan and Gouffier (more dukes and

---

20 See J. J. Supple, *Arms versus Letters: the Military and Literary Ideals in the 'Essais' of Montaigne* (Oxford, 1984), especially pp. 9–13.

21 cf. R. J. Knecht, *Francis I* (Cambridge, 1982), pp. 2–8 and D. Seward, *Prince of the Renaissance* (London, 1973), pp. 21–6.

22 cf. R. J. Knecht, 'New Light on Francis I', *Bulletin of the Society for Renaissance Studies*, XI (1994), 1–7.

23 *Histoire des choses admirables advenues du regne de Louis XII et François Ier*, in J. F. Michaud and J. J. F. Poujoulat (eds), *Nouvelle collection des mémoires*, 1ère série, tome 5 (Paris, 1836), pp. 7 sqq.

marshals) also encouraged the chivalric or militaristic side of his studies, no doubt persuaded that, as David Cowling's paper reminds us, 'militer c'est le propre du roy'. One indication of the literary interests François acquired is provided by the inventory of the royal library drawn up by Budé's predecessor, Guillaume Petit, in 1518; his travelling library ('les livres que le roy emportoit ordinairement') consisted mostly of books on hunting and ancient military history, together with a good number of romances, *La Destruction de Troye la Grant, Le Chevalier Deliberé, Le Rommant des Deduiz,* and *Romuleon historié.*[24] Of course François did make use of humanist scholars, employing them as draftsmen, envoys, readers, physicians, confessors, and tutors to his own children; but it is hard to know how far they influenced his moral development.

Charles of Hapsburg, incidentally, also enjoyed a chivalric upbringing at the hands of Guillaume de Croy, a typical Burgundian cavalier, who supplanted the pious Adrian of Utrecht (later, as Hadrian VI, one of the few saintly Renaissance popes) as Charles's tutor, and had him reading romances and hunting furiously from the age of ten. Erasmus was suspicious of de Croy, and in his educational writings alludes frequently to the pernicious effects of the 'stupid and tyrannical fables of King Arthur'; this is more than mere literary snobbery.[25]

Erasmus clearly felt that such tales condoned thoughtless bloodshed, and his denunciation of princely violence, and especially of war, was one of few original elements that sixteenth-century Evangelical humanism brought to the traditional genre of the Mirror of Princes. All humanists hoped, in general terms, that injections of calming Stoicism and detached Platonism might tame the warrior aristocracy, but Erasmus's predecessors, wedded to a classical ethic founded on self-esteem, still allowed princely virtue to be a means to earthly fame as well as to heavenly glory. Erasmus's fundamentalist Christian ethic preached humility to all, but especially to the most exalted: one has only to read his adage on the eagle and the dung-beetle.[26]

Budé, on the other hand, endorsed Cicero's dictum that true glory lies in the esteem won by distinguished public service, and thus advocated a Christianity that permitted full participation in public life. Just as God claimed the glory of being acknowledged as Lord, he said, so might princes aspire to majesty in the sinful terrestrial realm, to inspire both

[24] E. Quentin-Bauchart, *La Bibliothèque de Fontainebleau* (Paris, 1891; reprint, Geneva, 1971), pp. 8–9.

[25] On all this, see J. D. Tracy, *The Politics of Erasmus* (Toronto, 1978), pp. 59–69.

[26] *Scarabeus aquilam quaerit (Adagia* III. vii. 1); see M. M. Phillips, *The Adages of Erasmus* (Cambridge, 1964), pp. 233–40.

awe and shame in their subjects and lead them into better paths. The pursuit of glory and the fear of public shame are of course fundamental motifs of chivalry. In the *Institution*, at least, Budé voiced his suspicions about the cult of humility and contempt for the world, the 'guilt culture' of Christian asceticism.[27]

Budé also made a case for certain kinds of 'just war' (Erasmus said that all wars were just — in the eyes of those who started them), and specifically condoned war 'contre les infidelles, occupateurs et injustes detenteurs de nos limites' (p. 145). Music to the ears of François, who was still posing in 1519 as the champion of Christendom, before he was forced into his expedient alliance with the Turks. The extermination of infidels was of course a feature of the *chansons de geste* and *romans de chevalerie*, in which Christian knights habitually made a thousand Muslim widows with one sweep of their sword.

Erasmus, by contrast, was notorious for his tolerance towards the Turks, whom he describes in an adage as 'half-Christian'; he deplores all kinds of crusading in the *Institutio*.[28] At the opposite extreme from his cosmopolitan, irenic, Evangelical, and idealistic tract is its contemporary, Claude de Seyssel's *Grant Monarchie de France*.[29] This is in essence a panegyric of Seyssel's master Louis XII, but also a constitutional essay and perhaps a manual of advice for the youthful François Ier, to whom it was presented in manuscript in 1515; it was printed first in 1519. It is a pragmatic and unheroic book, thus resembling its hero Louis XII. Like Machiavelli, Seyssel saw bloodshed not as the path to glory but as the instrument of power. Three of the five books deal with 'the necessity of strife': the third with warfare and armies, the fourth with diplomacy and the just war, and the fifth with conquests and how to retain them.

Seyssel's practical if not cynical approach is clear in his remark that princes rarely have the time or inclination to read the well-meaning educational treatises aimed at them:

> Mêmement des gens qui sont en tel degré, lesquels communément sont occupés ès grandes affaires s'ils sont sages et vertueux, tellement qu'ils n'ont guères de temps oisif pour employer en la litture [sic] de longues écritures; ou

---

27 He did, however, publish a treatise *De contemptu rerum fortuitarum* (Paris, *c.* 1520): see McNeil (n. 8 above), pp. 58–9; but this was another standard topic of rhetoric.

28 See my *Crusading Commonplaces* (Geneva, 1986), p. 89, and CWE, 27, p. 287.

29 References are to the edition by J. Poujol, *La Monarchie de France et deux autres fragments politiques* (Paris, 1961).

s'ils sont jeunes et volontaires sont adonnés à lubricités ou autres choses vaines et voluptueuses.

(p. 132)

Seyssel, a humanist *à ses heures*, enumerates a good many of these *longues écritures*, from Antiquity onwards, but his own *institution* is limited to a single chapter on 'les choses plus necessaires' (II, 2, pp. 130–2). If not original, at least his advice is brief; he summarises in two hundred words several chapters of Erasmus, on making laws, setting a moral example, appointing magistrates, and practising liberality. As for political ethics, 'il n'y faut autre remède...fors que le roy et monarque soit bon'. But he implies that the necessary 'sens, experience et prudence, accompagnées du bon vouloir' are rarely to be found together in one individual (p. 130), and thus confines himself to what we should call short-termism, to particular solutions to specific problems. Characteristically, when using the simile of the 'body politic' beloved of political commentators down the centuries, Seyssel as 'doctor to the state' will give advice only on particular diseases, 'sans parler plus avant du régime qu'ils ont à tenir en général pour la santé universelle du corps' (p. 133).

Budé, by contrast, does try to provide universal solutions based on humanist learning and emphasised by an epigrammatic style: his original title was *Recueil d'Apophthegmes*. Erasmus's *Institutio* has a similar subtitle and the preface to his *Apophthegmata* recommends the style to those wishing to gain the ear of princes.[30] The great advantage of the apophthegm is that it can be recycled *ad infinitum*, and this is vital to Budé's central preoccupation with oratory, in his eyes the supreme instrument for resolving conflicts in the councils of kings. The eloquent prince is the successful prince. Rabelais develops this theme in the episode of Eudémon the page (*Gargantua*, chapter XIV), though one may suspect parody when the object of his ideal panegyric, in itself a kind of mini-*Institutio*, is the ghastly Gargantua, bellowing like a cow into his bonnet. More relevantly to our theme here, Rabelais exposes the limitations of political rhetoric in the speech of Ulrich Gallet to the tyrant Picrochole (chapter XXIX), which is, to put it mildly, ineffective in preventing war.

The traditional reading of *Gargantua* has Rabelais combining the learning of Budé with the ethics of Erasmus and a dash of Seyssel's pragmatism. Stylistically it is, of course, a wholesale parody of the

---

[30] *Opera omnia Desiderii Erasmi*, edited by J. Leclerc (Leiden, 1703–6), IV, cols 87–8.

chivalric romances[31] — an indication of their popularity. But the ambiguities of humour prevent us making an unambiguous judgment on Rabelais's attitude towards the genre; his promotion of an aristocratic, almost chivalric, synderesis in the Abbaye de Theleme (chapter LV) must also give us pause.

What do the others have to say, more directly, about this *déclassé* medieval fiction, with its glorification of war? Budé is by no means hostile. In the *Institution*, he only mentions medieval writing once, to complain about the turgid, unreadable monastic style of the *Chroniques de France*, which has condemned many a valiant French deed to near-oblivion. Typically, he turns this into another plea for royalty to subsidise eloquence (pp. 62–3). Heroic fiction — if well-written — can inspire heroic deeds: did not Alexander the Great sleep with the *Iliad* under his pillow (p. 46)? In his *De philologia*, Budé seems even to admire the element of fantasy in chivalric romance and patriotically champions this primitive national literature. It makes an interesting contrast with Roger Ascham, who condemned the *Morte d'Arthur* for its gratuitous slaughter and sneaky adulteries. But in Budé's pedagogy the only *histoires* that can really teach us anything are classical or mythological.[32]

Erasmus, by contrast, puts these 'illiterate and foolish old wives' tales' on a par, ethically if not stylistically, with the ancient histories of such 'great raging bandits' as Achilles, Alexander, and Julius Caesar, and condemns both genres as incitements to tyranny and bloodshed.[33] Bad literature makes strange bedfellows, since our favourite reactionary Noël Béda joined Erasmus in denouncing the immorality and wickedness of the romances.[34] Perhaps it was to spite Béda that Rabelais allowed his giant prince to listen to them at mealtimes.[35]

Such attacks continued throughout the sixteenth century, as we shall see shortly; one of the most illuminating later criticisms was that the tales promoted a simplistic view of life. This could be applied particularly to the education of the hero, to which the humanists devoted so much ink and so much paper — and usually to so little purpose. We have seen what some of the educators thought about chivalry and its literary expression; what did the romances have to say about education?

---

[31] cf. M. A. Screech, *Rabelais* (London, 1979), pp. 33–4.

[32] On all this, see Tracy (n. 25 above), pp. 60 and 166, n. 99. Ascham is quoted by Seward (n. 21 above), p. 25.

[33] *Institutio*, CWE, 27, pp. 250–1.

[34] Screech (n. 31 above), p. 34.

[35] In *Gargantua* (n. 15 above), p. 146, l. 71.

If only all princes could have received the upbringing of Ogier le Danois![36] He was so big at birth that, as was traditional, he suffocated his mother, but no fewer than six fairies took over his education and gave him, at midnight on his first day, all the moral and physical qualities required in a knight. The first gave him bravery, the second an endless supply of battles in which to exercise it; lest this seem risky, the third fairy made amends with her gift, invincibility. The fourth made him 'beau, doux et gracieux plus que nul autre', the fifth, like the second *mutatis mutandis*, gave him an endless supply of ladies on whom to exercise his charms. The last fairy, rather self-interestedly — but as a plot-device — granted 'qu'il ne meure jamais — jusques à ce qu'il ayt esté mon amy par amours' (f. a, ii^v). Thus Ogier is fully equipped for life as a knight by the time he is one day old.

There is a similar scenario in the most popular of all romances, *Amadis de Gaule*,[37] whose guardian sorceress, Urgande La Descogneue, like-wise grants the hero the twin gifts of success on the battlefield and in the boudoir. But we do get an account of Amadis's training, which sounds remarkably like that of François Ier. Once he has been rescued (rather like Gulliver escaping from Brobdingnag) from a box adrift at sea, Amadis spends six years at the unlikely court of King Languines of Scotland, 'et si n'avoit passetemps pour lors qu'à tirer de l'arc, nourrir chiens, ou aller à la chasse' (f. XII^r); his long-lost brother is similarly trained, by a kidnapping giant, 'à bien piquer d'estriers, escrimer, et faire tous actes [qui] convenoient à ung chevalier'(f. XXXVII^v).

Des Essarts, the translator, dedicated the book to François's son, Charles of Angoulême, emphasising the sheer 'passe temps et plaisir' to be found in its 'rencontres chevaleureuses' and 'infiniz propos d'amours' (Prologue, unpaginated). It was this mindless escapism that made *Amadis* a particular target of criticism later in the century. La Noue, in a famous chapter of his *Discours*, thundered against its seductive blend of impossible victories and adulterous liaisons, all spiced with magic; such stuff, together with its medieval predecessors, was more pernicious to the young than the reading of Machiavelli by the old.[38] Brantôme, no

---

[36] References are to the edition of A. Lotrian (Paris, *c.* 1530), BL 1074 k 5. For the bibliography of *Huon de Bordeaux* and *Ogier le Danois,* see G. Doutrepont, *Les Mises en prose des épopées et des romans chevaleresques du XIVe au XVIe siècle* (2nd ed., Brussels, 1969), pp. 139–45 and 168–76.

[37] References are to the first edition of the first book, translated by N. de Herberay des Essarts (Paris, 1540).

[38] François de La Noue, *Discours politiques et militaires*, edited by F. E. Sutcliffe (Geneva, 1967), VI, pp. 160–176. The preceding *Discours V* is, by contrast, La

stranger to spicy tales himself, nonetheless agreed about the immorality of *Amadis*. Montaigne included it among the useless 'fatras de livres' that he had been spared as a child, and René de Lucinge mocks his own youthful infatuation with 'cette fadaise'.[39]

Apparently *Amadis*, being pure entertainment and the most successful soap-opera of its time, has no redeeming features. But some of its predecessors do lay claim to moral respectability. The prologue to *Ogier le Danois*, for example, hopes piously that the book will 'donner exemple de vertueusement vivre en ce mortel monde ainsi que ont faict ceulx dequoy nostre matiere fera mention' (f. a, ii[r]). The text is full of familiar exemplary figures, such as odious flatterers, wise counsellors, and head-strong princes; Charlemagne has frequently to be restrained by virtuous and eloquent courtiers (e.g. f. a, v[r]). Ethically, it is a rather confusing mixture of the shame culture embodied by chivalry and the guilt culture enshrined in Christianity. For example, the pious young hero prays that God will not allow his own and his father's honour as knights to be besmirched (f. a, iv[v]), and a noble paladin with whom Ogier lodges recommends Christian humility, even quoting Psalm 119, as an aid to earthly advancement (f. a, vi[v]).

It is thus possible to extract from *Ogier* the rudiments of a moral system; more explicit and rather surprising is a passage about the upbringing of another of the fictional *pairs de France*, Huon de Bordeaux.[40] His mother (having — surprisingly — survived childbirth) raises Huon and his brother at home, despite the noble children's natural desire to go to learn chivalry at court. Finally she does send them to Charlemagne. But ringing in their ears is her advice, worth quoting at length because, remarkably, it echoes to the letter — but succinctly — much of the advice given by princes' pedagogues from Plutarch onwards:

> Accompaignez vous de tous nobles hommes que vous verrez bien condictionnez, ne soyez jamais en lieu où mauvaise parole soit dite ou mauvais conseil basty, fuyez la compagnie de gens qui n'ayment point honneur ne verité, n'ouvrez vos oreilles pour ouïr n'escouter menteurs, raporteurs ou flateurs, hantez souvent l'Eglise, et donnez pour Dieu

Noue's *Institution*, built, like those of Erasmus and Budé, around the apophthegms of Plutarch.

39 Brantôme is quoted by Sutcliffe in his edition of La Noue, p. 161, n. 2; Montaigne, *Essais*, I, xxvi and II, x; Lucinge, *La Maniere de lire l'histoire*, edited by M. J. Heath (Geneva, 1993), p. 67.

40 *Histoire de Huon de Bordeaux, pair de France et Duc de Guyenne*, edition of P. Rigaud (Lyon, 1611).

largement: soyez larges et courtois, donnez aux pauvres chevaliers, fuyez la
compagnie des jongleurs, et tous bien[s] vous en adviendront.

(p. 11)

Erasmus in a nutshell. But perhaps we should not be too surprised to
find these elements of moral guidance even in pulp fiction. We know that
the distinction between history and fiction was blurred.[41] Many
romances revolve around historical figures like Charlemagne or Roland;
perhaps the most remarkable is *Perceforest*, where Alexander the Great
rubs shoulders with the knights of the Round Table. No wonder they trip
over one another in Rabelais's Underworld (*Pantagruel* XXX)! But this
is not just a one-way process: historians took liberties too. Seyssel
remarks, for instance, that Xenophon's influential *Cyropaedia* describes
Cyrus's deeds 'non pas telles qu'elles furent à la vérité, mais telles
qu'elles doivent être en un sage roy et accompli' (p. 131). Similarly but
more recently, Bayard's *Loyal Serviteur* gave an account of his master
which may be considered 'faction' rather than biography. Fleurange's
account of François Ier's upbringing may belong in the same category.
For many contemporaries, no doubt, François himself was more like a
fictional stereotype than a man of flesh and blood.[42] Beyond mere
entertainment, tales of chivalry often claimed to inspire emulation, and
we are sometimes told — however unreliably — that they actually did, as
with Alexander and the *Iliad* under his pillow. For instance, the marquis
of Pescara, one of François Ier's most redoubtable foes, attributed his
extraordinary deeds of arms against the French to the inspiration of the
romances.[43] Again, Bayard's father brought him up on these tales, with
obvious results. But if that was sufficient to inflame his military ardour, it
is interesting that, according to the *Loyal Serviteur*, Bayard's *mother* sent
him to court with three pieces of ethical advice remarkably similar to that
given to Huon de Bordeaux:

La première, c'est que, devant toutes choses, vous aimiez, craigniez et serviez
Dieu, sans aucunement l'offenser, s'il vous est possible...La seconde, c'est
que vous soyez doux et courtois à tous gentilshommes, en ôtant de vous tout
orgueil. Soyez humble et serviable à toutes gens. Ne soyez médisant ni
menteur. Fuyez envie, car c'est un vilain vice. Ne soyez flatteur ni rapporteur,
car telles manières de gens ne viennent pas volontiers à grande perfection...
Soyez secourable à pauvres veuves et orphelins, et Dieu le vous récom-

---

[41] A wide-ranging recent study is P. G. Bietenholz, *Historia and Fabula: Myths
and Legends in Historical Thought from Antiquity to the Modern Age* (Leiden,
1994).

[42] See A.-M. Lecoq, *François Ier imaginaire: symbolique et politique à l'aube de la
Renaissance française* (Paris, 1987).

[43] See my edition of Lucinge, *La Maniere* (n. 39 above), p. 10.

pensera. La troisième que, des biens que Dieu vous donnera, vous soyez
charitable aux pauvres nécessiteux…[44]

The confusion of fiction and fact, of legend and history, hints at one
way of reconciling arms and letters, of being at the same time *le roi
chevalier* and *le père des lettres*. The most striking defence of chivalric
romance comes from René de Lucinge, quoted earlier only as a critic. In
La Maniere de lire l'histoire he admits that as a youth he could not get
enough of them, and he gives us a delightful glimpse of the errant
schoolboy:

> J'y estoy si fort acharné que j'y employoy les nuictz; j'en cachay les livres
> sous la couverte, de peur que le pedant ne me surprist, employant mal son
> uyle…
>
> (p. 66, variant)

But he also presents the romances, only partly in self-defence, as an
apprenticeship in the study of history proper, because they sharpen our
moral judgement and our critical faculties. Almost everyone agreed that
the most vital component in the education of the aristocrat was a
knowledge of history, however defined. But Lucinge found moral
edification even in *Amadis de Gaule*:

> Les loix de chevallerie…l'honneur et le support que les chevaliers doivent aux
> dames, le soulagement des oppressez, [tout ce] qui oblige [les princes] au
> respect, à la foy et à la loyauté, y sont merveilleusement bien depeincts.
>
> (p. 66)

Not merely depicted, but *bien depeincts*…Thus pleasure and profit are
mingled, and we may ask — only slightly tongue-in-cheek — whether
that is not a more memorable foundation for an apprenticeship in public
duties than the platitudes of the pedants, whether at Amboise or
Gordonstoun. It is worth remembering that that bloodthirsty tyrant
Alexander was taught by Aristotle, and the even bloodier Nero by
Seneca. Perhaps it was just as well that the humanist pedagogues do not
seem to have got very close to their sovereigns.

---

[44] *Histoire du gentil seigneur de Bayard, composée par le Loyal Serviteur*, edited
by L. Larchey (Paris, 1882), pp. 3 and 12 (the quotation).

4

Le Mythe de François Ier, de Clément Marot à André Thevet

Frank Lestringant

François Ier est d'ordinaire évoqué euphoriquement dans la période ascendante de son règne, qui correspond au temps de la cristallisation du mythe, lorsque se fixe le 'François Ier imaginaire' dont a parlé Anne-Marie Lecoq.[1] Je voudrais ici évoquer ce mythe au contraire sous le signe de la perte et de la mélancolie. Le mythe de François Ier n'est pas seulement prospectif, machine de propagande destinée à l'éblouissement des princes rivaux — Charles Quint ou Henri VIII — et à l'émerveillement des intellectuels dûment stipendiés par 'l'Apollon gaulois'. Il est aussi largement rétrospectif, entretenu bien après la décrépitude et la mort du roi, au temps des guerres de Religion, quand la confiance envers les souverains successifs s'est trahie et que, par contraste avec la situation présente, le long règne du fondateur de la branche des Valois-Angoulême apparaît comme une sorte d'âge d'or révolu.

Certes le souvenir que l'on garde de François Ier dans la seconde moitié du XVIe siècle est étrangement flou, même chez les intellectuels et les historiens qui devraient être pourtant les plus aptes à distinguer la suite des temps. L'éloge de François Ier repose invariablement chez les prosopographes sur le lieu commun de l'alliance, particulièrement réussie chez ce prince, des armes et des lettres — des armes, qui viennent en premier, et des lettres, qui illustrent et pérennisent celles-là. Fait chevalier sur le champ de bataille de Marignan 'par le Capitaine Bayard', il a mérité aussi, par sa munificence et sa générosité envers les bons esprits — à preuve les 'six mil francs' donnés à Pierre Gilles d'Albi pour acquérir des manuscrits au Levant — le titre envié de 'pere des lettres'. C'est ainsi qu'André Thevet, dans sa *Cosmographie univer-*

---

[1]   Anne-Marie Lecoq, *François Ier imaginaire: Symbolique et politique à l'aube de la Renaissance française* (Paris, Macula, 1987).

selle, puis dans les *Vrais Pourtraits et Vies des hommes illustres*, déclare sans grande originalité que 'ce Roy François a flory tant aux armes qu'aux lettres',[2] et qu'il 'n'a point esté seulement un Mars victorieux, ains aussi le Pere nourrissier et amateur des bonnes lettres'.[3] Ce Mars, sans doute, a connu de cinglants revers, comme en témoigne la désastreuse journée de Pavie, mais cette Providence des doctes n'a jamais failli.

Figure faste et tutélaire, que l'on crédite du renouveau intellectuel et artistique qui accompagne l'essor de la Renaissance en France, François Ier est tiré par chacun des deux camps en sa faveur. Les catholiques comme Belleforest ou Thevet voient en lui, non sans quelque raison, un adversaire résolu de l'hérésie de Luther, laquelle, de son temps, 'commença d'entrer en France'. Et presque aussi heureux que Panurge, envié et révéré, comme l'on sait, des Papimanes, pour avoir successivement vu trois Souverains Pontifes,[4] le roi François

en personne veit deux Papes, l'un à Marseille, et l'autre à Nice, pour avec eux conferer du moyen qu'il y avoit de remettre l'Eglise Chrestienne en son premier honneur, et faire revenir à icelle ceux, qui imbuz d'heretiques opinions s'en estoient distraits.[5]

Autre son de cloche du côté protestant: Théodore de Bèze, dans ses *Vrais Pourtraits des hommes illustres en pieté et doctrine* (1581) rallie François d'Angoulême au combat réformé, le plaçant avec sa sœur, la pieuse Marguerite, en tête de la cohorte des théologiens et des martyrs qui ont permis en France le renouveau de l'Évangile. Marguerite d'Alençon, reine de Navarre, joue un peu le rôle de truchement ou de chaînon manquant dans cette annexion pour le moins forcée à la Cause.[6] Certes l'on ne cache pas au lecteur protestant que François Ier a été un 'adversaire de la pure doctrine'. Mais par le soutien constant

---

2   André Thevet, *La Cosmographie universelle* (Paris, L'Huillier et Chaudière, 1575), f. 625^v.

3   André Thevet, *Les Vrais Pourtraits et Vies des hommes illustres* (Paris, veuve J. Kerver et G. Chaudière, 1584), livre IV, ch. 6, f. 210^v.

4   Rabelais, *Quart Livre*, ch. 48, édition G. Demerson des *Œuvres complètes* (Paris, Le Seuil, 1973), p. 709: 'Ouy, ouy (respondit Panurge), ouy dea, messieurs, j'en ay veu troys, à la veue desquelz je n'ay gueres profité.'

5   A. Thevet, *La Cosmographie universelle*, loc. cit.

6   Théodore de Bèze, *Les Vrais Pourtraits des hommes illustres en pieté et doctrine* (Paris, Jean de Laon, 1581; rééd. Genève, Slatkine, 1986), pp. 132–3: 'François, Premier de ce nom, Roy de France'; pp. 134–5: 'Marguerite de Valois, sœur du Roy François Premier, et Roine de Navarre'.

qu'il a apporté aux humanités, il doit être considéré comme un allié objectif de la Réforme. Ce Prince, en effet, mérite d'être loué, d'autant qu'il a remis 'en honneur les langues Hebraique, Grecque, Latine, et les bonnes sciences, pour estre les portieres du temple de la vraye Religion', et qu'il a 'chassé l'ignorance laquelle empeschoit la verité de venir en avant'.[7] On pense à l'allégorie du Rosso ornant la Galerie François Iᵉʳ de Fontainebleau et montrant le roi en empereur romain, armé du glaive et du livre, entrant dans le temple de Jupiter Capitolin illuminé, après avoir terrassé les monstres de l'ignorance qui tâtonnent et titubent dans l'ombre, les yeux bandés.[8] Dans le détournement habile proposé par Théodore de Bèze, la Réforme rend ici un magnifique hommage à l'humanisme, dont elle retrouve un instant l'esprit.

On comprend du reste la logique d'une telle récupération: la Cause réformée n'est pas seulement spirituelle, elle est aussi temporelle. Elle a besoin, pour être autorisée dans le siècle, de cette figure paternelle qui retient encore quelque chose de la sacralité de l'onction et vient confirmer parmi les hommes le juste choix de Dieu. Monarque héréditaire, François Iᵉʳ n'en est pas moins l'Oint du Seigneur. Il a reçu d'en haut cette grâce et cette élection qui en font le guide providentiel de son peuple, le bon berger, le nouveau Christ. Déjà chez Marot, dans les derniers vers de *L'Enfer*, le roi François, de retour de la captivité de Madrid, est appelé à descendre dans les abîmes du Châtelet, s'identifiant au Christ venu libérer les âmes des justes enfermées dans les Limbes:

> Car ta prison liberté lui seroit,
> Et comme Christ, les Ames pousseroit
> Hors des Enfers, sans t'en laisser une ombre.[9]

C'est en ces termes que, plein de foi et d'espérance, le prisonnier s'adresse au Juge d'Enfer, le rébarbatif Rhadamantus.

On voit par là le rôle dévolu au mythe de François Iᵉʳ dans son usage rétrospectif. Il fonde en droit et en autorité une origine. Il la rapporte à un temps historique proche encore, mais irréversiblement perdu, et dont les vivants, dans la conscience aiguë et douloureuse de la tragédie présente, sont mélancoliquement séparés.

---

[7] Théodore de Bèze, op. cit., p. 133.
[8] Pour la signification allégorique de cette fresque (VII Sud), voir Françoise Joukovsky, 'L'Empire et les barbares dans la Galerie François Iᵉʳ', *Bibliothèque d'Humanisme et Renaissance*, L (1988), 7–28, et notamment pp. 22–5.
[9] Clément Marot, *L'Enfer*, vv. 441–3. Voir mon édition de *L'Adolescence clémentine* (Paris, Gallimard, 'Poésie', 1987), p. 382, note 49.

Le même flou onirique enveloppe la place de François Ier dans l'histoire des lettres en France. Il suffit de rappeler le 'rolle' — la liste — qu'Agrippa d'Aubigné dans l'une de ses épîtres dresse 'des Poëtes de son temps'. Tout commence avec 'le Roy François'. 'Tout ce qui a escript en France auparavant' mérite de sombrer dans l'oubli, en raison de 'leur barbare grosserie'.[10] Ni Alain Chartier, jadis pourtant estimé d'une Reine de France, ni le *Roman de la Rose*, dont quelques modernes prétendent tirer 'de belles et doctes inventions', ne valent la peine qu'on les exempte de l'opprobre général. Rien que d'attendu dans cette condamnation par la Renaissance à son déclin des ténèbres qui l'ont précédée. La surprise vient ensuite, de ce que d'Aubigné embrasse dans 'la premiere bande' des poètes français, qui a fleuri 'de la fin du Roy François et du regne de Henry second', des talents aussi divers que Du Bellay, Salel, L'Hospital, poète néo-latin, Jodelle, Baïf, Scève, Marot, et Théodore de Bèze, disciple du précédent. Cette troupe est regroupée sous la guide paternelle de 'M. de Ronsard que j'ay cogneu privement',[11] chef de la bande qui a 'battu' le chemin des lettres nouvelles.

Guère moins déroutant est le jugement porté par Du Bartas dans *La Seconde Semaine*, au *Second Jour*, dans le livre consacré à 'Babylone' et à la multiplication des langues à partir de Babel. Point de départ du renouveau littéraire en France, Marot revêt les traits d'un grand ancêtre un peu décati. L'alerte Quercinois est à proprement parler devenu une ruine:

> Marot que je revere ainsi qu'un Colisée
> Noircy, brisé, moussu: une medaille usée:
> Un escorné tombeau, non tant pour la beauté
> Que pour le sainct respect de leur antiquité.[12]

Singulière hyperbole, à mille lieues de la pochade trop fameuse de Boileau, et qui confère au Virgile français, comme lui nommé *Maro*, le poids, l'autorité et le respect sacré et vaguement terrifiant dû aux monuments enfouis, aux inscriptions illisibles!

---

[10] Agrippa d'Aubigné, 'Lettres sur diverses sciences', XI, in *Œuvres*, éd. H. Weber (Paris, Gallimard, 'Pléiade', 1969), p. 859.

[11] Ibidem, p. 860.

[12] Guillaume de Saluste Du Bartas, *La Seconde Semaine* (1584), *Second Jour*, livre VI: 'Babylone', vv. 653–6. Édition Y. Bellenger *et al.* (Paris, STFM, 1992), t. II, p. 358.

Le comble est sans nul doute atteint avec André Thevet. Dans un chapitre d'histoire littéraire de la *Cosmographie universelle*, ce dernier date 'du temps de François premier, restaurateur des bonnes lettres (duquel temps y a eu une belle vollée d'hommes sçavans en toutes sciences, comme Grec, Latin et Hebreu)', 'Alain Chartier et Jean de Meun, qui ont escrit de beaux livres'. Molinet, Octovien de Saint-Gelais, 'Jean Marot, qui a escrit le voyage de Loys douzieme à Genes: et puis Clement Marot son fils qui eut l'esprit poëtique de son pere' sont alignés d'une seule venue. [13] Thevet se serait-il laissé abuser par l'édition donnée par Marot du *Roman de la Rose,* [14] œuvre qu'admirait de toute évidence le Quercinois et qu'il a butinée non seulement dans le *Temple de Cupido*, mais jusque dans la Chanson VII [15] et dans *L'Enfer*? Toujours est-il que François Iᵉʳ, souverain mythique, entraîne tout le passé littéraire de la France dans son aura. C'est là une origine absolue, parce qu'elle englobe tout ce qui l'a précédée.

À vrai dire, la confusion de Thevet trahit une certaine ambiguïté de sens et d'intention. Faire de Jean de Meun le contemporain de Molinet et de Marot qui l'ont adapté et publié, mais aussi de l'humaniste Guillaume Budé, et l'un des poètes représentatifs du règne de François Iᵉʳ, ne revient-il pas à rejeter ce dernier dans un passé lointain et quelque peu obscur? L'Apollon gaulois apparaît moins alors comme un rénovateur ou un initiateur que comme la figure de synthèse de la culture nationale, le résumé complet d'un passé glorieux sans doute, mais auquel le présent peut-être n'est pas inférieur. Figure récapitulative d'un âge antérieur, François d'Angoulême appartient de toute évidence à un monde disparu.

De ces quelques témoignages du mythe de François Iᵉʳ au déclin du siècle, on peut conclure à une révérence pour le moins ambiguë envers l'illustre fondateur d'une dynastie bientôt éteinte. Comme le Colisée marotique évoqué par Du Bartas sur le ton épique — image si étrangement inappropriée qu'elle ne saurait être le fruit du simple hasard — le chef de la dynastie est renvoyé à l'univers des antiquités de Rome et des regrets humanistes.

Mais ce François Iᵉʳ monumental n'est pas pour autant figé ou intouchable. La matière mythique dont il est composé est malléable,

---

13 André Thevet, *La Cosmographie universelle*, op. cit., f. 642ʳ.

14 *Le Roman de la Rose, dans la version attribuée à Clément Marot (1526)*, publié par Silvio F. Baridon, 2 vols (Milan–Varèse, Istituto Editoriale Cisalpino, 1957).

15 Clément Marot, Chanson VII, in *L'Adolescence clémentine*, éd. cit., p. 223.

susceptible d'adaptations et de bricolages. J'ai mentionné en passant la tentative de récupération orchestrée par Théodore de Bèze pour le parti protestant. Plus subtil peut-être, car plongeant dans les tréfonds d'une histoire personnelle et d'une enfance commune, je voudrais évoquer à présent le cas d'André Thevet, dont on a seulement pu apprécier jusqu'ici la culture littéraire toute personnelle.

Il faudrait parler à cet égard d'un François Iᵉʳ imaginaire au second degré, l'image reconstituée se situant au point d'intersection de l'imaginaire royal officiel et d'un imaginaire personnel, celui d'André Thevet, cosmographe des derniers Valois, que le hasard ou plutôt la Providence a fait naître en 1516 à Angoulême, le berceau de la dynastie qui règne depuis lors sur la France. De cette coïncidence heureuse, Thevet va tirer un profit symbolique, en détournant à lui le prestige qui émane de la ville d'apanage, qui est en même temps sa petite patrie. Dès lors ce qui peut apparaître comme autant de marques d'un chauvinisme indiscret et le plus souvent déplacé tend à souligner, de lieu en lieu, une allégeance et à rappeler le lien originel qui unit le cosmographe courtisan à la famille régnante.[16]

Les protestations de fidélité envers le site nourricier se multiplient tout au long de la volumineuse *Cosmographie universelle* de 1575, surgissant dans les contextes les plus inattendus. Au cœur d'une description de l'Afrique et de l'Asie, se profile, par une sorte de réminiscence tenace, la silhouette escarpée de l'acropole natale, ceinte de remparts et assiégée. À l'orgueilleuse 'tour de Babylone', confondue avec Babel, se superposent 'les murailles d'Angoulesme, lieu de ma naissance', qui, à l'exemple de la cité antique, 'furent abattues miraculeusement, lors que le Roy Clovis en approchant, luy voulut donner l'assaut'.[17] Dévêtue soudain du tour de ses remparts, la nouvelle Jéricho s'offre à son conquérant et se donne à son roi, le fondateur de la monarchie des Francs, scellant ainsi l'alliance qu'a depuis confirmée le surgeon royal des Valois–Angoulême. Babel ou Jéricho, qu'importe au

---

[16] Je m'inspire librement, à partir d'ici, d'une étude naguère esquissée sous le titre: 'La Ville d'Angoulême et ses métamorphoses dans l'œuvre du cosmographe André Thevet', *Mémoires de la Société archéologique et historique de la Charente* (1977–8), 29–50. Pour la biographie de Thevet, je renvoie une fois pour toutes à mon livre: *André Thevet, cosmographe des derniers Valois* (Genève, Droz, 1991). Voir en particulier le chapitre Iᵉʳ, pp. 19–32.

[17] A. Thevet, *La Cosmographie universelle,* op. cit., t. I, livre X, ch. XII, f. 354ʳ. L'anecdote touchant la ruine miraculeuse des remparts d'Angoulême à l'époque de Clovis est rapportée une seconde fois plus en détail dans le même ouvrage, t. II, livre XIII, ch. V, f. 519 ᵛ.

demeurant: Angoulême, de toute évidence, est à la hauteur des cités légendaires de l'Ancien Testament. C'est aussi, comme on verra, la clef de la Terre promise.

Par une métaphore continuellement reconduite — en prenant le mot dans son sens étymologique de déplacement — la patrie d'Angoulême va s'adapter tour à tour aux lieux les plus divers, de la Babylone asiatique à tel promontoire écarté du Nouveau Monde. Rien d'étonnant à ce qu'apparaisse en Nouvelle-France un lac d'Angoulême traversé par le Saint-Laurent,[18] un Promontoire d'Angoulesme à la place de la baie de New York,[19] ou qu'un 'Mont Angoumoisin' se dresse sous l'équateur au large des côtes du Brésil.[20] Le toponyme migrateur combine de la sorte l'ancrage immobile à un lieu de référence et le déplacement inhérent à toute entreprise de description du monde. Réaffirmant constamment son lien à Angoulême, Thevet ne cesse néanmoins de se déplacer, et sa ville natale l'accompagne en des circumnavigations qui décrivent la totalité du champ des connaissances. Au terme, la petite patrie est devenue universelle comme la cosmographie elle-même.

Les Cygnes de la Touvre

Dans la *Cosmographie de Levant*, le pèlerin, parvenu après maintes avanies au Saint-Sépulcre de Jérusalem, ne sait en comparer la basilique romane qu'à la cathédrale Saint-Pierre d'Angoulême, pareillement voû-

---

18 A. Thevet, *La Cosmographie universelle*, II, f. 1011ᵛ. Cette appellation remonte au deuxième voyage de Jacques Cartier en 1535–6.

19 A. Thevet, *La Cosmographie universelle*, II, f. 1009ᵛ. Ce toponyme vient du voyage de reconnaissance de Giovanni da Verrazano en 1524, mais Thevet en détourne la nomination à son profit. Voir sur ce point mon article 'La Ville d'Angoulême et ses métamorphoses...', art. cit., pp. 42–6.

20 A. Thevet, *Le Grand Insulaire et pilotage*, t. I, MS fr. 15452, f. 206ʳ. Il est question de l''Isle des Rats': 'Ceste Isle gist à quatre degrés de latitude, et trois cens trente six de longitude..., elle est montaigneuse en quelques endroits, entre autres de la part du Sud, là où se voit au bord de la marine une asses haute montaigne, faite quasi en pyramide, laquelle est peuplée d'arbrisseaux. Je l'ay monté avec grand peine, a cause des incommodités, qui y sont, et y ay compté deux nuicts, pour contenter mon esprit. Je la nommie [*sic*] le Mont Angoumoisin. C'est de ceste montaigne, que je vis les estoiles, qui sont proches du cercle Arctique....'

tée 'et quasi de la [même] grandeur'.[21] En fin de parcours, le voyage renoue avec son origine, et le tombeau du Christ, terme de la série d'épreuves qualifiantes affrontées par le cordelier, le ramène, touchant à peine au but, à l'ombre des tours de sa ville natale, dans son couvent.

Un peu plus tard au cours de son périple levantin, et alors que s'amorce la volte du retour, l'excursion à un abîme naturel près d'Antioche devient le prétexte à un éloge pour le moins chauvin de la Touvre, 'environné[e] d'un territoire le plus beau et le plus amene qui soit au demourant du monde'.[22] Emporté par une euphorie toute patriotique, Thevet n'hésite pas à comparer ensuite les crues bénéfiques de la Charente à celles d''un second Nil'. Et la même rivière se voit élevée à la dignité du Jourdain, puisque, à l'instar du fleuve béni, elle procède de deux fontaines réunies en un seul cours, le Charannat et la Touvre, elle-même résultant de la Tardoire et du Bandiat. En conséquence, l'Angoumois est assimilé tour à tour à la féconde Égypte et à la Terre promise des Hébreux.

Le *locus amoenus* de la patrie lointaine, que Thevet préfère au paysage somme toute aride du Levant et à ses rivières par comparaison peu poissonneuses, s'ouvre enfin sur le spectacle — souvenir personnel ou incrustation topique — de deux cygnes se battant jusqu'à la mort, mais bientôt réconciliés par quatre de leurs congénères accourus. Cette scène édifiante, que le narrateur qualifie de 'prodige', se déroula sous les fenêtres de Monsieur de Hauteclaire, maître des requêtes du roi, dont Thevet était sans doute l'hôte. Insérée dans la pérégrination orientale, l'évocation idyllique de la fontaine de Touvre, séjour apprécié du Roi et des Grands, se rattache à une féconde lignée poétique, dont les illustrations vont de Clément Marot au père François Garasse, en passant par Ronsard et Belleforest.[23] La page de Thevet eut des lecteurs attentifs autant qu'attendris en François de Corlieu, l'historien d'Angoulême,[24] et en Étienne Pasquier, dont une lettre, datant du début

---

21 A. Thevet, *Cosmographie de Levant* (Lyon, J. de Tournes et G. Gazeau, 1554 et 1556; rééd. par F. Lestringant, Genève, Droz, 1985), ch. XLVIII, p. 175. Voir ma note 175, 4 sur ce passage.

22 A. Thevet, op. cit., ch. LII, pp. 191–2.

23 Sur le mythe poétique de la Touvre au XVIᵉ siècle, voir Pierre Du Chambon, *Les Cygnes de la Touvre. Avec les ornements d'Abel Brunyer* (Ruffec, Dubois éditeur, 1928), pp. 12 sqq.

24 François de Corlieu, *Recueil en forme d'histoire de ce qui se trouve par escrit, de la ville et des comtes d'Engolesme, party en trois livres* (Angoulême, Jean de Minieres, 1576), I, 1: 'André Thevet, cosmographe du roy, homme de singulier

des années 1590, célèbre la rivière 'pavée de truites, tapissée de cygnes et bordée d'escrevisses'. [25] Amplifiant le tableau déjà hyperbolique de la *Cosmographie de Levant*, Pasquier égale à nouveau la Charente au Nil, et l'Angoumois, dont les productions agricoles sont énumérées, à un Paradis terrestre qui ignorerait 'le fruict de science qui perdit Adam'.

Bien plus, la Charente réunit à présent en elle les quatre fleuves du Paradis: 'Ceste grande riviere incogneue, qui passoit au travers de l'ancien paradis terrestre, s'est transformée en celle de la Charente, laquelle depuis la ville d'Angoulesme jusques à S. Savinien, où elle va fondre en la mer, est bordée de prez'. [26] À la différence de la 'malgisante Loire', la Charente ne déborde que 'pour le profit du païs', ainsi que le Nil en Égypte. Dans cette lettre du temps des guerres civiles qui s'attardent — Pasquier a échappé non sans peine aux soldats de la Ligue qui tiennent le plat pays — le magistrat entasse à plaisir les références les plus diverses qui signifient l'abondance et la prospérité, manière de faire étalage de sa culture érudite, mais aussi de conjurer, par l'accumulation de citations euphoriques, le désastre persistant du présent. Sans doute avec Pasquier, le mythe de l'Angoumois, lequel, plus que la Touvre, mérite le titre de 'jardin de la France', tend-il au florilège savant: l'Éden, l'Égypte, la Campanie, et Capoue sont résumés et confondus dans ce microcosme béni des dieux. Mais le mythe garde quelque chose de sa fécondité originelle, si efficace et si profuse qu'on en arrive à

---

entendement, raconte une histoire memorable de deux cygnes de la Touvre que je ne repeteray point icy.'

25 Étienne Pasquier, *Lettres*, livre XIV, lettre VII, éd. D. Thickett des *Lettres familières* (Genève, Droz, TLF, 1974), p. 218. La formule, proverbiale au moins depuis Marot, comme on verra plus loin à la note 27, se rencontre également dans *Les Discours non plus melancoliques que divers, de choses qui appartiennent a notre FRANCE: et a la fin la maniere de bien et justement entoucher les Lucs et Guiternes* (Poitiers, Enguilbert de Marnef, 1556; émission en 1557: BN, Z. 7143), ch. 20, p. 89: 'et vous diront les Engoumoisins de la beauté d'icelle et fertilité, que c'est la riviere couverte de Cygnes, pavee de Truites, et bordee d'Anguilles et Escrevisses.' Ce chapitre, inséré dans un recueil composite, qui est une fabrication du libraire E. de Marnef, a pour auteur probable Élie Vinet, et se retrouve, avec quelques variantes, sous la forme d'une publication séparée ayant pour titre *Engoulesme* et pour sous-titre *De la Touvre, et quelques autres rivieres d'Engoumois, et d'un sepulchre na-gueres trouvé soubs terre audit païs* (Poitiers, E. de Marnef, 1567; BN, Rés. 4° Lk7-23518 -2). Pour la bibliographie d'Élie Vinet, on se reportera à Louis Desgraves, *Élie Vinet humaniste de Bordeaux (1509–1587)* (Genève, Droz, 1977), p. 53, notices 11 et 14.

26 Étienne Pasquier, ibidem.

oublier que les abords de la Touvre ont été saccagés, le 'pavé de Truitte' réellement détruit, comme le prophétisait sans le savoir Clément Marot dans l'*Eglogue sur le trespas de Loyse de Savoye* (1531),[27] et les cygnes massacrés et mangés par les reîtres noirs lors de la troisième guerre de Religion (1568).

Tel que le dessine la *Cosmographie de Levant* de Thevet, le mythe d'Angoulême comporte toutefois sa part de menaces. Dans la proximité immédiate de la Touvre s'étend 'l'espouventable' forêt de Braconne, peuplée de monstres mi-hommes mi-bêtes, ces 'anthropithiriens inophiles' que Thevet répute 'ennemis de toutes sciences' et qui, méprisant la vertu et 'bonne doctrine', mènent une 'vraye vie bacchanale'.[28] S'agit-il là, comme le veut un lecteur de Thevet, d'une communauté de moines débauchés, sacrifiant à leur ventre plutôt qu'à Dieu et méritant l'épithète d''inophiles' en raison d'un amour immodéré de la boisson?[29] Toujours est-il que l'Angoumois imaginaire du cosmographe est structuré par le fort contraste régnant entre le jardin protégé des abords de la Touvre, berceau sacré des divins cygnes, et la forêt sauvage ouverte aux maléfices et aux plus noires turpitudes.

L'antithèse formée par les oiseaux d'Apollon, messagers de concorde et symbole de pur amour, et les 'ordures' qui peuplent la forêt ténébreuse, se trouve illustrée ensuite dans l'histoire d'Angoulême. L'Éden précaire de la Touvre sera violé, ses hôtes célestes tués, comme nous l'apprennent les témoignages convergents de Thevet, Belleforest, et François de Corlieu, postérieurs aux premières guerres de Religion.[30]

---

[27] Clément Marot, 'Eglogue sur le trespas de ma Dame Loyse de Savoye, mere du Roy Françoys, Premier de ce nom' (1531), vv. 163–4, in *Œuvres poétiques* de Clément Marot, éd. Gérard Defaux (Paris, Bordas, 'Classiques Garnier', 1990), t. I, p. 228:

> La pauvre Touvre arrousant Angolesme
> A son pavé de Truites tout destruict.

Pour le commentaire de ces vers, cf. Pauline M. Smith, 'Marot et la Touvre (Eglogue I)', *Bibliothèque d'Humanisme et Renaissance*, XLIX (1987), 367–9.

[28] A. Thevet, *Cosmographie de Levant*, op. cit., ch. LII, p. 192.

[29] Note marginale d'un certain 'Les Fossez' sur l'exemplaire de la Bibliothèque nationale de Paris (Rés. G. 1037). La mauvaise réputation de Braconne s'est poursuivie au-delà de Thevet, renforcée par le crime de François Ravaillac, le régicide, qui était originaire de Touvre. Voir notamment le roman d'Ardouin-Dumazet, *Les Brigands de Braconne*, (rééd., Ruelle (Charente), Université populaire de Ruelle, 1984).

[30] Thevet, *Cosmographie universelle*, t. II, livre XVI, ch. 6, f. 660ᵛ, à propos d'une province de l'Écosse: 'La ville principale est Elghen, pres d'un Lac appellé l'Espine, tout chargé de Cygnes, comme nagueres estoit la Touvre

À vrai dire, cette dystopie est déjà inscrite dans l'*Eglogue* déplorative de Clément Marot. L'idylle est menacée, le vert paradis d'Angoulême enténébré par la mort qui rôde et vient frapper la 'Bergère' éponyme, la duchesse d'Angoulême. À cette idylle détruite, au pavé disjoint des truites de la Touvre, la Corneille, le Corbeau, et la comète ('l'Estoille à la grand queue') apportent bientôt une funèbre confirmation. Mais pour finir, la promesse des 'champs Elisiens' retourne cette vision funeste en son envers radieux.[31] Le diptyque se referme alors sur le Printemps éternel promis aux âmes élues.

On observe ainsi une sorte d'échange entre le mythe et la réalité, entre la création littéraire et les bouleversements de l'Histoire. La Touvre est visitée par la cour en voyage qui pique-nique sur ses bords un beau jour du mois d'août 1565: c'est l'une des étapes les plus sereines du tour de France royal de Charles IX et de Catherine de Médicis. Le roi 'se feit amener devant luy bien huict ou neuf vingt Cignes tout en une troupe'.[32] On prend les truites à pleines nasses pour les porter sur la table royale. Trois ans plus tard, l'oasis heureuse est devenue le symbole du désastre national.

La Dépouille du comte Jean

Angoulême au XVIe siècle connaît une fortune inopinée, suivie d'une décadence sans retour. Le contraste géographique se transporte à l'histoire, opposant le temps des commencements, après l'avènement

---

d'Angoulesme'; François de Belleforest, *La Cosmographie universelle de tout le monde* (Paris, Chesneau et Sonnius, 1575), I, col. 193: '[cet] abisme admirable du Touvre, qui a sa largeur plus grande que le Charente..., couverte jadis de Cignes (ainsi que j'ay veu) et (comme l'on dit) pavée de Truites, des meilleures, et mieux saulmonées qui se mangent en France'; François de Corlieu, *Recueil en forme d'histoire...*, op. cit., 1576, I, 1: 'Ce fleuve de Touvre est celebré par nos poëtes françois pour sa beauté, et un infiny nombre de cygnes que les comtes d'Angoulesme y avoient d'ancienneté affranchy, deputans officiers pour la garde et entretenement d'iceux, chose qui estoit grandement belle à voir: mais à present la race en est perdue pour l'injure des guerres.'

31 Clément Marot, 'Eglogue...', v. 191, op. cit., p. 229.

32 Abel Jouan, *Recueil et Discours du Voyage du Roy Charles IX. de ce nom à present regnant, accompagné des choses dignes de memoire faictes en chacun endroit...* (Paris, pour Jean Bonfons, 1566), f. 55r, à la date du 16 août 1565. cf. Jean Boutier, Alain Dewerpe, et Daniel Nordman, *Un Tour de France royal: le voyage de Charles IX (1564–1566)* (Paris, Aubier, 1984), ch. X.

inespéré, le premier janvier 1515, de François d'Angoulême à la couronne de France, à l'époque funeste des guerres civiles, lorsque la cité est disputée par des adversaires également incapables de s'assurer une victoire définitive. Deux fois assiégée et prise d'assaut, en 1562 et en 1568, deux fois saccagée par les troupes huguenotes, la ville ducale verra non seulement ses murailles abattues — accident fréquent, au dire de Thevet — mais ses églises profanées, ses couvents violés, les moines et prêtres pendus, émasculés, ou jetés dans les puits et par-dessus les remparts. Thevet rappelle à ce propos que 'plusieurs de [ses] amis, parents et alliez y ont les premiers passé le pas'. Et de filer le parallèle avec 'les Canibales, ou Margageas' du Brésil tropical, 'la felonnie desquels je vous ay autrefois fait imprimer en l'histoire de mes Singularitez de la France Antarctique'.[33]

Le pire est que la cité est détruite jusque dans ses fondations symboliques. La profanation des tombeaux de la cathédrale Saint-Pierre, dont certains étaient révérés par le populaire, brise le lien sacré qui unit la cité à ses origines mythiques. Non seulement la soldatesque huguenote s'en prend aux 'corps saincts canonisez', détestables reliques favorisant l'idolâtrie des foules, mais dans sa rage cathartique et par haine de toute image, elle traite avec la même férocité les tombes des

---

[33] A. Thevet, *La Cosmographie universelle*, op. cit., f. 519ᵛ. Et plus haut: 'Au surplus, je ne pense point, que jamais ceste ville souffrit plus de persecutions, ne fut son païs voisin plus abandonné, du temps des Goths, Ostrogoths, et Vvandales, voire des Romains et des Anglois, qu'il a esté l'an de grace mil cinq cens soixante huict, lors qu'elle fut assiegee des Huguenots, ny qu'il s'y fist jamais plus de cruautez, tant envers les Prestres, Moynes, Nonnains, que autres Catholiques: jusques à brusler et demolir les Temples, et desenterrer les corps saincts canonisez, et autres bons personnages morts de mon temps. Car qu'ainsi soit, il resta bien peu desdits Moynes et Prestres, qui ne fussent pendus, les autres eurent les parties honteuses coupees, autres jettez dans les privez, dans les puits, et precipitez et culbutez du hault en bas des murailles de la ville, apres avoir long temps esté tenuz en une extreme langueur: et, qui plus est, lors qu'on exerçoit telles miseres, chacun crioit à haute voix (j'entens ceux qui homicidoient) Vive, Vive, Vive l'Evangile: n'y ayant composition et accord, signé tant d'une part que d'autre, pour la reddition de la ville, qui empeschast tels massacres et voleries....' À l'époque de la séparation de l'Église et de l'État, les déportements des troupes huguenotes lors du siège de 1568 connurent une nouvelle publicité, comme l'atteste l'ouvrage de l'abbé Louis Fourgeaud, *Origine et introduction du protestantisme en Angoumois: séjour de Calvin à Angoulême, son influence et ses résultats, ravages des protestants* (Angoulême, 1909). Le propos est affiché d'emblée: 'Je vais raconter le séjour de Calvin en Angoumois et montrer combien fut déplorable l'influence qu'il exerça dans notre région.'

grands ancêtres. C'est ainsi que le cadavre du comte Jean, mort en odeur de sainteté, et devenu après sa mort l'objet d'un culte officieux, est exhumé et décapité en 1562, 'desmembré et mis en pieces' six ans plus tard. Est alors détruite l'efficace d'un corps qui produisit après sa mort plusieurs miracles, 'soulageant les femmes en leurs accouchementz et faisant concevoir les steriles', ainsi que le rapporte Jean du Port dans son essai d'hagiographie.[34] Or le comte Jean, qui, après Azincourt, fut détenu en Angleterre trente-deux ans comme otage, n'était pas seulement un héros national. C'était 'le grand homme de la famille',[35] 'un autre saint Louis', dont l'aura sacrée était appelée à rejaillir sur toute la dynastie.[36] Ce personnage de sainte vie, vêtu 'de drap commun, couleur de cendre', sauf aux fêtes solennelles,[37] multipliait les aumônes, édifiait, à son retour de captivité, par sa volonté d'apaisement et mourut au château de Cognac, là même où devait naître plus tard son petit-fils François. Dès 1515 et jusqu'en 1523, date de la mort de l'évêque d'Angoulême, la famille royale tenta d'obtenir du pape la canonisation. C'est enfin du comte Jean que vint la salamandre, promue emblème royal, avec la fortune que l'on sait.

Le plus grave aux yeux de Thevet, qui ne s'arrête guère aux croyances d'un vain peuple, c'est qu'en dispersant les restes du comte Jean, les huguenots, 'mal affectionnés à la race des Valois', ont voulu en abolir 'le sacré tige'.[38] Par-delà le crime de lèse-majesté et l'atteinte portée à 'l'Apollon gaulois', Thevet dénonce dans ces 'vieillaqueries'[39] une entreprise délibérée d'effacement des origines. C'est aussi le mythe d'Angoulême qui est menacé par un tel sacrilège. La cité éponyme a perdu son palladium, et la dynastie régnante s'en trouve du même coup

---

34 Jean du Port, *La Vie de tres-illustre et vertueux Prince, Jean Conte d'Angoulesme, aïeul du grand Roy François, dediée à Monseigneur le Duc d'Espernon, Par Jean du Port, sieur des Rosiers, Conseiller du Roy en la Seneschaucée et siege Presidial d'Angoulmoys* (Angoulême, Olivier de Minieres, 1589), p. 151. Dans une perspective plus politique qu'hagiographique, cf. Jean Papire Masson, *La Vie de tres-illustre Prince Jean Comte d'Angoulesme et de Perigueux, yssu de la Maison Royale de France, mise de Latin en François* [par I. Masson] *et dediée au tres-chrestien Roy de France et de Navarre Louys XIII* (Paris, Guillaume Marette, 1613). Le démembrement de la dépouille par les huguenots est longuement narré aux pages 13–17.

35 Anne-Marie Lecoq, *François Iᵉʳ imaginaire*, op. cit., p. 40.

36 Anne-Marie Lecoq, op. cit., p. 112.

37 Jean Papire Masson, op. cit., p. 12.

38 Thevet, *La Cosmographie universelle*, II, f. 521ʳ; *Les Vrais Pourtraits*, II, livre IV, ch. 30, f. 303ʳ. Le mot 'tige' est du masculin au XVIᵉ siècle.

39 Thevet, *Vrais Pourtraits*, f. 303ᵛ.

frappée dans son principe. En 1587 le célèbre *Theatre des Cruautez des heretiques de nostre temps*, ouvrage de propagande catholique sorti des presses de Plantin à Anvers, consacre aux malheurs d'Angoulême, de son clergé, et de sa cathédrale, pas moins de six planches sur un ensemble de trente. [40] Au passage, la profanation de la tombe du comte Jean est mentionnée avec horreur et rapprochée du sort analogue réservé à la dépouille de Louis XI exhumée de la sépulture de Notre-Dame de Cléry près d'Orléans.

Entraîné par cette déconfiture symbolique, Thevet perd pied, et s'emploie à trouver une nouvelle assise à ce mythe personnel intimement lié à la fortune dynastique. En premier lieu, il convient de dédramatiser l'événement traumatisant. Là où la *Cosmographie universelle* rapporte nûment le forfait des séditieux, le chapitre des *Vrais Pourtraits* que Thevet consacre à 'Jean d'Orleans Comte d'Angoulesme' tente de leur trouver des excuses: c'est 'la fureur de la guerre', et non point le fanatisme religieux, qui est seule responsable de l'infortune advenue à la dépouille vénérée. [41] Le sacrilège est imputé au malheur des temps et illustre l'adage selon lequel 'il y a bien affaire à tenir bonne bride à Mars, quand il est esbourgeonné'. Quitte à se rendre suspect de sympathie pour les princes protestants, Thevet les décharge presque de la faute dont les accablent les apologistes catholiques, qui 'exaggerent... fort ceste matiere'.

Le singulier détachement que manifeste Thevet en 1584 et qui contraste avec le pathos exprimé une dizaine d'années plus tôt dans les pages de la *Cosmographie universelle*, tient peut-être au recul des événements. Il s'explique aussi par la volonté de retirer à l'acte iconoclaste toute charge affective. En neutralisant, pour ainsi dire, les restes du comte Jean, et en innocentant par voie de conséquence les profanateurs, Thevet parvient à limiter les effets du désastre symbolique de 1568.

---

[40] Richard Verstegan, *Theatre des Cruautez des heretiques de nostre temps* (Anvers, Adrien Hubert, 1588; réédition, Paris, Michel Chandeigne, 1995). C'est Charles Ruelens, 'Un publiciste catholique du XVIᵉ siècle: Richard Versteganus', *Revue catholique*, XII (1854), p. 480, note 1, qui estime que le texte 'semble sortir des presses de Plantin'.

[41] Thevet, ibidem.

La Sépulture antique de Vars

La *Cosmographie* avait adopté une stratégie différente, quoique con-
vergente. La destruction du symbole rencontrait sa compensation immédiate, l'archéologie fantastique prêtant à une histoire déficitaire un
secours inespéré. À la place de la dépouille comtale, un second corps
est 'inventé', de beaucoup antérieur au précédent, puisqu'il proviendrait
de l'antiquité gréco-latine, et tout aussi intact que celui du comte
d'Angoulême avant la décollation de 1562. Il s'agit en l'espèce de la
sépulture antique découverte en 1541, 'en la terre de Vars, à trois lieües
d'Angoulesme'.[42] Élie Vinet, dans le chapitre sur Angoulême et la
Touvre inséré en 1556 dans les anonymes et composites *Discours non
plus melancoliques que divers*, avait consacré à cette découverte un
récit alerte et passablement irrévérencieux. Les sauts des crapauds
jaillissant du sépulcre heurté par la charrue d'un laboureur, la cupidité
de l'évêque dépêchant aussitôt ses officiers sur place pour s'assurer du
trésor escompté, les dévotions spontanées du 'pauvre peuple' persuadé
'que c'estoit là le tombeau et corps de saint Jaque, je ne sçay du petit ou
du grand saint Jaque apostre de Jesuchrist',[43] tout cela contribuait au
divertissement d'un lecteur prié d'entrée de laisser mélancolie. Plus
gravement, Thevet entreprend de restituer à cet épisode curieux sa
dimension symbolique. Se fondant sur l'analogie existant entre l'exhu-
mation du comte Jean et celle de l'apôtre supposé, il découvre dans ce
dernier une figure de substitution. Les deux opérations de mise au jour
des corps ensevelis sont productrices de sacré, mais d'un sacré dont
l'efficace s'inverse d'un exemple à l'autre: si le corps de Jean, en
définitive, se révèle tabou, et qu'il ne saurait manifester le miracle de sa
chair incorruptible que dans la profanation, la dépouille du Pseudo-
saint-Jacques, en revanche, réclame d'être arrachée à son 'coffre de
plomb' pour devenir objet de culte.

Sans doute Thevet, avec plus de netteté encore que Vinet, se
désolidarise-t-il des croyances superstitieuses du 'simple peuple des
environs', avide de reliques et coutumier de se tromper.[44] Mais il
corrige aussitôt l'identification du mort antique avec l'apôtre Jacques,
par une seconde hypothèse, où la mythologie politique retrouve ses
droits. Le mort inconnu sera 'quelque Prince Grec', comme l'atteste la
lame d'or couverte d'inscriptions trouvée sur sa poitrine et dont le sens

---

[42] Thevet, *La Cosmographie universelle*, II, f. 519ᵛ.
[43] *Discours non plus melancoliques que divers,* op. cit., 1556, p. 91.
[44] Thevet, *La Cosmographie universelle*, II, f. 519ᵛ.

n'a pu être déchiffré par les amis du cosmographe. Le passage qui suit, dans lequel Thevet s'emploie, conformément à une légende nationaliste des plus tenaces,[45] à démontrer l'antériorité de la langue et de la culture gauloises par rapport à celles des autres nations, assure le lien avec l'actualité d'Angoulême. En effet, le prince 'aux characteres Grecs' n'est point réellement grec, mais gaulois, puisque, à en croire Thevet, 'lesdits Gaulois ont usé les premiers' d'un tel alphabet.[46]

Vinet, pour sa part, se montrait beaucoup plus circonspect, jusqu'à mettre en doute le sexe du défunt, lequel, à en juger par la stature et par le crâne, 'ressembloit quasi plus à une femelle'.[47] Dans le récit plaisant des *Discours non plus melancoliques ...*, apparemment retouché par un libraire en mal de publicité et visant le plus large auditoire possible, aussi bien que dans la version plus déférente de l'*Engolesme* de 1567, l'auteur se gardait bien de toute identification hâtive. L'examen attentif de la lame d'or remplissait les dernières pages du chapitre. Vinet y découvrait l'évidence même. Le grimoire ne donne pas à lire un texte, mais une sorte de grille logique. Sur chacune des sept lignes de l'inscription sont disposées les sept voyelles de l'alphabet grec, d'abord dans l'ordre, puis à rebours; ensuite, avec un décalage progressif d'une lettre en partant des deux premières lignes, la suite vocalique est reprise en 'boustrophédon'. Le tout compose un carré de sept par sept, où le commentateur voit un 'meslinge' inspiré des rêveries pythagoriciennes. Le chapitre des *Discours* se concluait par une moquerie à l'adresse du lecteur qui se serait opiniâtré 'à vouloir deviner que c'est'.[48]

Thevet, qui reproduit dans sa *Cosmographie* le mystérieux carré, en lui ajoutant le support ornemental d'un rouleau (fig. 1), ne paraît guère goûter le sel de la plaisanterie risquée par Vinet ou son libraire. Ce dernier proposait en effet de considérer dans la lame une énigme factice, un vain casse-tête imaginé à quinze siècles de distance pour le désespoir des modernes archéologues. Prenant au contraire la chose fort au sérieux, Thevet s'est enquis vainement, cela va sans dire, auprès 'des plus doctes de nostre France', de 'l'interpretation' de ces 'beaux characteres Grecs'. Il lui déplaît qu'ils puissent ne rien signifier. Dans le *Grand In-*

---

[45] Voir Claude-Gilbert Dubois, *Celtes et Gaulois au XVIe siècle: le développement littéraire d'un mythe nationaliste* (Paris, Vrin, 1972).

[46] A. Thevet, *La Cosmographie universelle*, II, f. 520r: 'Ce sont donc des tesmoignages assez suffisans, pour monstrer que lesdits Gaulois en ont usé les premiers, et tousjours ont esté preferez aux autres nations és lettres et sciences, et par especial aux Grecs, et à leurs Roys Philippe et Alexandre son fils.'

[47] *Discours non plus melancoliques que divers...*, op. cit., 1556, p. 91.

[48] Ibidem, p. 94.

sulaire et pilotage, ouvrage inachevé de la vieillesse, Thevet reviendra à la charge, s'en prenant aux 'regratteurs', qui ont voulu 'se gaber de nostre monument Angoumoisin, lequel ilz pretendent estre supposé, pource qu'il n'y a aucunes consonantes, qui puissent accoupler le son des mots'.[49] Or ce défaut de consonnes ne suffit pas à faire reculer l'intrépide cosmographe, résolu de lire dans l'énigmatique suite vocalique, sept fois variée, un message à déchiffrer. Et d'appeler pour garant 'l'authorité Premierement du grand Roy François, en apres de l'Evesque d'Angoulesme qui a eu fort long temps ceste lame en sa puissance'.[50]

L'œuvre de symbolisation est achevée: la terre de Vars renferme l'origine deux fois millénaire de la dignité princière en Angoumois. À l'ancêtre démembré lors des guerres civiles, s'est substitué, en une sorte d'ellipse chronologique, le corps intact de 'l'ancêtre de l'ancêtre'. Gain manifeste: l'autorité des comtes d'Angoulême, dont Thevet ordonne implicitement la lignée depuis une sépulture réinventée, s'accroît d'une origine légendaire et de plusieurs siècles d'existence.

De plus, par delà l'effacement posthume du comte Jean, deux figures symétriques vont pouvoir entrer en relation de part et d'autre de la dépouille absente. Au prince antique arborant les caractères grecs, répond le petit-fils de Jean, 'restituteur des bonnes lettres en France' et, en particulier, des études grecques, le roi François Ier.

La sépulture de Vars contenait une énigme: celle de la mystérieuse lame gravée. Une question était ainsi posée, à des siècles d'intervalle, à l'histoire présente. Thevet, lui seul, et presque à son insu, a découvert la réponse à cette interpellation du passé. Aux indéchiffrables voyelles, c'est la personne même de l''Apollon gaulois', restaurateur de l'hellénisme en France, qui constitue la réponse longuement différée. Nul doute que l'éloge de la culture 'gauloise' ne doive être ainsi compris. Le Roi François Ier a le premier permis l'illustration de cette thèse surprenante: durant son règne, il a apporté la preuve que les Gaulois l'emportaient dans la connaissance des bonnes lettres sur toute autre nation, y compris sur les Grecs!

On comprend qu'en dépit de son admiration proclamée pour Vinet, 'homme tres-docte et tres-eloquent, [s]ien bon Seigneur et amy',[51]

---

[49] Thevet, *Le Grand Insulaire*, t. I, BN Ms fr. 15452, f. 36[r] (cf. *La Description de plusieurs Isles*, BN Ms fr. 17174, f. 15[v]). Dans cette version ultime, le cosmographe identifie le mort comme étant 'quelque Capitaine Goth'.

[50] Thevet, *Le Grand Insulaire,* ibidem.

[51] A. Thevet, *Les Vrais Pourtraits*, livre VI, ch. 86 : 'Ausone, Bourdelois', f. 490[r]; cf. IV, 26, f. 284[r].

Thevet ne puisse adopter sur la singularité de Vars le regard distant et réservé du savant bordelais — qu'il pille au demeurant sans vergogne. Il lui fallait adhérer à ce mystère souterrain, pour y scruter le secret de sa propre origine et le point de départ de sa stupéfiante carrière de cosmographe gyrovague.

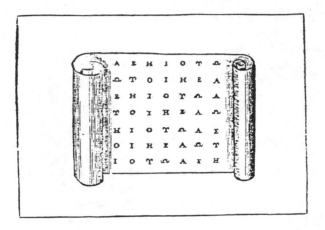

Fig. 1

5

'Suyvant le naturel du sexe fœminin':
The Representation of the Feminine in
Les Angoisses douleureuses qui procedent d'amours

Elizabeth Guild

Helisenne de Crenne's *Angoisses douloureuses qui procedent d'amours*, first published in 1538, was initially very successful, and yet was soon muffled by humanist developments that overtook it.[1] For Étienne Pasquier, for instance, writing some twenty years later, her style was as inept as that of Rabelais's 'escolier Limosin', a cautionary example of 'un langage escorche-latin'.[2] However, I want to suggest that this text is not inept in its use of the discourses with which it engages; rather, it interrupts and unsettles them. The discourses I have in mind are Arthurian romance, the lover's discourse, and prevailing discourses of the female body. Exploration of the combination of the second and third of these discourses suggests that function and representation of the body in this text is markedly different from the woman's body in male-authored lover's discourse, where 'feminine', 'nature', and 'body' tend to be equated with each other.

What the body in this woman's story reveals is a sense of embodiment and of relation to the body different both from the prevailing philosophical and physiological models of the feminine, and from the traditions of representation and rhetoric that these models subtend. The first are determined by an irrefutable 'nature'; the second, which are propped up by the concept of nature, are determined to metaphorise and fragment the supposedly natural female body. Helisenne de Crenne's writing offers us a version of the body that insists on its materialisation

---

[1] All references are to Paul Demat's edition of the first volume of *Les Angoisses douleureuses qui procedent d'amours* (Paris, Les Belles Lettres, 1968).

[2] Étienne Pasquier, 'A Monsieur de Querquifinen Seigneur d'Ardivilliers', in P. Rickard, *La Langue française au seizième siecle: Étude suivie de textes* (Cambridge, CUP, 1968), 240–4, p. 242.

— without materialisation being equated with nature.[3] The body which is represented in these terms is *not* what determines a woman's way of being. Against the odds, that is, the feminine here is not simply biologically determined; and along with this, the constraining conceptual oppositions between body and mind, nature and culture, are temporarily unsettled. Her narrator's self-representation is one of embodiment: but this is not a reproduction of the conventional discourse of female nature, where nature and the body are equated; rather, it exposes the profoundly unnatural — ideological — functions of 'nature' in a discourse which insists on possessing the meaning of the term, claiming that the meaning ascribed is 'only natural', that is, fixed irrefutably and essentially as 'nature' determines.

The text presents itself as a warning to virtuous women against illicit passion. A reminder of the narrative may be useful: for brevity, and also as a reminder of how the text has come to be represented, the following account is useful: the first volume 'recounts Helisenne's infatuation for a young man of lower rank than herself, ends in her incarceration by her husband...the other two sections...describe the endless experiences of the young man and his friend in their search for the heroine and remind us of Arthurian romance, with the male lover spiritualising his emotions by a series of travels and lengthy frustrations'.[4]

Helisenne de Crenne was writing at a distance from the Court, in a style which was soon to be disparaged, telling a story which does not immediately resonate with the preoccupations and narrative concerns of its moment. It is difficult to locate her work, and we might wonder who read it. Her narrator emphasises that she writes for other women. This does not exclude men, and of course, our reading has to understand the text in relation to what men were writing. However much men may have represented women, may have seemed to be writing about women, were they not primarily writing for other men? Helisenne de Crenne's appeal to women readers may be read not so much as an answer to what men were writing, but as an interruption of the flow of words between men. This invocation of a community of women readers, like Louise

---

3   I owe the term 'materialisation' to Judith Butler, in *Bodies that Matter* (London & New York, Routledge, 1993). She writes: 'What I would propose in place of ...conceptions of construction [of the body] is a return to the notion of matter, not as site or surface, but as *a process of materialization that stabilizes over time to produce the effect of boundary, fixity, and surface we call matter*' (p. 9). It is the translation of this into a specific historical instance that is mine.

4   I. D. McFarlane, *Renaissance France, 1470–1589* (London & Tonbridge, Ernest Benn, 1974), p. 169.

Labé's Preface addressed to Mademoiselle Clémence de Bourges Lyonnaise, gestures towards an alternative culture — not exclusively, but primarily, feminine.

A set of terms, namely body, voice, or speech, representation and construction, will ground my reading of the text, all of which circulate around a central term: *angoisse*. However significant the concept of 'voice' in Helisenne de Crenne's narrative may be (as we shall see shortly), it is none the less important to start with the body, for two reasons: to remind that voice is embodied, and to remind of the body's significance as a site of representation and construction of identity. To start with the body is to *not* sidestep the problem of essentialism raised by the prevailing discourse of sex and sexuality at the time of writing.

Reference to the body locates this text within the economy of the gaze, which was so preoccupied with the female body at the time. And it is this that connects this otherwise peripheral text with the theme of the Colloquium: for construction (or fashioning) and representation of the body is so compelling an aspect of humanism in the reign of François Ier, that is, of a humanism which is an overwhelmingly masculine culture. The relations between men that underpin and saturate humanist culture determine the fashioning and representation of the body, particularly of the female body. Women are objects of representation between men — even when an erotic relationship between a man and a woman is the apparent object of representation.

The body acts as a site of representation. It is used, not least, by the monarch — generations before Louis XIV's spectacular, self-mythologising self-production.[5] Think of that portrait of François Ier by François Clouet (now in the Louvre): the very semblance of the humanist prince. Here the body as represented by the portraitist is above all symbolic, represented for maximum cultural intelligibility and consumption, a body manipulable by and for the purposes of authority and power. Think, too, of the body in Castiglione's *Cortegiano*: the culture endorsed here is one of the perfectly formed and managed body, a body whose gestures and performances and presence are so regulated as always to correspond perfectly to, or represent, what the courtier wishes. In Castiglione's text men and women come together in conversation to exchange views on their culture of representation; the more usual scene, however, is that women are exchanged both as persons and bodies and as images, ideas, fantasies, between men, and have little

---

5   See, for instance, J.-M. Apostolidès, *Le Roi-machine: Spectacle et politique au temps de Louis XIV* (Paris, Minuit, 1981).

chance of joining in the conversation. Represented, not representers. Think, for instance, of love lyric; and, closer to the court as a cultural centre, think of the range of visual representations of men and women, and the disparity between them, as François Clouet's *Bain de Diane* (now in Rouen) so dramatically illustrates. Diana and her nymphs, nude, occupy the foreground of the canvas; top left, hapless Actaeon, in contemporary doublet and hose, nothing exposed or erotogenic about *his* body.[6] Here the female body is not only the object of the spectator's gaze, but also already figures within a narrative of the gaze and its dangers.

A culture of representation, a culture of the gaze; such is the connection I am suggesting between this text and the 'cult of humanism'. Along with this — witness Castiglione's emphasis on self-fashioning — let us remember that the humanist subject of representation is a voluntarist subject; his mark is choice. To this culture I want to put the question: what would the gazed-on woman's story be, the woman who, it seems, unlike her humanist father, brothers, or husband, has no choice but is subject to their choices for themselves, and is exchanged literally and discursively between men?

Helisenne de Crenne's cautionary story interrupts this exchange, and tells us that, despite a woman's subject status, there is a margin of choice in terms of the forming of her subjectivity. She is not necessarily just subject to nature or to her nature; not even when she seems to say she is, when she reproduces the terms of the prevailing discourse of the 'nature fœminine', using such terms as: 'audace fœminine' (p. 26) or 'lascivité fœminine' (p. 71). For these terms, used here *by* rather than *of* a woman, thereby undergo revision. As Irigaray suggests in *Speculum de l'autre femme*, when a woman speaks, reproducing the terms which habitually fall within the system of representation to which she is subject as silent object of desire (as if nature and her nature dictated that this were her proper place), her *mimétisme*, her unsettling repetition, is enough to expose what is unnatural, constructed, and imaginary in a culture or system which represents itself as 'natural'.

Thus Helisenne de Crenne's representation of a woman in the *Angoisses douleureuses qui procedent d'amours* both reproduces and

---

6 What is, of course, equally striking about this representation is its ambiguity: the female body is the object of the gaze and desire of the (male) spectator inside and outside the canvas; but the representation also warns of the dangers of the gaze, for it brings within the field of vision the spectacle of Actaeon's terrible death.

differs from the masculine economy of representation of feminine subjectivity. The site of difference, and choice, is the body, a body which is materialised rather than served up in metaphorical morsels. But before going on to look at the detail of this representation of the body, there are two related metaphors which need some attention: first, writing, and second, voice, both of which are contexts for reading this text, and which both converge on the concept of cure.

That writing cures is an idea which has quite some currency in sixteenth-century France and beyond: writing cures, or heals, we might say, by making or remaking links, reconnecting what had become disconnected. This text begins by creating a connection between itself and its women readers, and between them: it dedicates itself to them, as an exemplary tale for them, cautioning against passion. But as well as its prophylactic purpose, it offers the possibility of cure for its narrator's pain, although not unconditionally so; it must, so the text goes, have the right reader(s), and such may be the pain remembered by the narrator as she writes that the process of writing is interrupted.[7] The narrator claims that she writes primarily to exorcise, to caution, and to heal; but diegetically the cure demanded turns out to be not so much the end of love, as claimed, as the return of the lover, on whose presence her life depends. She writes so as to reach her absent lover, in the hope that he will rescue her from her captivity, as he does in the third volume. In so doing he proves himself worthy of her, and proves, too, the redeeming power of love — for it is love that transforms the would-be lover from being an early modern Essex man into a perfect lover-knight.

The more significant form of connection in this text is, however, its refusal of metaphorisation, a process which seems to transform its object, by making imaginary connections, playing on connotations. But in many of the representations of women at the time the process begins in effect with *dis*connection, and in its transformation(s), baffles the brute eloquence of more raw matter, particularly when the matter is pain, *angoisse* or *douleur*. Helisenne de Crenne's text, by contrast, gives pain a voice, and is rooted in pain which is always more than metaphor.

---

7 'A l'occasion des griefves et insuperables douleurs interieures, la parolle m'estoit foreclose; mais peu après grand multitude de souspirs vuydoient de mon estomach, et m'intervint diverses et merveilleuses fantasies si cruelles et ignominieuses que la recente memoire rend ma main debile et tremblante, en sorte que par plusieurs foys y laissay et infestay la plume; mais pensant qu'il me seroit attribué à vice de pusillanimité, je me veulx efforcer de l'escripre' (p. 34).

Writing, then, is represented as one form of cure for pain; so too is talk, possibly, in the form of confession. But more insistently, talk is represented as seduction, and, just as powerfully, as disease, as a destructive currency that circulates between men at women's expense, misrepresenting them. Misrepresentation by men's talk is more dangerous than what is usually cast as *the* danger, that is, women's talk. [8]

It has become something of a feminist critical commonplace to celebrate women, not just writers, not just early modern women, in terms of their voice, the voice or voices that have dared to speak out of centuries of silence. To speak is to become a subject. This text seems to invite a reading of this sort: here a woman decries her lot, and her cry can unite and speak for other women, habitually so isolated in their subject silence. And besides, it is a text that does not allow what the notion of voice sometimes allows, problematically: that is, that voice becomes a rather disembodied concept, rather too much a metaphor. For the text insists on the relations between voice and body, and so allows a direct confrontation of the prevailing humanist model of the feminine, which essentialised woman as man's other, as nature to his culture, body to his mind or soul. That the body was cast as being determinant does not mean that the only way to think differently about the feminine, or read its representations differently, is to locate it elsewhere than in the body, for instance in a metaphorical 'voice'. It remains important to explore the representations of the supposedly 'natural' body for what traces they bear of construction, and thereby of the construction of feminine subjectivity, and to think about voice in this embodied context.

This voice and body — speaking body, embodied voice — here interrupt the silence which surrounds the habitually represented body, as read by men. Take the *blason*, for example: here a part of the woman's eroticised body is a mastered fragment, on which love has written for the poet to read — as in Scève's: 'Front apparent, afin qu'on peut mieux lire / Les lois qu'amour voulut en lui ecrire' (*Le Front*), as a blank which the poet will fill with his meanings, or indeed, in a *blason* by François Sagon, as the poet-seducer's bait:

---

8   On the dangers of women's words, see, for instance, Francesco Barbaro, *De re uxoria* (1416), and for discussion, see A. R. Jones, *The Currency of Eros: Women's Love Lyric in Europe, 1540–1620* (Bloomington & Indianapolis, Indiana University Press, 1990), and E. D. Harvey, *Ventriloquized Voices: Feminist Theory and English Renaissance Texts* (London & New York, Routledge, 1992).

Mais si tu veux permettre à mes deux yeux,
Voir le tétin où l'on te connait mieux,
Le corps, la cuisse où ta beauté se livre,
J'aurai sujet de toi faire un beau livre.[9]

The body-part becomes *topos*; it falls within a rhetoric grounded in the mirror model of knowledge, which speaks of seeing as knowing, and privileges presence as meaning, whilst at the same time disregarding a woman's presence. It presumes that the speaker (male) sees clearly, and it falls within a dualist economy which works with a supposed distinction between body and mind — in this case, her body, his mind.

Helisenne de Crenne's representation unsettles this dualism and fragmentation, despite the presence early in the narrative of some apparently congruent rhetoric of love, for instance: 'l'ardente flamme qui me brusloit et consumoit' (p. 24), and: 'combien que mon corps se departe, mon amoureux cueur fera residence avecques mon amy jusques à la separation du corps et de l'ame' (p. 44). The inclusion of such *topoi*, which will subsequently be left behind, helps to mark the development in the text of a different discourse.

It is also marked by its contrast to the two loudest male voices in the text: the husband's and the would-be lover's. Their rhetoric falls on each side of a dualist divide: on the one side, the husband, all jealousy and rage and patriarchal possessiveness, defending his brutality with the alibi of honour. His version of his wife is essentialist through and through; he insists that she is subject to her bodily nature, and that nature makes her lascivious, disorderly, irrational; his 'cure' for her passion is brutally literal attacks on her body.[10] On the other side is the lover, whose speech is all rhetorical, figurative excess, for instance: 'Las, le mal qu'il fault que j'endure…est violent et insuperable; c'est une playe que nulle medecine ne peult soulder, c'est ung feu par nulle puissance d'eau inextinguible, c'est une ardeur que nulle glace ne pourroit refrigerer'(p. 54). It is up to *her* words to play across the man-made

---

[9] Both quotations are from the selection of *blasons* in F. Charpentier (ed.), *Louise Labé: Œuvres poétiques & Pernette du Guillet: Rymes* (Paris, Gallimard, 1983).

[10] For example: '"O meschante et malheureuse creature remplie d'iniquité, qui ne desire que l'execution de ton appetit desordonné, comment t'ose tu trouver en ma presence? N'as tu crainte que je convertisse mon espée par juste ire en ta poictrine?" En proferant telz motz, par si grand fureur et impetuosité me donna si grand coup qu'au cheoir je me rompiz deux dentz, dont de l'extreme douleur je fuz longue espace sans monstrer signe d'esperit vital' (p. 34).

divide, to destabilise the distinction between literal and figurative language that the two men uphold.

Like the women's bodies that figure in masculine representation, the body in this text is represented as being readable, or as a site of representation; but here both the readings, and the relation to the represented body are different. Here the body is readable in a variety of ways: I shall concentrate on the three grounding representations, two of which run together, namely its formation (in relation to whom or what), and its erotogenic rather than organic presence; and thirdly, its pain. Some of these representations reproduce familiar masculine readings, others differ, others implicitly and explicitly question them.

The narrative begins with an account of the early life of the narrator, and dwells on the formation of her body. The embodied person she comes to be is formed through her loving relationship with her mother, then her husband, and then, later, in the triangular relationship with her would-be lover and her husband. Desire, the narrator confides at the outset, is what made her beautiful; it also made her ill, for she was married at the age of just eleven, too young, the narrative implies, for sexual pleasure. However, she is initially cavalier about this, prepared to sacrifice health for happiness. Although here she makes light of it, it is an important disjunction which will come to have much more significance in her narrative. By thirteen, she claims, 'en perseverant en telles [ardentes] amours…j'estoye de forme elegante et de tout si bien proportionnée que j'excedoye toutes aultres femmes en beaulté de corps' (p. 3). She is quite clear, it is her body that is beautiful, not her face; she represents this self-perception as corresponding exactly and untroubledly to what others see, and talk about: '"Voyez là le plus beau corps que je veis jamais". Puis après, en me regardant au visaige, disoient "Elle est belle, mais il n'est à accomparer au corps".' What is clear in the narrator's first representations of herself is that she imagines there is a match between what others see and either envy or desire, and what she sees; and that if seeing is libidinal, the body that is seen is already a body produced by, quite as much as inhabited by, desire. This represented body is already far from being a 'natural', organic body, far from being immediately known to her: it is formed and informed by desire, it is imaginary, and belongs in the order of language: each of these relations to it, constructions of it, are quite as much hers as they are others', and it is through representation that her body materialises.

There is a missing term in this summary of relations to the body: namely, that there is a narcissistic aspect. The narrator delights in her beauty, in being the object of others' desire: for instance: 'tout le monde jectoit son regard sur moy, en disant les ungs aux aultres: "Voyez là la creature excedant et oultrepassant toutes aultres en formosité de corps." Et après qu'ilz m'avoient regardée, ilz alloient appeler les aultres... C'estoit une chose admirable de veoir le peuple qui s'assembloit entour moy'(p. 22); her would-be lover's gaze sends her back to her mirror; and his beauty acts as a mirror for her own. Even the use of examples in the narrative, which supposedly caution against love, reminding of passion's havoc and destructiveness, is nonetheless narcissistic, for the narrator is comparing herself with, amongst others, Helen, Penelope, Medea, Dido, Guinevere, and Iseult.

What seems important in the narrator's representation of her body is that it recasts the relationship between desire and the body: this is not the terrifyingly random, all-consuming, organic female desire of so many masculine representations. It seems, rather, to coincide with a different conceptualisation, namely, that 'the subject can perceive her own body only by way of...symbolization of her desire', and that 'the field of jouissance is formed through an organization of signifiers but realized in a body'.[11]

In the terms of these quotations, drawn from a recent study of psychoanalytic theories of hysteria, this sixteenth-century narrator is a hysteric; that is, a specific hysterical structure is in play. This is a valuable idea, for it moves beyond the early-modern model of generalised hysteria: that is, if female by nature, then hysterical. It is clear that the structure of desire in this text is other than hysterical in that sense: the organic body is not the source. The narrator's descriptions have to do with the body as a site of self-representation, a subjectivity inseparable from social, libidinal, and discursive con-struction. On the other hand, it is also important to recognise the way that this representation preserves rather than unsettles prevailing representations: the narrator's narcissism props up the economy of the gaze, expresses how a woman's desire is entangled in this economy to which she is subject, in which she is object — and which, despite this, she enjoys. But for all that this representation in part serves the *status quo*, it none the less takes us beyond an analysis of the sexual and cultural economy in terms of simple opposition: subject and subjected or object, active and passive.

---

[11] M. David-Ménard, translated by C. Porter, *Hysteria from Freud to Lacan: Body and Language in Psychoanalysis* (Ithaca & London, Cornell University Press, 1989), p. 44, and N. Lukacher, Introduction to the same study, p. xiii.

Desire makes the body beautiful; but desire's more acute and pro-found impact on the body is pain. The *angoisses douloureuses* of the title are emotional and psychical, and realised in and on the body. The narrator's experience of pain is in marked contrast to that of the two chief male figures in the text, the husband and the would-be lover. The husband feels rage and jealousy, and inflicts violent pain on his wife's body. The would-be lover's pain operates on the level of a rhetoric, and both in its own clumsy excess and its contrast to the narrator's 'real' pain, is shown up as being vacuous and disconnected. For instance, after the husband has — yet again — brutally beaten the narrator, he says:

> Depuis hier, Madame, que parlay à vous, j'ay continuellement consumé le temps en merveilleuse solicitude, craignant que monsieur vostre mary ne vous eust molestée ou mal traictée, sans ce que eussiez sceu evader son impetueuse ferocité, que je comprendz estre grande, par ce qu'il m'a veu parler à vous. Las, si je pensoye qu'à l'occasion de moy eussiez souffert quelques precipitations ou peines, *ce me seroit douleur pire que la mort.*
>
> (p. 61, my emphasis)

His rhetoric of life and death — and this is just one example — might be described as not knowing what it is saying, all the more so when the disjunction between his words and the materialisation of her pain — and brutally, the husband's — is so patent.

The would-be lover has already lamented that there is no medicine for his wound ('une playe que nulle medecine ne peult soulder' (p. 54)). Metaphorical wound, metaphorical medicine: his words sit squarely on one side of the literal/metaphorical divide. Medicine and the ills it might cure are much more poignant in the narrator's discourse. Her ills are physical, emotional and psychical, and no medicine in the form of a pill or a potion can cure them; even the talking cure which the narrative advocates offers only temporary relief. Her version of illness and treatment is homeopathic: her disease is love, the sight of her would-be lover the cause of her disease, and the only medicine for it, the sight of that same man. This might seem to fall within the same order of rhetoric as that of her incurable would-be lover; true, it is figurative medicine, but the representation of her ills is so much more fully materialised in terms of the body, and her embodied representation in the text already from the outset has so much more force, that just as the physiological and the psychical supplement each other inextricably, so do literal denotation and metaphorical connotation. Where this continuity is even more importantly clear is in the function of pain, the *angoisses douloureuses* of the title. Their very definitions bring the posited two orders, physical and psychical, into communication, implying some sort of homogeneity, without its necessarily meaning that the physical is all-determinant. Pain and the passion it communicates are more than corporeal, but their corporeality is irrefutable.

Huguet offers little help with either *angoisse* or *douleur*: *douleur* is neither glossed nor given any synonyms — just a few examples are listed; and *angoisse* is given as meaning: *étroitesse* and *serrement*.[12] Cotgrave is more useful.[13] *Douleur* generates the following list: 'griefe, sorrow, anguish, sadnesse, teene, heaviness, ache, pain, smart, sorenesse, a throw, throbbing, wringing' — that is, a mixture of the physical, the emotional, and the psychical. The meanings of *angoisse* are similar: 'anguish, griefe, sorrow, agonie, perplexitie, vexation of mind or body'; and *angoisser* gives us: 'to vex, grieve, afflict, perplex, fill with anguish, *almost choake with sorrow*' (my emphasis). What Cotgrave reveals about usage supports the function of the terms in this narrative, as I shall now describe in more detail.

'Almost choake with sorrow': as the narrator repeatedly records, pain interrupts her, and silences her: for instance: 'l'extreme destresse de ma douleur interrompoit ma voix' (p. 9), and: 'la parolle me fut forclose au moyen des regretz qui anticipoient ma voix' (p. 42); and at these moments, loss of voice must be read as a bodily impossibility of speaking: in both instances her silencing is accompanied by other physical symptoms: anorexia, trembling, terrible chill: 'je commençay à trembler, et entra une si extreme froideur dedans mes os que pour la douleur que je souffroys, la parolle me fut forclose' (p. 42). As the romance takes its disastrous course, and as her desire is forbidden and frustrated, emotional pain increasingly produces illness, where, before, it had been satisfied desire which made her ill.

> Je continuay celle penible et douleureuse vie, qui me causa une maladie qui m'accompaignera jusques à la mort (p. 49);

and, after her husband has threatened to imprison her far away and detailed the tortures he is going to inflict on her would-be lover, before killing him and presenting her with the body, illness is again her recourse:

[12] E. Huguet, *Dictionnaire de la langue française du seizième siècle*, 7 vols (Paris, 1925–67).

[13] R. Cotgrave, *A Dictionarie of the French and English Tongues* (London, 1611), facsimile, English Linguistics, 82 (Menston, 1968).

Telles variables ymaginations m'estoient tresgriefves et quasi insupportables
…et me causoient une fiebvre si tresfroide, avecq la crainte que j'avoye, que
je m'esvanouyssoye. (p. 66)

She later falls so ill that her life is in danger: 'une insidieuse fiebvre…
en si grand extremité me detenoit que je n'avoye esperance aulcune de
mon salut' (p. 77). The narrator is quite clear: excessive pain causes her
illness. Her representation of her body is in marked contrast to her
husband's reading of it. That her husband misreads is revealed by his
belief that her illnesses are organic: he insists on the need for doctors
and their medicine, whereas she is clear: 'il n'y avoit que une seulle
medecine qui me peust guarir…veoir mon amy' (p. 49)…'j'estoye
autant travaillée des passions de l'ame que de maladie corporelle'
(p. 77).

The hinge is 'autant': her pain is materialised in her body — and her
body is materialised in this pain. The physical, the emotional, and the
psychical are inseparable; and what equally seems clear is that, far from
thinking the body in terms of essence, as matter which is given by
nature and immediately known, this is a body which gains substance
and meaning through processes of representation, repetition, and
materialisation. Pain is the key example. As Judith Butler argues in
Bodies that Matter, bodily pain is one of a number of 'primary and
irrefutable experiences…But their irrefutability in no way implies what
it might mean to affirm them and through what discursive means'
(p. xi).

The narrator's pain affects both her body and her speech; when she is
at a loss for words, 'almost choked with sorrow', her pain is realised in
her body, and communicates in ways such as blushing, pallor, sighs,
involuntary gestures, trembling, and illness. All of these are within the
bounds of cultural intelligibility: what is unusual is their materiality. In
comparison to her pain, the figurative currency which speaks of passion,
makes metaphors of life and death, may seem insubstantial and
nerveless — for instance: 'O front, tu es une table d'attente / Où ma vie
est, et ma mort très-patente' (Scève, *Le Front*). The emotional stakes as
represented by Helisenne de Crenne are of a different order; the
conventional rhetoric which figures in the early part of the narrative,
such as 'mon entendement fort blecé au moyen de l'ardent amour'
(p. 5), soon gives way to a more forceful representation: the narrator
represents herself as dying of and for love; and were her desire to be
realised, her lover would die for love, violently at her husband's hand.
She, too, would suffer whatever violence he chose to inflict.

The text reminds us, if only for a moment, of the sorts of violence to which a woman was subject: it is not just love's metaphorical violence that causes fear and pain. Men's idle talk about the narrator violates her honour; she is also the object of the violence that is rhetorical excess; and within the home there is no escaping her husband's physical violence.

This love story unsettles the conventions of the discourse of love. Not, though, by excess or shortfall: these terms suggest a shared economy rather than the possibility that within this narrative are terms which articulate differences. It interrupts the ruling discourse, in two converging ways, namely its refusal of metaphorisation, and the grounding and reiteration of this refusal in its representation of 'nature fœminine', which will not conform to the ruling discourse of female nature.

6

Un chancelier humaniste sous François Ier: François Olivier (1497–1560)

Jean Dupèbe

(he became Chancellor of France in May 1545)

Thus McFarlane Buchanan p.114

(PTO for Dupèbe's date: 28 April 1545!)

Si les lettres et les arts connurent sous le règne de François Ier un essor remarquable,[1] ce fut en grande partie grâce à l'industrie d'une bourgeoisie éclairée, qui, pendant plusieurs générations, mit son ambition et sa culture au service de l'État et de l'Église. Nombreuses furent ces familles qui, du quatorzième au seizième siècles, s'élevèrent par degrés, souvent du fond d'un négoce provincial et de charges municipales, jusqu'aux offices et aux bénéfices les plus prestigieux.[2] Formés au droit civil et, dès la seconde moitié du quinzième siècle, aux 'lettres d'humanité', avides d'honneurs et de savoir, leurs enfants apparaissent, de Charles VIII à François Ier, comme les vrais champions de l'humanisme français; protégés par le prince et les grands, ils jouèrent, à leur tour, le rôle de mécènes pour nombre de lettrés de petite fortune, avocats, régents de collèges ou de facultés. On peut citer, parmi tant de noms, les Budé, les Briçonnet, les Ruzé.[3] Ajoutons les Olivier auxquels le Chancelier François Olivier donna un lustre tout particulier. Pourtant, les historiens ne se sont guère intéressés au personnage ni à sa famille. Ses prédécesseurs, Antoine Duprat et Guillaume Poyet, ont eu plus de

---

[1] Voir R. J. Knecht, *Renaissance Warrior and Patron: The Reign of Francis I* (Cambridge, CUP, 1994), chap. 22, 'Patron of the Arts', pp. 425–61, et chap. 23, 'Father of Letters', pp. 462–77.

[2] Voir le cas du Chancelier Antoine Duprat, Albert Buisson, *Chancelier Antoine Duprat* (Paris, Hachette, 1935), pp. 17–40.

[3] Sur la famille Budé, voir Madeleine Foisil, 'Guillaume Budé (1467–1540)', in Roland Mousnier et collaborateurs, *Le Conseil du roi de Louis XII à la Révolution* (Paris, PUF, 1970), pp. 277–92; sur les Ruzé voir Philippe Hamon, 'Culture et vie religieuse dans le monde des offices: les Ruzé dans la première moitié du XVIe siècle', *Bibliothèque d'Humanisme et Renaissance*, LIII (1991), 49–64.

chance.[4] Il reste que, contrairement à eux, de son vivant comme après sa mort, Olivier fut admiré pour sa culture et ses qualités d'homme d'état. Ainsi Jacques Auguste de Thou ne tarit pas d'éloges sur les vertus du Chancelier, le seul homme, dit-il, qui, au milieu de courtisans uniquement soucieux de leurs intérêts, songeait au bien public et à la justice.[5] Montaigne, qui se plaît à rapporter une anecdote peu flatteuse sur Poyet, écrit: 'Les plus notables hommes que j'aye jugé par les apparences externes, ce ont esté…pour gens suffisans, et de vertu non commune, Olivier et l'Hospital, Chanceliers de France.'[6] Jugement intéressant: il associe deux hommes qui furent en effet très liés et qui eurent les mêmes idées politiques. La sympathie de Montaigne pour Olivier se révèle encore quand il cite un bon mot de ce grave magistrat: il nous dit que, lui, Montaigne s'est défait de toute ambition, se souvenant 'de ce mot du feu Chancelier Olivier, que les François semblent des guenons qui vont grimpant contremont un arbre, de branche en branche, et ne cessent d'aller jusques à ce qu'elles sont arrivées à la plus haute branche, et y montrent le cul quand elles y sont'.[7]

On comprend aisément le silence ou l'oubli dont François Olivier est aujourd'hui victime. Il est nommé par le roi Chancelier de France le 28 avril 1545. Deux ans après François Ier meurt, le 30 mars 1547. Olivier

---

4   Voir, outre A. Buisson sur Duprat, déjà cité, Charles Porée, *Un parlementaire sous François Ier: Guillaume Poyet (1473–1548)* (Angers, 1898); cf. Denis Richet, *La France moderne: l'esprit des institutions* (Paris, Flammarion, 1973), p. 88: 'Le XVIe siècle connut de très grands chanceliers: un Poyet, un Michel de L'Hospital.'

5   Sur les témoignages de mépris et de haine à l'égard de Duprat et de Poyet, voir, par exemple, BN MS Dupuy, f. 150r: 'De improbis Gullielmi Poyeti moribus' et f. 150v 'Gullielmi Poyeti epitaphia'; f. 153r–v, 'De Anthonio de Prato': 'Huic patre mercatore sat locuplete orto Aruernia patria fuit…Summa vindictae auiditas, vilissima auaritia, ambitio plusquam humana qua etiam pontificios apices ausus est cogitare; virorum summus despectus, foeminarum autem complexus, summa erga prostratos atque afflictos immanitas.' Voir aussi le mépris des humanistes: L. Clément, *De Adriani Turnebi regii professoris praefationibus et poematis*, (Parisiis, 1899), pp. 54–5. Voir enfin Philippe Hamon, *L'Argent du roi: les finances sous François Ier* (Paris, 1994), p. 533. Sur de Thou et Olivier voir *Historiarum sui temporis Partis Primae tomus I* (Parisiis, 1604; BN Rés, La20, 7d), III, 215 (1547): 'Is unus, dum ceteri fere in aula rebus priuatis intenti erant, pro regni dignitate & publica utilitate excubabat.' Cf. tome II, XVI, 703, (1559) et XVII, 857.

6   *Essais*, II, 17; sur Poyet, incapable d'improviser une harangue latine, I, 10.

7   *Ibidem*, II, 17.

reste donc à peine deux ans à son service: on peut penser à bon droit qu'il compte peu dans l'histoire politique de ce règne. Sous Henri II, sa carrière est aussi brève: les sceaux lui sont retirés par lettres patentes du 2 janvier 1551. Il garde, il est vrai, le titre de l'office avec ses privilèges, gages et pensions. C'est néanmoins une disgrâce; il se retire de la cour. À l'avènement de François II, on lui rend les sceaux et il est de nouveau Chancelier de France, mais il meurt à peine un an plus tard le 30 mars 1560.[8] Carrière mouvementée, qui se signale surtout par ses échecs. Ce sont pourtant ces revers qui nous semblent intéressants: ils annoncent ceux de son successeur et ami, Michel de l'Hospital. On peut parler à cet égard de la faillite politique d'un certain humanisme incarné par Olivier. Il nous faut donc étudier l'aspect à la fois culturel et politique de cet humanisme à la fin du règne de François Ier, de 1545 à 1547.

Il convient de dire d'abord quelques mots de la famille.[9] Le goût des lettres d'humanité ne résulte pas seulement d'un choix personnel: la culture est aussi une sorte de capital familial qui se constitue et se développe par les multiples réseaux d'une parentèle riche et influente. Mais il lui faut, au départ, une solide assise sociale. Pour un jeune bourgeois gradué en droit, le Parlement ouvre les chemins les plus sûrs vers les brillantes carrières. Telle est en gros, à l'époque qui nous intéresse, l'histoire des Olivier. Ne parlons pas d'une famille 'illustre'.[10] Elle est récente. Elle arrive de La Rochelle sans doute avec le grand-père, Jacques, vers le milieu du quinzième siècle.[11] On se souvenait encore, au

---

[8] La date de la mort du Chancelier est soit le 30 mars soit, selon certaines sources, le 28: Émile Dupré Lasale, *Michel de L'Hospital avant son élévation au poste de Chancelier de France (1505–1558)*, vol. II (Paris, 1899), p. 189.

[9] Seule étude jusqu'ici: Françoise Lehoux, *Gaston Olivier, aumônier du roi Henri II (1552). Bibliothèque parisienne et mobilier du XVIe siècle* (Paris, L'auteur, 1957): analyse élargie du testament et de l'inventaire après décès du cousin germain du Chancelier: Archives Nationales, Minutier Central, XIX 188, 271 (Trouvé). Notre étude s'appuie aussi sur les études XIX, CXXII, VIII, ainsi que sur BN MSS Pièces originales, 2142 'Olivier de Leuville' et sur le fichier Picot, MS nouvelle acquisition française 23249.

[10] F. Lehoux, op. cit., p. 10.

[11] Les historiens, à partir du dix-septième siècle, prétendent que la famille est originaire de Bourgneuf, village près de La Rochelle. Jean Imbert, natif de La Rochelle, écrit dans l'épître dédicatoire au Chancelier Olivier de sa *Paraphrase en Langage Francoys du premier livre des Institutiones forenses* (Paris, Simon de Colines, 1545), qu'ils ont tous deux une origine commune: '...ex una & eadem regione ductae originis paternae communis inter nos necessitudo. Nam illustrissimum illum patrem tuum, ex se ortum & oriundum urbs agerque Rupellanus in maximis suis laudibus iactant & gloriantur.' Si le père de François, Jacques (II),

milieu du siècle suivant, de l'origine provinciale du chancelier. Les débuts sont donc modestes. Jacques Olivier est à sa mort, vers 1489, procureur au Parlement, ce qui n'a rien de brillant; mais il est parvenu à une réelle aisance: il habite un vaste hôtel comprenant quatre corps de logis, rue de Jouy, dans la paroisse Saint-Gervais,[12] à côté d'un confrère, Étienne de Noviant, procureur à la chambre des comptes,[13] dont il a sans doute épousé la fille, Jeanne de Noviant.[14] Il possède en outre les seigneuries de Leuville et de Ballainvilliers.[15]

Avec l'un de ses six ou sept fils, Jacques II,[16] le père du chancelier, l'ascension sociale est rapide. Docteur ès droits, avocat au Parlement, pensionné par le duc d'Orléans, futur Louis XII, il gravit, grâce à la faveur de ce prince, tous les échelons des honneurs: nommé chancelier du duché de Milan en 1510, il devient en 1517, premier président au Parlement. Grâce à sa première femme, Geneviève Tuelu, qui est la mère du chancelier François Olivier, il pénètre dans les cercles de l'humanisme parisien. Elle serait en effet, si l'on en croit Claude

---

est né à La Rochelle, son oncle Jean, évêque d'Angers, est né à Paris. Voir *infra* n. 29.

[12] Selon F. Lehoux, p. 10, il serait mort 'avant le 5 mai 1488', mais voir BN MSS P.O., 2142 n° 2 (28 février 1489 n. st.). Sur l'hôtel, Lehoux, pp. 10, 16–21, 103: la maison de Jouy devient l'hôtel de Mancy, puis en 1601, l'hôtel de Fourcy: il est aujourd'hui situé aux n° 9, 9 bis, 9 ter de la rue de Jouy, dans le Marais.

[13] Lehoux, p. 18, n. 83. Voir aussi E. Compardon et A.Tuetey, *Inventaire des Registres des Insinuations du Châtelet de Paris: Règnes de François Ier et de Henri II*, (Paris, 1906), n° 1312 (Y 89, f. 249ʳ) et n° 4297 (Y 97, 4 et 22 juillet 1552, f. 455ᵛ) sur l'emplacement de l'hôtel.

[14] Voir, par exemple, Archives nationales (AN) MC XIX 14 (13 novembre 1499), XIX 20 (17 mai 1503), XIX 31 (30 janvier 1508).

[15] Voir, par exemple, BN MS PO 2142 n° 3 et AN MC XIX 14 (15 mars 1500 n. st.).

[16] Selon Lehoux, p. 10, Jacques I a sept fils. Je n'en connais que six, que j'indique dans un ordre quelconque: Jacques II, Guillaume, Claude, Étienne, Jean, seigneur de Mancy, et Jean, abbé de Saint-Médard à Soissons. Il a deux filles: Nicole, femme de Germain Valin, avocat au Parlement, et Jeanne, femme de Jacques Rapouel, marchand, bourgeois de Paris. Voir le poème de Bernardino Dardano 'In aduentum clarissimi ac prestantissimi domini Iacobi Oliverii I.V. Doctoris ac Senatus Mediolani moderatoris', publié à la fin de Jean Bouchet, *La Deploration de l'Eglise militante* (Paris, Guillaume Eustace, 1512; BN Rés. Yc 1635; et séparément dans Rés. G. 2805). Voir BN MS PO 2142 n° 7, 8, 9, 10, 12, 13; AN MC XIX 10 (2 mai 1495) et XIX 14 (13 novembre 1499): il est avocat au Parlement. Voir aussi *Catalogue des Actes de François Ier*, IX, 151: troisième président (2 janvier 1515) et premier président (29 mai 1517) et R. Delachenal, *Histoire des avocats au Parlement de Paris, 1300–1600* (Paris, 1885), p. 273.

d'Espence, la nièce du chancelier de Louis XII, Jean de Ganay (*c.* 1450–1512).[17] Le degré de parenté est douteux, mais la parenté est réelle. Elle est encore plus étroite, quand l'une de ses filles, Catherine, épouse Nicole Boylève (Boileau), neveu de la femme du Chancelier, Jehanne Boylève.[18] En tout cas, Jean de Ganay est une personnalité du premier ordre: c'est, au dire du médecin humaniste Guillaume Cop, un esprit encyclopédique, tourné vers les lettres et les sciences, passionné surtout de mathématiques, de géographie, d'architecture.[19] En 1494, lors de l'expédition de Charles VIII en Italie, il a rencontré Ficin à Florence.[20] Son frère cadet, Germain de Ganay, est plus connu. Ce prêtre, conseiller clerc au Parlement, évêque de Cahors, puis d'Orléans, est surtout un mystique, curieux de tous les arcanes de la théologie néoplatonicienne, disciple de Ficin et de l'abbé Trithemius,[21] ami et protecteur de Lefèvre et de Budé, ainsi que des principaux humanistes du début du siècle. C'est dans un tel milieu qu'on doit situer le président Olivier. Quand il part pour Milan, il est salué par un poète italien, Bernardino Dardano, qui, jouant, comme tout le monde après lui, sur le nom 'Olivier', chante le

---

[17] On voit dans AN MC XIX 48 (27 mars 1520 n. st.) et XIX 57 (9 février 1525 n. st.) que François est fils de la première femme de Jacques II, Geneviève Tueleu. Claude d'Espence, *Oraison funebre es obseques de feu Messire Francoys Olivier* (Paris, Michel de Vascosan, 1561), p. 14.

[18] Geneviève Tueleu est la fille de Jean Tueleu, procureur au Parlement, et de Denise de Ganay dont la parenté avec Jean de Ganay n'est pas clairement établie: MC XIX 58 (25 avril 1525). Je conjecture que Nicole Boyleve (Boileau, Boileaue) est le neveu de Jeanne Boyleve parce qu'il est son héritier en VIII 15 (29 mars 1518 n. st.): 'Noble homme maistre Nicole Boyleau, seigneur de Persant, conseiller du roy en son grand conseil et heritier de feue dame Jehanne Boyleau femme de feu Me Jehan de Ganay en son vivant chancelier de France.' Sur ce Nicole Boyleve, mari de Catherine Olivier, sœur de François, voir MC XIX 48 (27 mars 1520 n. st.). Voir aussi Ernest de Ganay, *Un chancelier de France sous Louis XII, Jehan de Ganay* (Paris, 1932), p. 7. Jean de Ganay et Jeanne Boyleve n'eurent pas d'enfant.

[19] Voir l'épître dédicatoire à Jean de Ganay de sa traduction d'Hippocrate, *Praesagiorum libri tres* (Paris, Henri Estienne, 1511; BN. Rés. Td21 1). C'est surtout un spécialiste de Vitruve.

[20] Voir Ficin, *Opera* (Bâle, 1576), I, 987, 988.

[21] Voir A. Renaudet, *Préréforme et humanisme à Paris pendant les premières guerres d'Italie (1494–1517)*, 2e éd. (Paris, 1953), p. 413, et E. Rice, *Prefatory Epistles of Jacques Lefèvre d'Étaples* (New York & Londres, Columbia University Press, 1972), pp. 20–1.

protecteur de la paix et le nourrisson de Pallas et des Muses.[22] Ces éloges emphatiques prouvent surtout que Dardano cherche un mécène,[23] mais ils seraient ridicules s'ils ne s'adressaient pas à un homme connu pour sa culture. On comprend dès lors pourquoi Charles de Bovelles, le disciple de Lefèvre, lui dédie en 1515 ses *Conclusiones theologicae*.[24] Enfin, quand il meurt en 1519, l'avocat au Parlement, Me Nicolas Versoris, note dans son *Livre de Raison*, qu'avec lui disparaît un 'homme bien lecttré et expert en son office'.[25]

Plusieurs de ses frères, oncles du chancelier, doivent nous arrêter un instant: d'abord, au début du siècle, Étienne, prêtre licencié en décret, chanoine de l'église collégiale Saint-Merry à Paris et titulaire de plusieurs bénéfices à La Rochelle, personnage d'ailleurs obscur; ensuite, Jean, seigneur de Mancy, qui, par sa charge de notaire et secrétaire du roi, se trouve anobli; de plus, fait notable pour l'histoire de la famille, il est attaché à la maison de Foix et de Navarre; il est dit, dans un acte notarié de 1500, 'secrétaire de Monsieur de Foix', c'est-à-dire du neveu du roi, Gaston de Foix, duc de Nemours, gouverneur du Dauphiné et de Milan; après la mort de ce dernier en 1512, il est au service de sa sœur, Germaine de Foix; il se présente en effet comme 'procureur général et ayant le gouvernement et administration des terres et seigneuries que très haulte et puissante princesse ma dame Germaine de Foix, reyne de Navarre et douairière d'Arragon a ou royaulme de France'.[26] Un autre frère, Claude, seigneur de Ballainvilliers, est receveur ordinaire du duché de Nemours[27] et secrétaire de l'Infant de Foix ou de Navarre, c'est-à-

---

[22] Dans le poème déjà cité 'In aduentum': 'O cui pacifere imposuerunt Oliue: / In gremio teneris sibi quem formauit ab annis / Pallas et Aonie gratissima turba sorores / fouere….'

[23] À la fin du poème: '…nec dedignere…me, licet indignum, in numero ascripsisse tuorum.'

[24] *Theologicarum conclusionum libri decem* (Paris, Jodocus Badius, 1515; BN Rés. m.D.16).

[25] *Mémoires de la société d'Histoire de Paris et de l'Ile-de-France*, XII (1885), p. 104.

[26] Étienne: AN MC XIX 14 (13 novembre 1499, 2 février 1500 n. st., 24 octobre 1500); Jean, seigneur de Mancy et de Morangis (Marne), 'secretaire de Monsieur de Foix': MC 14 (15 mars 1500 n. st.); procureur de Germaine de Foix: XIX 45 (20 décembre 1517; 20 mars 1518 n. st.; 22 mars 1518 n. st.); il est dit aussi 'secretaire de hault et puissant seigneur messire Charles de Luxembourg'; XIX 45 (2 février 1518 n. st.). Voir A. Lapeyre et R. Scheurer, *Les Notaires et secrétaires du Roi sous les règnes de Louis XI, Charles VIII et Louis XII (1461–1515)* (Paris,1978), vol. I, n° 496, p. 240; vol. II, planche LXXVI.

[27] AN MC XIX 36 (27 octobre1511).

dire, du fils aîné de Catherine de Foix, Henri d'Albret, futur mari de Mar-guerite d'Angoulême, sœur de François Ier. Après un accord avec ses frères, c'est Jean qui s'établit dans l'hôtel paternel de la rue de Jouy; c'est encore lui qui, à la mort de Jacques II, en 1519, devient le tuteur de son neveu François, le futur chancelier, alors mineur.[28] On peut voir dans ce détail une raison des liens étroits qui semblent avoir uni le chancelier à son cousin germain, Gaston, fils de Jean.

C'est pourtant un autre oncle Jean, sans doute le plus jeune des frères,[29] qui a exercé sur la culture et la spiritualité de ses neveux une influence décisive. Ce moine bénédictin érudit et humaniste, savant dans les trois langues, illustre parfaitement l'idéal de renouveau culturel et religieux qui anime l'Église à la fin du quinzième siècle. Il sort rapidement de l'obscurité d'un monastère provincial: nous le trouvons au début du siècle à l'abbaye royale de Saint-Denis où il est aumônier, dignité qu'il garde toute sa vie. En 1510, il devient abbé des deux abbayes de Soissons, Saint-Médard et Saint-Crépin. À ses charges pastorales s'ajoutent sans nul doute les faveurs du roi, puisqu'il compose à sa mort, en 1515, on ne sait à quel titre, une longue épitaphe en vers latins toute à la gloire de Louis XII.[30] Sa culture et son crédit lui attirent les hommages de quelques humanistes qui voient en lui à la fois un pair et un protecteur. Dès 1512, Bovelles lui dédie les dix livres de ses *Physica elementa*.[31] Le poète Bernardino Dardano, client du Président Olivier, se lamente longuement dans un poème latin de l'absence mo-mentanée de l'abbé, son unique refuge et secours.[32] Sa culture grecque

---

28 AN MC XIX 48 (27 mars 1520 n. st.). François n'a pas 25 ans en 1520. Selon Claude d'Espence, *Oraison funebre*, p. 69, il est mort à 63 ans en 1560. Il est donc né en 1496/7. Jean devient aussi tuteur d'Antoine, fils de Jacques II et de sa deuxième femme, Madeleine Lullier: MC XIX 57 (3 avril 1524).

29 Jean, seigneur de Mancy, est dit 'l'aisné': MC XIX 14 (15 mars 1500 n. st.). Jean, l'abbé de Saint-Médard, est donc le plus jeune. De plus, il est né à Paris, sans doute dans la seconde moitié du quinzième siècle. Sur ses dignités ecclé-siastiques voir par exemple MC XIX 57 (9 février 1525 n. st.); XIX 70 (12 juin 1532); XIX 151 (2 mars 1539 n. st.); XIX 152 (9 mars 1540 n. st.): il est dit évêque d'Angers et 'aulmosnier de l'eglise et abbaye Mgr St Denis en France'.

30 Papirii Massoni, *Annalium libri quatuor* (Lutetiae, Apud Nicolaum Chesneau, MDLXXVII), IV, 532–3; cf. Dr Dumont, 'Jean Olivier, Évêque d'Angers de 1532 à 1540', *Mémoires de la Société Académique du Maine-et-Loire*, XIII (1863), p. 35.

31 *Physicorum elementorum libri decem. Vaenundantur in aedibus Ioannis Parui & Iodoci Badii Ascensiani* (Paris, 1512 ; BN Rés. R 905).

32 *Dardani Epigrammata* (Basileae, Apud Io. Frobenium, MDXVIII), pp. 41–5: 'Desperatio ad Io. Oliverium abbatem Suetionensem.'

est particulièrement prisée: un helléniste, Jacobus Musurus Rhodius, lui offre son édition grecque des *Sentences des sept sages*, publiées chez Gourmont, en le saluant comme un homme 'très savant en toutes sortes de sciences, surtout en grec et en latin'.[33] On connaît un manuscrit grec de prières et d'hymnes, conservé à Berne et qui porte, en grec, de la main de l'abbé, sa propre devise.[34] Ses connaissances dans ce domaine sont encore prouvées par ses relations avec le jeune Allemand, Gunther d'Andernach, fraîchement arrivé à Paris et reçu bachelier en médecine: il lui dédie notamment en 1528 sa traduction latine d'un traité de Galien.[35] La réputation de l'abbé est donc arrivée jusqu'à ce jeune disciple du lecteur royal Jacques Thouzat. Mais Jean Olivier est aussi instruit en hébreu et en chaldéen, comme l'atteste l'inventaire de la bibliothèque qu'il a léguée à son neveu, Gaston: il mentionne une cinquantaine d'œuvres écrites en hébreu, en chaldéen, et en arabe.[36] Au reste, Guillaume Postel dédie au prélat en 1538 sa *Grammatica Arabica* et dans l'épître dédicatoire il vante 'sa passion et sa parfaite connaissance des trois langues', 'linguarum trium ut summus amor ita etiam summa cognitio'.[37]

Cet abbé érudit est aussi un lettré, amateur de poésie néolatine, selon la mode du temps. Rien d'étonnant qu'il soit en commerce littéraire avec Salmon Macrin. Peut-être même est-ce à l'instigation de ce dernier, comme le suggère I. D. McFarlane,[38] que le prélat compose, on ne sait à quelle date, un poème allégorique chrétien intitulé *Pandora*, publié par Étienne Dolet, en 1541, avec des hendécasyllabes de Bernardino Dardano, puis deux fois traduit en français en 1542 et en 1548.[39] Vers 1540,

---

[33] Voir Henri Omont, 'Essai sur les débuts de la typographie grecque à Paris (1507–1516)', *Mémoires de la Société de l'Histoire de Paris et de l'Ile-de-France*, XVIII (1891), p. 37. Épître pp. 108–9: 'Longe uerendo in Christo patri D. Ioanni Oliuerio Diui Medardi Suessionensis abbati dignissimo Regisque chronographo prudentissimo omnifaria disciplina tum graeca tum latina cumulatissimo…' (Mazarine 10487 (7)).

[34] H. Omont, 'Georges Hermonyme de Sparte maître de grec à Paris', ibidem, XII (1885), p. 79: MS grec Berne 703.

[35] *De sectis ad Medicinae candidatos opus* (Paris, Simon de Colines, 1528).

[36] Lehoux, pp. 39, 85–7.

[37] Parisiis, Apud Petrum Gromorsum: exemplaire utilisé, British Library, 622 g 16(3).

[38] 'Jean Salmon Macrin (1490–1537)', *BHR*, XXI (1959), p. 337; cf. p. 63.

[39] Voir Joseph Denais, 'L'épitaphe du poète Jean Olivier, Évêque d'Angers', *Revue de l'Anjou. Nouvelle série*, XIX (1889) (BN 8° Lc9 12), pp. 89–90: traduction de Guillaume Michel (Paris, A. & C. Les Angeliers, 1542; BN Rés. p.Yc 1838 (3)); *Pandore, œuvre latin de Jean Olivier, en son vivant evesque d'Angiers, traduict*

dans sa vieillesse, il adresse au même Macrin une ode latine.[40] Si l'on songe à l'épitaphe latine de Louis XII, aux quatre épitaphes qu'il a pris soin de composer pour son tombeau, on ne peut douter qu'il n'ait voué, tout au long de sa vie, un culte fervent aux Muses latines, sans d'ailleurs se soucier de publier une œuvre dont il ne reste que des fragments. Il cultive également la compagnie des poètes: il aide de ses libéralités Nicolas Bourbon, qui chante la piété, la science, et la générosité de son protecteur.[41] On ne se trompera pas si l'on voit dans ce bénédictin un partisan de Lefèvre, d'Érasme et de Budé, si l'on pense que ses sympathies doctrinales et politiques vont aux humanistes proches de Marguerite de Navarre, comme Guillaume et Jean du Bellay. C'est ce prélat acquis aux idées évangéliques que le roi honore en lui donnant en 1532 le siège épiscopal d'Angers, qu'il quitte à sa mort, huit ans plus tard, en 1540.[42]

Cet humaniste est aussi, selon l'esprit de l'époque, un bâtisseur, épris de beauté et de luxe: son nouveau palais épiscopal excite l'enthousiasme de Nicolas Bourbon.[43] De même, sa somptueuse sépulture, qui s'élevait dans la chapelle Saint Michel de la cathédrale d'Angers et qu'on pouvait admirer jusqu'à la révolution avec ses épitaphes latines gravées dans le marbre, témoigne des goûts de cet homme de la Renaissance.[44] C'est aussi un réformateur. Théodore de Bèze nous dit que sous son pontificat l'évangile 'fut reçu avec grande avidité'; il ajoute ces mots sur l'évêque lui-même: 'Cestuy-ci estant de bon savoir…et de gentil esprit, favorisoit

---

en françoys (Poictiers, [Jean et Enguilbert de Marnef], MDXLVIII): traduction de Pierre Bouchet de La Rochelle (British Library, 39c65). Pour le texte: *Pandora Iani Oliverii Andium hierophantae* (Lugduni, apud Steph. Doletum, 1541; BN Rés. m. Yc 775; ex libris 'Jo Vulcob Biturigensis kai tôn philôn 1558'); hendécasyllabes de Dardano, p. 50: Jean est encore abbé de Saint-Médard de Soissons.

40 Salmoni Macrini, *Hymnorum selectorum libri tres* (Parisiis, ex officina Roberti Stephani, MDXL), p. 114. Voir I. D. McFarlane, art. cit., p. 338.

41 *Tabulae elementariae, pueris ingenuis pernecessariae* (Apud Simonem Colinaeum, 1539), p. 40.

42 Il meurt le 12 avril 1540: voir les articles cités du Dr Dumont et de Joseph Denais. Voir aussi BN MS Anjou-Touraine, XVI, 'Évêques d'Angers' (collection Dom Housseau), f. 258ᵛ.

43 *Nugarum libri octo* (Lyon, Apud Seb. Gryphium, 1538), III, n° CXV, pp. 191–2, VI, n° XV, p. 329. D'après l'ép. dédicatoire de Jacobus Musurus il était aussi historiographe du roi. Voir aussi *Historiae literariae ordinis S. Benedicti* (Augustae Vind. et Herbipoli, MDCCLIV), IV, p. 455. Je n'ai pas trouvé la preuve qu'il fut grand aumônier de la reine de Navarre comme le disent la *Gallia Christiana* et F. Lehoux.

44 J. Denais, art. cit., pp. 86–90.

en ce qu'il pouvoit ceux de la religion.'[45] Il nomme alors le poète angevin Germain Colin, poursuivi pour luthéranisme en 1539, condamné à l'humiliation de l'amende honorable, à la torture et au bûcher, finalement sauvé par un appel au Parlement de Paris et peut-être en 1545 grâcié par le roi. On ne peut s'empêcher de penser à l'efficace protection de l'évêque.[46] Peut-on pour autant soupçonner Jean Olivier de luthéranisme? Un historien a remarqué que, dans les statuts synodaux d'Angers de 1532 à 1540, on ne trouve aucune condamnation des livres luthériens, distribués pourtant en grand nombre partout en France, sans cesse dénoncés et condamnés par les autorités diocésaines.[47] Mais il serait imprudent, alors que la situation religieuse est encore incertaine, que les choix sont loin d'être fixés, de prétendre définir le credo d'un homme de la génération de Lefèvre et de Budé. Pourtant comment comprendre que l'une de ses épitaphes, celle qui débute par ces mots: 'Inquiris, hospes, quis siem…?', ait eu une remarquable célébrité? Souvent recopiée et citée, traduite en français par des poètes aussi peu orthodoxes que Germain Colin et Clément Marot, par un certain Pierre Bouchet, de La Rochelle, personnage mal connu, elle apparaît, sous une forme agréable, comme un petit testament spirituel, pénétré de certaines idées chères aux réformés; à ses qualités littéraires s'ajoutent quelques audaces doctrinales: le néant de l'homme, essentiellement pécheur, qui ne peut rien sans Dieu; le mépris des honneurs ecclésiastiques, que vient d'ailleurs curieusement démentir la magnificence du tombeau; la nécessaire lecture des Écritures; un silence délibéré sur le purgatoire, remplacé par un 'repos' de l'âme avant la résurrection des corps; enfin l'unique confiance dans la grâce de Dieu.[48]

---

[45] *Histoire ecclésiastique des Églises réformées au Royaume de France*, éd. G. Baum et E. Cunitz (Paris, 1883), I, p. 80. Bèze se trompe en faisant de l'évêque d'Angers le frère du Chancelier. En tout cas, il montre une grande estime pour les deux.

[46] Voir J. Denais, *Un émule de Clément Marot: Les Poésies de Germain Colin Boucher Angevin, secrétaire du Grand-Maître de Malte* (Paris, 1890); Émile Picot, *Supplément aux poésies de Germain Colin* (Paris, 1890), pp. 6–14; N. Weiss, 'Germain Colin et la réforme à Angers (1535–1545)', *Bulletin d'Histoire de la Société du Protestantisme français*, XL (1891), pp. 57–73. Citation de Bèze p. 62.

[47] *Le Diocèse d'Angers*, sous la direction de François Lebrun (Paris, Beauchesne, 1981), p. 104.

[48] Selon Dr Dumont, art. cit., p. 35, il y avait au moins quatre épitaphes latines: trois sont citées, pp. 29 sqq. Voir aussi J. Denais, art. cit., pp. 87 sqq., et Abraham Gölnitz, *VLISSES Belgico-Gallicus* (Lugduni Batavorum, 1581), pp. 273–4. Ce témoin visuel, après avoir cité l'épitaphe 'Ianus Olivarius iaceo…' ajoute: 'Praeter

L'influence de l'évêque sur certains membres de sa famille, sur ses neveux en particulier, est indéniable. On ne peut ignorer que le soupçon de luthéranisme pèse sur eux. Prenons d'abord le parent le plus éloigné, mais le plus connu, le poète Antoine Héroet (Hérouet). C'est le frère de Georges Hérouet, seigneur de Carrières, conseiller du roi et trésorier de ses guerres, mari de Madeleine Olivier, la demi-sœur de François Olivier.[49] Avec l'auteur de *La Parfaicte Amye* nous retrouvons la cour de Marguerite de Navarre et le cercle de poètes, suspects de luthé-ranisme, Marot, Fontaine, Macrin. Ces soupçons prennent quelque consistance quand on connaît les relations de parenté et, si l'on peut dire, d'affaires entre Héroet et le demi-frère du chancelier, Antoine Olivier, prêtre, maître des requêtes, abbé commendataire de l'abbaye du Valasse, évêque de Digne puis de Lombez. On sait qu'Antoine Héroet, lui-même prêtre, longtemps abbé de Cercanceaux, succède à Antoine Olivier à l'évêché de Digne, après en avoir été, pendant un an, 'l'économe et administrateur'.[50] Ce sont là de bons procédés fréquents entre parents et familiers, soucieux de garder dans la famille les bénéfices lucratifs. Or,

hoc sunt plura alia', et il cite l'épitaphe 'Inquiris, hospes, qui sim…?'; éd. 1635, pp. 245–6; Jean Hirelius, *Des Antiquitez d'Anjou* (Angers, 1605), pp. 214–15. Copies du XVIe siècle dans BN MS lat. 4813 f. 262r et dans Dupuy 736, ff. 157v–158r; copie du XVIIe siècle dans BN MS Anjou-Touraine, XVI, ff. 212r et 258v. Voir aussi Clément Marot, *Œuvres poétiques*, éd. G. Defaux (Paris, 1993), vol. II, 1183–4. Il existe trois traductions françaises de cette épitaphe: celle de Marot, éd. cit., II, pp. 397–8; celle de Germain Colin, BN MS lat. 4813, éd. J. Denais, op. cit., n° CCXCVII, p. 269; celle de Pierre Bouchet dans sa *Pandora* de 1548: J. Denais, art. cit., *Revue de l'Anjou*, XIX (1889), pp. 89–90; ce n'est qu'un plagiat de la traduction de Germain Colin. Celle de Marot est la plus exacte.

49 Lucien Grou, 'La Famille d'Antoine Héroet', *Revue d'Histoire littéraire de la France*, VI (1899), 277–82. Grou confond deux 'Madeleine Olivier', p. 280: l'une est en fait la demi-sœur de François, fille de Jacques II et de sa seconde femme, Madeleine Lullier, et mariée à Georges Hérouet (voir par exemple AN MC CXXII 1344, 26 juin 1547; XIX 55, 5 juillet 1523; XIX 57, 9 février 1525 n. st.); la seconde est la fille de Jean, sieur de Mancy et de Perrette Lopin, et la femme de l'avocat au Parlement, Socin de Vitel: MC XIX 70 (9 septembre 1539); XIX 160 (28 avril 1541; 16 mars 1542). Je n'ai pas trouvé la preuve formelle que Georges Hérouet est le frère d'Antoine. Voir aussi Antoine Héroet, *Œuvres poétiques*, éd. F. Gohin (Paris, 1943), pp. VIII–X.

50 AN MC XIX 160 (20 décembre 1541); XIX 185 (18 octobre 1551) 'économe et administrateur': lettres de commission signées du roi à Anet le 7 octobre 1551. Antoine Olivier est aussi seigneur de Villemaréchal (Seine-et-Marne), conseiller au grand conseil, prieur du prieuré de Saint Eutrope de Saintes, membre dépendant de Cluny: MC CXXII 1341 (29 février 1545 n. st.); CXXII 1344 (27 septembre 1547); XIX 176 (16 décembre 1548).

Antoine Olivier, lui-même un lettré, est lié au cercle de Nicolas Bourbon qui l'admire tout particulièrement. Surtout nous savons que, sans doute vers la fin des années 1550, il s'oriente vers la réforme; il meurt dans la religion réformée à Montargis en 1571.[51] Trois autres neveux de Jean Olivier choisissent la voie ecclésiastique de leur oncle, à Angers ou à Soissons. Nous connaissons déjà Gaston, sieur de Mancy, une relation de Nicolas Bourbon, qui lui adresse dans ses *Nugae* de 1538 deux distiques grecs, preuve que ce neveu de l'évêque était, lui aussi, un helléniste. Il devient chanoine et grand archidiacre d'Angers. Il est, de plus, très lié à l'humaniste luthéranisant, Charles de Sainte-Marthe, poète, jurisconsulte et théologien, protégé de Marguerite de Navarre.[52] Nous trouvons ensuite un frère de Gaston, Pierre, qui est grand aumônier de Saint Denis et abbé commendataire de Saint Médard de Soissons. Il meurt prématurément en 1541.[53] Un frère de François, Jean Olivier, doyen de Beauvais, chanoine de Notre-Dame de Paris, est aussi archidiacre de Blois et d'Angers; il meurt en 1533, sans nul doute, dans la force de l'âge.[54] Enfin un Jacques Olivier, cousin de Gaston et l'un de ses héritiers, apparaît souvent dans les documents notariés: c'est un fils de Claude et c'est sans doute lui qui est désigné dans un acte où l'on voit 'Révérend Père en Dieu Jehan Olivier, évêque d'Angers comme soy disant auoir l'administration et gouvernement des biens et personne de maistre Jaques Olivier, son nepveu, escollier estudiant en l'université d'Angers, prevost de Villedommange lez Reims, membre deppendant de

---

51 Testament: BN MS Clairambault 1100, ff. 43r–44r (28 mai 1571 à Montargis). Il fait des legs à ses deux nièces, filles de sa sœur Madeleine, épouse de Georges Hérouet, Madeleine et Diane. Il fait aussi un don 'aux pauvres de la Religion réformée de ceste ville, de laquelle il fait profession'. Il lègue sa bibliothèque à 'Me Mathieu Béroald, professeur public, Jehan Desouches ministre de ceste ville, et Me Jehan Foucault, advocat au Parlement et conseiller de Madame la duchesse de Ferrare, dame dudict Montargis'.

52 Lehoux, p. 39; *Nugae* (1538), VI, n° XXXIII, p. 345. Voir Charles de Sainte-Marthe, *In Psalmum nonagesimum pia admodum & Christiana Meditatio* (s. l. n. d. [1550]) (BN A 630): ép. dédicatoire à Gaston Olivier, seigneur de Mancy; voir C. Ruutz-Rees, *Charles de Sainte-Marthe*, traduction française (Paris, 1919), pp. 114, 117–18, 331–3.

53 AN MC XIX 156 (10 octobre 1540); Lehoux, p. 13 n. 43; *Gallia Christiana*, IV, 403, n° XLIV.

54 BN MSS PO 2142 n° 33–46; AN LL 139, pp. 146–7 (15 novembre 1533) exécution du testament de Jean Olivier.

l'abbaye de Charoux en Poictou'. Il devient archidiacre d'Outre-Maine et chanoine à la cathédrale d'Angers.[55]

* * *

De quelque côté que l'on se tourne, on n'aperçoit dans la parentèle du Chancelier Olivier que des notables lettrés, bien en cour, attachés à la maison de Navarre, établis, grâce à une entraide familiale habile, à des postes honorables de l'État et de l'Église. On peut élargir encore le clan en y ajoutant les Mondoré, alliés aux Ganay,[56] ainsi que les de Thou, apparentés aux Tuelu.[57] Ainsi Pierre de Mondoré, conseiller du roi en son grand conseil, garde de sa librairie, helléniste, mathématicien, astrologue, ≡ astrologer poète néolatin, converti à la réforme, appartient, de loin, à la famille Olivier, tout autant que le père de Jacques Auguste de Thou, Christophle de Thou, seigneur de Cély, premier président en la cour du Parlement.

tout autant (que) : just as much (as)   appartenir
                                                      to belong to

---

55 AN MC XIX 151 (2 mars 1539 n. st.): il est le frère de Jeanne Olivier, femme de
    Pierre Le Bossu (XIX 197, 2 mars 1555 n. st.), fille de Claude Olivier, seigneur
    de Ballainvilliers et de Marie Mangné (XIX 60, 12 janvier 1527 n. st.). Il est
    mentionné dans le testament de Gaston Olivier, Lehoux, pp. 47–9: MC XIX 188
    (17 août 1552): il donne à 'Me Jacques Olivier archidiacre d'Outremaine en
    l'église d'Angers son cousin toute sa chapelle d'argent doré et les aornements
    d'icelle'. Il y avait trois archidiaconés dans le diocèse d'Angers: le grand
    archidiaconé, dont Gaston était titulaire, l'archidiaconé d'Outre-Loire, et
    l'archidiaconé d'Outre-Maine, échu à Jacques Olivier, son cousin: BN MS
    Anjou-Touraine, XVI, f. 518.

56 Pierre de Mondoré est le fils aîné de Jacques de Mondoré, sieur du Rondeau,   aîné
    notaire et secrétaire du roi, et de Perrette Barthomier, dont l'un des frères, Pierre   elder /
    Barthomier, sieur d'Olivet, est marié à Antoinette de Ganay, l'une des sœurs de   eldest
    Jean de Ganay: MC XXXIII 23 (19 novembre 1540), XLIX 13 (21 novembre
    1540) VIII, 69, f. 111r (20 août 1541) 70, f. 364r (13 décembre 1542); 74, f. 149r
    (31 août 1547); Ernest de Ganay, op. cit., p. 102. Pierre de Mondoré est né vers
    1510: il a trente ans environ en 1540: MC VII 180 (15 septembre 1540). Voir
    aussi sur lui Dupré Lasale, op. cit., I, p. 326. Il meurt à Sancerre en 1570.

57 Le président Christophle de Thou (1508–82) est marié à Jacqueline Tuelu, fille
    de Jean Tuelu, procureur au Parlement et seigneur de Cély (Seine-et-Marne) et
    de Jeanne Chevalier: BN MSS PO 2895 n° 2–8, Compardon-Tuetey, op. cit.,
    n° 3029 (AN Y 94, f. 269v) et René Filhol, *Le Premier Président Christofle de
    Thou et la Réformation des Coutumes* (Paris, 1937), pp. 14–15, qui s'appuie sur
    BN MS Dupuy 638 f. 68r. Christophle de Thou est l'un des exécuteurs du
    testament de Gaston Olivier, le cousin germain du Chancelier: Lehoux pp. 31, 49.
    Voir aussi MC VIII 88 (24 janvier 1564), VIII 110 (7 décembre 1580).

[p 89, n. 8]

François Olivier, quant à lui, en se mariant, peut-être dès 1538,[58] à Antoinette de Cerisay, entre dans la puissante *gens* des Bohier.[59]

En dépit d'une jeunesse dissipée, selon son ami le théologien Claude d'Espence,[60] le chancelier reçut une éducation très soignée: son père y fut très attentif, comme François lui-même, à son tour, veilla scrupuleusement à la formation de ses enfants.[61] C'est là un trait de mœurs qui montre clairement les valeurs de cette bourgeoisie parlementaire. Si l'on en croit un avocat à Fontenay-le-Comte, natif de La Rochelle, Jean Imbert, qui semble bien le connaître, François apprit les trois langues: le latin, le grec, et l'hébreu. Ce qui n'est guère surprenant: songeons à son oncle, l'évêque d'Angers, à son cousin Gaston, ou à un juriste tel que Charles Dumoulin, helléniste et hébraïsant.[62] On peut être sûr que le

---

58 Le 14 mai 1538, précisent Moréri, *Le Grand Dictionnaire historique*, VIII, 58 et le P. Anselme, *Histoire de la Maison royale*, VI, 484. La date de 1550 retenue par F. Lehoux, p. 11 n. 27, d'après la fiche Picot, est évidemment fausse; on trouve de nombreux actes d'Antoinette de Cerisay, épouse du Chancelier, dans les années 1540, par exemple MC CXXII 1341 (24 juin 1545): mention d'une procuration du 1er mai 1542 pour 'Dame Anthoinette de Cerisay, femme de noble homme & seigneur Messire Francoys Olivier, chevalier, conseiller du Roy en son prive conseil, president en sa court de Parlement a Paris, chancelier d'Alencon et garde des sceaux de France'. De plus, leur fils aîné, Jean, est né bien avant 1550: le 27 août 1550 il est notaire et secrétaire du roi, BN MS PO, 2142, n° 109.

59 Anthoinette de Cerisay est la fille de Nicolas de Cerisay et d'Anne Bohier: MC VIII 182 (4 juin 1542). Les Bohier sont alliés aux Briçonnet et aux Duprat: Albert Buisson, op. cit., pp. 36–9; P. Hamon, *L'Argent du roi*, pp. 178–9 et *passim*.

60 Claude d'Espence, *Oraison funebre*, p. 16.

61 Voir Jean Imbert, *Paraphrase en Langage Francoys* (1545), qui, parlant du père, Jacques II, écrit dans l'ép. dédicatoire: '(pater) te non solum paternis artibus liberaliter institutum, uerum etiam aliis ingenuae totius encyclopediae disciplinis (quas ille per suorum iniuriam temporum nancisci non licuerat) & praeterea trium linguarum omnium maxime nobilium, Hebraicae nimirum, Graecae, & Latinae, summa ornatum facultate in forum ueluti proscenium produxisset....' C'est Daniel d'Auge qui nous informe, en se flattant naïvement d'ailleurs, du soin qu'a pris le Chancelier de l'éducation de ses enfants: il l'a nommé précepteur: '...me iampridem in tuam asciueris familiam potissimumque delegeris, cui tuos liberos, quorum educationem tam sanctè procuras, instituendos commendares', *D. Gregorii Nyssae De immortalitate animae* (Paris, Gilles Gourbin, 1557).

62 Voir son *Tractatus Commerciorum et usurarum* (Parisiis, 1555: 1ère éd. 1546/7): il cite des versets en hébreu, pp. 3 (il approuve la traduction de Santes Pagnini), 692, 785. Jean-Louis Thireau, *Charles du Moulin (1500–1560)* (Genève, Droz, 1980), p. 142, lui accorde seulement 'quelques rudiments' d'hébreu.

chancelier possède une forte culture et notamment, sans nul doute, dans le domaine de l'Écriture Sainte. Joachim du Bellay, quelques années plus tard, affirme qu'il est helléniste et qu'il cultivait, dans sa jeunesse, la poésie néolatine,[63] témoignage confirmé en partie par George Buchanan.[64] De cette œuvre il ne reste que quelques poèmes latins manuscrits sur la mort de la mère du roi, Louise de Savoie.[65] Comme on doit les dater de 1531, au plus tôt,[66] on peut conclure que le futur Chancelier se mêlait encore de poésie au moins jusqu'à l'âge de trente-quatre ans. On ne saurait donc parler, en toute rigueur, d'un passe-temps de jeune homme: c'est l'activité favorite d'un magistrat de sens rassis. Il suffit de penser à ses confrères et amis, Michel de l'Hospital et Pierre de Mondoré, cités par Montaigne.[67]

Protégé par la sœur du roi, ce lettré parcourt rapidement la carrière des honneurs: après des études de droit, il exerce un temps le métier d'avocat au Parlement sous le patronage de Guillaume Poyet:[68] dès 1525, il est nommé par Marguerite chancelier de son duché d'Alençon, puis il devient maître des requêtes, président à mortier du Parlement; le 25 septembre 1544, le roi lui donne l'office de Garde des Sceaux et, le 28 avril 1545, celui de Chancelier de France.[69]

Avec François Olivier c'est, à bien des égards, le parti de Marguerite de Navarre qui accède à la magistrature suprême et pénètre dans les conseils du roi. Parti complexe, dont on peut énoncer ainsi les idées principales: il aspire à la réforme des abus dans l'État et dans l'Église, à la paix et au dialogue, à l'extérieur, avec les princes luthériens d'Allemagne,

---

63 *Œuvres poétiques*, VIII, éd. G. Demerson (Paris, 1985), *Xenia* 14, vv. 12–16, p. 75.

64 Philip Ford, *George Buchanan, Prince of Poets* (Aberdeen, Aberdeen University Press, 1982), p. 142, 'Eucharisticon', vv. 6–7; I. D. McFarlane, *Buchanan* (London, Duckworth, 1981), pp. 114, 115; voir aussi p. 94, une requête adressée à Olivier par Buchanan sans doute dès 1545 pour le collège de Guyenne.

65 BN MS lat. 8139, ff. 122v–124r: cinq pièces; l'essentiel a été publié par E. Dupré Lasale, op. cit., I, pp. 324–5.

66 Elle meurt entre le 22 et le 29 septembre 1531: *Journal d'un Bourgeois de Paris sous le règne de François premier (1515–1536)*, éd. Ludovic Lalanne (Paris, 1854), p. 426.

67 *Essais*, II, 17. De nombreux poèmes latins de Mondoré se trouvent dans BN MS lat. 8139 et quelques-uns dans le recueil de Janus Gruter, *Delitiae C poetarum gallorum*, (Francofurti, 1609), vol. 4 (BN Yc 8840 (4)), pp. 711 sqq.

68 Claude d'Espence, op. cit., p. 22.

69 *C.A.F.*, IV, 735 n° 14419; IX, 147, 152; BN MSS PO 2142, n° 18, 19, 20, 22, 23–32, 69–75, 78. (Oliver reçoit du roi les sceaux à la mort de François Errault, sieur de Chemans: 25 septembre 1544.)

à la tolérance et à la clémence avec 'les mal sentants de la foi', à l'intérieur du royaume: réforme, paix, clémence sont les principes politiques et religieux notamment de Guillaume et de Jean du Bellay. Dès 1543, Olivier est envoyé avec le cardinal du Bellay pour une ambassade, d'ailleurs avortée, à Spire.[70] Parmi ses amis, quelques noms suffiront à nous faire comprendre le sens de sa promotion: Michel de l'Hospital, le maître des requêtes François de Connan, le conseiller Barthélemy Faye, Jacques du Faur, Jean de Morel: ce sont tous des humanistes, disciples d'Érasme et de Budé.[71] Au grand conseil, citons d'abord son beau-frère, mort prématurément, Nicole Boylève, mari de sa sœur Catherine, son parent Pierre de Mondoré, Aymar de Ranconnet, qu'il peut connaître par Michel de l'Hospital.[72] Enfin les hellénistes, qui représentent l'élite des maîtres ès arts, sont nombreux autour de lui: Loys Le Roy, Pierre Bunel, Daniel d'Auge, précepteur de ses enfants, après avoir été au service de Ranconnet,[73] plus tard, Adrien Turnèbe. En 1541, Étienne Dolet, dans l'épître dédicatoire de la *Pandora*, fait savoir au chancelier d'Alençon qu'il désire se mettre à son service.[74] En 1550, dans son *Oraison*

---

[70] Claude d'Espence, op. cit., p. 26. Voir l'*Oratio de sententia Christianissimi Regis scripta ad Serenissimos...spectabiles uiros uniuersosque sacri Imperii ordines Spirae conuentu agentes* (Paris, Robert Estienne, 1544).

[71] Voir *Francisci Connani Parisiensis...Commentariorum iuris Ciuilis Tomus prior quinque libros complectens. Bartholomaei Faii...praefatio ad Franciscum Oliuarium Franciae Cancellarium...* (Parisiis, Apud Iacobum Kerver, 1553). Voir la préface de Barthélemy Faye et l'ép. dédicatoire de Connan à Olivier; autre édition, Vascosan, 1558. Voir aussi Dupré Lasale, I, chap. V, pp. 94 sqq., p. 186. Voir aussi Michel de l'Hospital, *Discours pour la majorité de Charles IX*, éd. Robert Descimon (Paris 1993), pp. 21–4 et J. Dupèbe et P. Hamon, 'Humanistes en famille: les Meigret', *Bibliothèque d'Humanisme et Renaissance*, LII (1990), 341–3. Faye devient, après 1560, hostile au calvinisme: Irena Backus, *La Patristique et les guerres de religion en France* (Paris, 1993), pp. 40–5 et *Le miracle de Laon* (Paris, 1994), pp. 131–64.

[72] Dupré Lasale, I, p. 95.

[73] Dupré Lasale, II, pp. 53–4. Voir Loys Le Roy, dit Regius, *Le Sympose de Platon* (Paris, Jean Longis et Robert le Mangnyer, 1558), f. 53r. Sur d'Auge voir notre article, 'Documents sur Jean Dorat', *BHR*, L (1988), p. 713. Il se peut que d'Auge ait été au service d'Olivier avant d'être chez Ranconnet; en tout cas, il restera attaché à la famille Olivier.

[74] *Pandora Iani Oliuerii Andium Hierophantae* (Lugduni, Apud Steph. Doletum, 1541). Le texte de l'épître dédicatoire au Chancelier d'Alençon se trouve aussi dans Étienne Dolet, *Correspondance*, éd. Claude Longeon (Genève, Droz, 1982), pp. 238–9. Bonaventure des Périers demande au Chancelier d'Alençon de l'inscrire sur l'état des pensionnaires de la duchesse, *Œuvres françoises*, éd. Louis Lacour (Paris, 1856) I, p. 153.

funèbre de Marguerite de Navarre Charles de Sainte Marthe fait son éloge. Dès 1538, avec Jérôme Groslot et ses amis, Jean Dampierre, Jean Truchon, Pierre Bouguier, Lubin Dallier, il compte des admirateurs à l'Université d'Orléans.[75]

Dans le concert d'éloges qu'a suscité son élévation à l'office de Chancelier, retenons les hommages les plus significatifs. D'abord, parmi les hommes de loi, fonctionnaires de la reine de Navarre, nous rencontrons Guillaume le Rouillé, qui dédie à François Olivier en 1546 sa *Préexcellence de Gaule et des Gaulois*, accompagnée de poèmes de Nicolas Bourbon et de Jean Frotté.[76] Nous trouvons encore le juriste humaniste François Le Douaren, admirateur de la reine de Navarre et du nouveau chancelier.[77] Plus significatif est l'hommage de Jean Imbert: il émane d'un homme qui est dans le camp de Marguerite et des frères du Bellay;[78] il est acquis très tôt, sans doute dans les années 1540, au calvinisme; il est, en tout cas, parmi les premiers fidèles de l'Église réformée de Fontenay-le-Comte en 1557;[79] il est en relations avec

---

[75] Voir Charles de Sainte-Marthe, *In obitum incomparabilis Margaritae Illustrissimae Navarrorum Reginae Oratio Funebris* (Paris, R. Chaudière, 1550), pp. 79–80; *Oraison funebre*, p. 75. Voir sur ce texte l'article de Michel Magnien dans *Travaux de littérature,* VII (Strasbourg, 1994), 65–90. Jérôme Groslot, *De usucapionibus libellus* (Paarisiis [!], Apud Ioannem Lodoicum Tiletanum, 1538; BN F 5423). Lubin Dallier est le premier mari d'Antoinette de Loynes, qui épouse en secondes noces Jean de Morel.

[76] Poictiers, à l'enseigne du Pelican, 1546 (BN Rés. 8° La2 15; ex libris 'De Saincte Marthe'; nombreuses notes manuscrites). 'Dixain de maistre Iean Frotté, Secretaire du Roy, a Maistre Guillaume le Rouillé, Conseiller ordinaire de la Royne de Navarre.' Plus loin poème latin de Bourbon, 'D. Guililemo Rubigineo Amico doctissimo'. L'ép. dédicatoire à François Olivier contient un passage sur Diogène au siège de Corinthe. Elle est datée du 20 avril 1544. Il n'est pas impossible que Rabelais, qui se trouve alors dans l'entourage de Marguerite de Navarre, ait eu connaissance de ce texte avant de composer son 'Prologue' du *Tiers Livre*, même s'il pouvait trouver l'anecdote dans Lucien et Budé.

[77] Voir dans ses *Opera quae ad hunc diem edita sunt* (Apud Audoënum Paruum, via ad diuum Iacobum, sub Lilio aureo, 1550), *De pactis*, 'Ad…Franc. Olivarium Curiae Parisiensis Praesidem:…Quantum enim inclytae et illustri Navarrae Reginae obstrictus sum, quae studia mea diu benignissime fouit, tantum me tibi debere lubens profiteor et agnosco' (Bourges, 1er décembre 1544).

[78] Voir ses *Institutionum forensium Galliae pene totius...libri quatuor* (Paris, R. Chaudière, 1535; BL 502 c 26), ép. dédicatoire à Jean et à Guillaume du Bellay.

[79] Benjamin Fillon, *L'Église réformée de Fontenay-le-Comte* (De l'imprimerie de Pierre Robuchon, 1872 ; BN Rés. F. Ld152 175), pp. 7, 15 (consistoire de mai

l'avocat Milles Perrot, l'ami de Bunel et de l'Hospital.[80] Un autre juriste, lui aussi partisan, dans ces années-là, de la Réforme, l'avocat Charles Dumoulin adresse en 1546 à Olivier son épais *Tractatus commerciorum et usurarum*, qui n'est d'ailleurs pas seulement sur les contrats, la monnaie et l'intérêt; il traite aussi de philosophie politique: l'épître dédicatoire, très élogieuse et très déférente, expose clairement les valeurs de cette classe d'intellectuels réformateurs. Dumoulin salue d'abord en Olivier un humaniste accompli, un grand érudit, qui est, en outre, orné des 'vertus héroïques d'un homme d'Etat'. Comme beaucoup d'autres, l'avocat se plaît à jouer sur le nom 'Olivier', symbole de la paix et de la sagesse, les deux attributs d'Athéna. Ce jeu d'humaniste recèle un idéal politique, que résume, à la fin de l'épître, un mot grec: le chancelier est 'philopolitês': il aime ses concitoyens; il a le sens du bien public. Telle est la plus haute vertu d'un homme d'État.[81] Parmi les réformes récentes, Dumoulin cite l'édit de Moulins d'août 1546 qui s'attaque à la multiplication des procès, à leur infinie longueur et 'embrouillements', et à tous les abus qui en découlaient.[82]

Cet édit est aussi vivement approuvé par Pierre Bunel dans une longue lettre admirative qu'il adresse au Chancelier en décembre 1546 à l'instigation de son 'maître' Jacques du Faur.[83] C'est, au fond, un exposé politique, proche de celui de Dumoulin, mais plus précis. Il se termine brillamment par une petite utopie qui résume parfaitement les aspirations de ces intellectuels. Bunel félicite Olivier d'avoir, au Conseil, commencé à remédier, avec l'approbation de tous, aux abus 'accumulés par l'injustice du passé'. Dans cette tâche, il s'inspire, selon l'humaniste, des

---

1558), 19 (avocat dès 1520, lieutenant criminel au siège royal en 1557 par la protection de Michel de l'Hospital; il meurt en décembre 1560).

[80] Poème latin de Milles Perrot dans les *Institutiones forenses* (1535) de Jean Imbert; on note aussi un poème latin de Jean Garifauld, avocat à Fontenay, beau-père d'Imbert (Fillon, p. 15), et, comme son gendre, protestant. Sur Milles Perrot et sa famille, voir Dupré Lasale, II, pp. 2–3, et pp. 217 sqq.; Perrot est apparenté aux Gohory; l'un des parrains de son fils aîné Louis est le docteur régent de Paris, Jean Tagault (p. 218); de sa fille Marie, Barthélemy Faye (p. 219).

[81] *Tractatus*, op. cit., f. aIIᵛ: 'Cumque inter praecipuas virtutes tuas *philopolitês* sis omnemque *dysnomian* et effrenatam litium multitudinem auerseris...'

[82] Isambert, *Recueil général des anciennes lois françaises* (Paris, 1828), XII, n° 418 (Moulins, août 1546), pp. 912–14.

[83] *Petri Bunelli familiares aliquot epistolae* (Paris, Charles Estienne, 1551), pp. 109–11; éd. Toulouse 1687, pp. 188–90; une copie du XVIᵉ siècle BN MS Dupuy 736, ff. 47ʳ–48ʳ, donne le lieu et la date: Toulouse 1ᵉʳ décembre 1546: '...Nuper, te consiliario impulsore, rex, bonis omnibus plaudentibus, edixit de sanandis uulneribus quae superiorum temporum iniquitate imposita fuerunt....'

leçons morales et politiques des anciens philosophes. Peut-être pourrait-on lui reprocher sa modération, mais, comme les mesures les plus justes rencontrent toujours la plus forte opposition, Bunel préfère parler de sagesse. Le récent édit est le meilleur exemple de cette attitude: dirigé contre la corruption de la justice, il protège les familles des menaces de ruine et les plus grands talents d'une indigne décadence.[84] Puis le propos s'élargit en un discours utopique. Les États ne seront heureux que lorsque les soldats détesteront les guerres, les médecins les maladies, les avocats et les juges, les procès. Car si personne ne cherchait à s'enrichir au détriment d'autrui, si personne ne prenait son bien dans le bien d'autrui, tout le monde ferait obstacle aux maux, dès qu'ils surviennent: les soldats couperaient court aux causes des guerres, les médecins prendraient soin que personne ne tombe malade, les magistrats et les avocats s'opposeraient aux disputes naissantes avec plus de zèle qu'ils ne mettent à les juger tout au long de leur vie. [85] Le sens de ce rêve est que les agents de l'État ne doivent plus s'enrichir du malheur des autres, guerres, maladies, procès. L'État doit rétribuer des fonctionnaires, militaires, médecins, juges et avocats, qui, au lieu d'être, comme aujourd'hui, de malfaisants parasites, seraient, avec une contribution de tous, responsables du bien public. [86] On peut trouver les germes de cette

---

84 Ibid., p. 110 (1551), p. 190 (1687): 'Quae uero ad immoderatam quorundam hominum frangendam ambitionem et lites restringendos in lucem protulisti, cur non summa cum laude tua commemoraremus? Nulla ratione, meo iudicio, Galliae melius prospicere potes, quam si controuersiarum seminarium, quoniam radicitus euelli non potest, magna ex parte circuncidas & amputes. Nulla enim capitalior est pestis hac rixandi consuetudine, qua non solum omnes fortunae absumuntur, verum etiam praeclara ingenia ad liberales artes percipiendas et res maximas gerendas idonea, foedissimo genere morbi exeduntur & extabescunt.' Voir le texte de l'édition Isambert, XII, pp. 912–13, qui contient ces idées.

85 Ibid.: 'Non dubitabo tamen pace hoc asseuerare tua: tum demum beatas fore ciuitates, cum milites a bello, medici a morbis, iudices a litibus abhorrebunt. Nam si nemo ex alterius damno quaestum facere studeret, si nemo ex alterius commodis suum pararet commodum, omnes aduenientibus malis, quoad fieri posset, occurrerent, rei militaris periti bellorum causas preciderent, nunquam nisi necessario et extremorum hostium iniuriis compulsi arma caperent, medici ne quis aegrotaret diligenter caueret, magistratus multo propentius concertationibus nascentibus obuiam irent, quam in eis iudicandis aetatem contererent.'

86 Ibid.: 'Quid? tu ergo hasce honestissimas hominum nationes fame necare uis? Imo uero in pace et otio, militibus stipendium persolui, medicis ab iis qui optima ualetudine uterentur mercedem exigere, causidicos et iudices ab iis qui non litigarent honorarium accipere iuberem.' Sur l'idée de 'bien public' et sur l'idéal du roi 'père de son peuple', voir les pages de Charles Dumoulin, *Tractatus,* op.

philosophie audacieuse chez Érasme et chez Budé. C'est elle, en tout cas, qui inspire le Chancelier dans les mesures qu'il prend le 16 juin 1546 à l'égard des mendiants et des pauvres valides: ces malheureux doivent être impérativement employés à des travaux d'intérêt général, moyennant un salaire.[87] Ainsi l'État doit prendre en main la pauvreté, non pas pour abolir la charité, mais pour user avec discernement de la charité publique, notamment quand il s'agit, comme ici, d'hommes valides.

En matière de religion, le Chancelier appartient au parti des novateurs: les noms que nous avons cités parmi ses proches, ses familiers, ses clients, et ses admirateurs le prouvent suffisamment. Il est néanmoins difficile de préciser davantage ses idées à la fin du règne de François Ier. On ne saurait voir en lui un adepte de la Réforme; le terme vague d''évangélique' serait plus approprié, comme pour beaucoup de ses partisans. Ainsi, en 1550, Sainte-Marthe affirme que la situation religieuse est désespérément confuse; il veut rester dans le sein de l'Église; il ne désavoue pas pour autant ses opinions personnelles.[88] Beaucoup évoluent: le demi-frère du Chancelier, Antoine, évêque de Digne, est engagé dans un long cheminement vers la rupture avec Rome. Un autre exemple de ces incertitudes doctrinales va nous montrer combien la Réforme exerce de séductions sur la famille Olivier et sur son entourage. Peut-être pourrons-nous deviner certaines croyances de François lui-même. L'un de ses parents, François Boylève, lui dédie, on ne sait à quelle date, une *Meditation sur le pseaulme 129*, c'est-à-dire sur le *De profundis*.[89] L'auteur, qui est Conseiller au Parlement puis au Grand Conseil, fonctionnaire du duché d'Alençon et, à ce titre, une accointance de Sainte-Marthe,[90] est, sans nul doute, l'un des frères de Nicole Boylève

---

cit., pp. 73 sqq.: le modèle est Néhémias dans l'Ancien Testament (Nehemias 5). L'éloge de Macrin, qui joue aussi sur le nom 'Olivier', doit dater de l'année 1546, voir J. Gruter, *Deliciae,* op. cit., III (BN Yc 8839 (3)) pp. 560–1.

[87] Isambert, XII, n° 407, p. 900 (16 janvier1546).

[88] *In psalmum nonagesimum,* op. cit.; voir à la fin sa lettre à Gabriel de Puyherbault: il veut rester dans le sein de l'Église et soumettre ses écrits à sa haute autorité, mais il tient quand même à garder sa liberté. Il revendique le droit pour un laïc d'écrire sur la religion: il veut qu'on juge non pas celui qui écrit mais ce qui est écrit.

[89] Bibliothèque Inguimbertine, Carpentras, MS 16. Je remercie la bibliothèque de m'avoir envoyé un microfilm du manuscrit. Le manuscrit est signalé dans la fiche Picot sur Olivier.

[90] *CAF*, IV 747 n° 14474; 761 n° 14542; VII 501 n° 26119; Compardon-Tuetey, n° 3442: Y 95 f. 356ᵛ (26 juin 1550); n° 4085: Y 97 f. 200ʳ (30 décembre 1551). Voir Charles de Sainte-Marthe, *In obitum incomparabilis Margaritae* (1550), pp. 80–1; *Oraison funebre*, p. 76.

(Boileau), le mari, mort prématurément, de Catherine Olivier.[91] Sa *Meditation* est d'inspiration réformée. Un laïc prétend écrire en langue vulgaire sur les psaumes. On sait que Marot, en les traduisant, a ouvert au public le plus large le trésor spirituel de ces chants sacrés et que l'Église réformée a popularisé cette traduction et ces cantiques. Pour un chrétien tenté par les nouveautés comme Sainte-Marthe, ces poèmes inspirés par l'Esprit Saint offrent le meilleur remède aux tribulations.[92] Boylève, pour justifier son entreprise, s'adresse au Chancelier comme à son protecteur et à son confident: il est absolument sûr de trouver en lui un lecteur attentif et bienveillant, car, dit-il, 'je n'ai pu rien offrir ni imaginer de plus saint ni de plus digne d'un chrétien, tel que, nous, nous professons tous de l'être, que ce petit présent'.[93] À l'en croire, Olivier professe donc le même christianisme que lui. Quel est ce christianisme? Nous venons de voir que ce laïc se targue d'une œuvre particulièrement 'sainte'. Il refuse en effet la division entre les fidèles et les prêtres: la communauté chrétienne est une. Il ne veut pas que la Parole soit con-fisquée par une minorité de clercs: 'Vous ne devez nullement supporter la doctrine, ou nous dirons plus justement l'erreur, de ces hommes, qui, après avoir enchaîné chacun à leurs artifices, écartent tout le monde, excepté une minorité, de cette profession du Christ, qui est commune à tous et qui est également efficace au salut de tous.' C'est en quelques mots énergiques se réclamer de la Réforme et inviter Olivier à s'y associer. La conséquence est claire: point n'est besoin d'une formation théologique poussée, réservée à une caste sacerdotale. L'Esprit Saint éclaire le cœur de tout homme qui sait, grâce à une authentique simplicité, être docile à la Parole. Car 'Celui qui ne peut jamais mentir a promis que

---

[91] Voir AN MC XX 50, f. 140^r (2 juillet 1556): on trouve les frères et les sœurs, François Boyleve, conseiller du roi en son grand conseil, Jehanne de Boilleve, femme de Roger (Oger) de Vaudetar, conseiller au Parlement, Nicolas de Boisleve, écuyer, seigneur de Bethemont, feu Nicole Boilleve, en son vivant conseiller du roi en son grand conseil et feue Katherine Olivier sa femme, Magdeleine Boilleve, *leur sœur*, veuve de noble homme Me André Bauldry en son vivant conseille du roi et président ès enquêtes. (On note que, dans un même acte, le nom des membres d'une même famille subit d'étonnantes variations orthographiques: Boyleve, Boilleve, Boisleve. On trouve aussi Boileau pour le mari de Catherine Olivier.) Voir aussi MC LXXIII 52, f. 494^{r-v} (24 décembre 1558).

[92] Sainte-Marthe, *In Psalmum nonagesimum*, f. 5^r; Boylève, MS 16, f. 2^r.

[93] f. 1^v: 'non in spem tantum, verum fiduciam certissimam plane adducor, laeto animo munusculum hoc nostrum "aequanimitatem tuam" suscepturam, quod eo neque sanctius neque uiro Christiano qual en nos profitemur omnes, dignius a me offerri excogitariue potuerit.'

sa douceur et son aide seraient toujours à notre disposition'. Le libre examen, cher à Luther et à Calvin, est hautement revendiqué. De dures épreuves personnelles, ainsi que la sollicitation d'une dame illustre, au cours d'une conversation roulant, entre gens très savants, sur la malheureuse condition humaine, l'ont conduit à composer cette *Meditation*, qui est un credo réformé. Boylève médite longuement sur le péché et la grâce, et sur la foi dans le Christ médiateur. Son texte est rempli de références à l'Écriture et aux Pères, qu'il cite d'ailleurs de mémoire, puisqu'il se plaint, dans l'épître dédicatoire, d'être 'éloigné de la compagnie si chère de sa bibliothèque'.[94] Il lui arrive même de citer le grec du Nouveau Testament. Ce magistrat est donc un humaniste qui possède une solide culture religieuse. Tel est aussi le cas, nous le savons, de François Olivier.

Peut-on dater approximativement cette *Meditation*? Sans doute faut-il la situer dans les années de disgrâce du Chancelier (1551–9). Retiré dans son château de Leuville, il écrit à l'Hospital en 1555: 'Ici je vis pour le Christ et pour moi.'[95] Boylève s'adresse donc à un homme qui, dans sa retraite, s'adonne à la méditation religieuse. Selon François Duchesne, 'entre les manuscrits qui sont dans la Bibliothèque de feu Monsieur le

---

94 Ibid.: 'Nam minime tibi ferenda eorum opinio, vel error verius videbitur, qui vbi suis quemque artibus astrinxerunt, ab hac, quae omnium communis est, omnibusque ad salutem aeque efficax, Christi professione, praeter paucos quosdam, omnes submouent. Cuius nobis eam esse naturam spiritus ille diuinus docuit, quae non animum magnis disciplinis instructum, non multis annis in ea perdiscenda detritum, requirat, sed eum dumtaxat, qui ingenua simplicitate facile se docilem praebeat. Illius sane lenitatem [f. 2r] auxiliumque nobis semper adfuturum pollicitus est is qui mentiri nunquam potest. At sane paucis hisce diebus, qui me summo maerore luctuque exercuerunt, eius in me solando ac vero undique colligendo vim eam sensi. Qua destituti, nec ipse, nec omnes qui uspiam terrarum degunt homines, calamitatem hanc fluctusque, qui nobis assidue impendent, sine summa rerum animique desperatione euasuri videamur. Ad eum igitur quoties opus erit (erit autem in hac vitae molestia fere semper) confugiemus, in eumque nos tanquam in tutissimum portum recipiemus. Porro eorum quae in hunc Psalmum meditati sumus, praeter meum illum animi dolorem anxietatemque, haec etiam occasio fuit. Nam cum nuper doctissimorum [f. 2v] hominum cetui interessem, ortusque forte esset inter eos de uitae huius calamitate sermo, quam nihil aliud quam cursum ad mortem, eumque perbreuem definiebant, rogauit me generis nobilitate, quae tum forte aderat, illustrissima mulier, at eadem ingenii dotibus non inferior, ut eam in rem aliquid scriberem eique primo quoque tempore offerendum curarem.' Plus loin f. 3r: '...neque enim solido adhuc cibo vescimur, neque, si vesceremur, solidius aliquid absentibus nobis a Charissimo Bibliothecae consortio mittere licuisset....'

95 BN MS lat. 8585, ff. 159v–160r: 'Hic Christo et mihi viuo.'

Cardinal de Richelieu, il y a un Traicté de la préparation de l'Ame pour Dieu, un commentaire de l'Oraison dominicale et une Introduction de sapience, composés par Monsieur le Chancelier Olivier, qui peuvent servir de tesmoignage de sa piété et de sa doctrine'.[96]

On peut donc conjecturer que ce magistrat très pieux, dont la mine sévère intimide Michel de l'Hospital,[97] est en totale sympathie avec Boylève. On cultive dans ce milieu de notables une religion savante, nourrie de l'Écriture, qu'on lit dans le grec, voire dans l'hébreu, nourrie aussi des Pères, religion tout intérieure, peu portée sur les cérémonies, centrée sur le Christ, dominée par l'idée du péché et de la grâce. C'est un christianisme austère, lié à une conception pessimiste de l'existence. 'La vie n'est qu'une course rapide vers la mort': telle est, selon Boylève, la conclusion de la compagnie savante, à laquelle il doit en partie le thème de sa *Meditation*.[98] Il faut garder à l'esprit la piété rigoriste de ces humanistes proches de la Réforme pour comprendre l'attitude de Charles de Sainte-Marthe, en 1550, dans sa méditation latine sur le psaume 90: cet admirateur du Chancelier, cet ami de son cousin Gaston, se range publiquement du côté de Gabriel de Puyherbault, moine de Fontevrault, qui, en 1549, dans son *Theotimus* attaque les 'mauvais livres' et dénonce Rabelais avec une particulière violence. C'est que Sainte-Marthe, au nom de sa propre foi, vise les mêmes adversaires, que dénonce d'ailleurs également Calvin, mais sans faire allégeance à Rome ou à Genève.[99] Un tel zèle réformateur, propre à cette classe de juristes érudits et pieux, inspire, quelques années plus tard, au magistrat humaniste Jacques de Vintimille ses deux épitaphes satiriques de Rabelais.[100]

* * *

---

[96] *Histoire des Chanceliers et des gardes des sceaux de France* (Paris, 1680), pp. 630–1.

[97] Janus Gruter, *Deliciae*, III, p. 4: 'Te sum perpetuo veritus, Francisce, tuumque / Triste supercilium mea semper Musa refugit.'

[98] f. 2^{r–v}: voir n. 93.

[99] *THEOTIMUS siue de tollendis & expungendis malis libris...* (Parisiis, Apud Ioannem Roigny; BN Rés. D 13460): violente sortie contre Rabelais, ses livres et ses mœurs, pp. 180–3. Calvin, *Des scandales*, éd. O. Fatio (Genève, Droz, 1984), p. 138. *In Psalmum nonagesimum*, f. 19^v: le passage vise sans doute Rabelais.

[100] Voir notre article 'Deux épitaphes de Rabelais par Jacques de Vintimille', *Équinoxe* (Kyoto, Rinsen-Books, 1987), I, pp. 91–5.

L'humanisme politique et religieux du Chancelier Olivier et de ses partisans subit, de 1545 à 1547, de graves revers. Il est partout, à l'intérieur
comme à l'extérieur, battu en brèche. La fin du règne de François Ier ne
lui est guère propice. La paix de Crépy-en-Laonnois (18 septembre 1544)
signée avec l'Empereur prévoit, dans une clause secrète, une action
concertée pour ramener les Protestants allemands dans l'Église et pour
favoriser la réunion d'un Concile général. L'heure semble donc être
venue d'une remise en ordre dans le royaume, dans l'Empire, et dans
l'Église. La cour est le théâtre d'une lutte entre deux factions autour d'un
roi vieilli et malade. Pour nombre d'observateurs, la fin est proche.[101]
Les lettres de l'historien allemand Johannes Sleidanus, agent du cardinal
du Bellay et ambassadeur des princes protestants de la Ligue de Smal-
kalde auprès de François Ier, nous apportent sur ces intrigues un
témoignage très vivant.[102] Le parti du cardinal du Bellay est aussi celui
qui soutient le Chancelier et qui réunit la sœur du roi, Marguerite de
Navarre, sa maîtresse, la duchesse d'Étampes, qui affiche des opinions
luthériennes, et son second fils, Charles d'Orléans, lui-même sympa-
thisant de la Réforme.[103] Ce parti préconise une politique de tolérance à
l'intérieur du royaume et une alliance, contre l'Empereur, avec les princes
protestants. Mais Sleidanus sent bien que son poids faiblit en face de la
faction adverse qui l'emporte au Conseil privé avec l'amiral Claude
d'Annebault et le cardinal de Tournon, auquel il adjoint le secrétaire des
finances Gilbert Bayard:[104] ce sont des ennemis acharnés de son protecteur: 'ces chancres', comme il les appelle énergiquement, 'poussent aux
bûchers et aux tortures'.[105] Depuis le début des années 1540, les persécutions religieuses se multiplient et s'aggravent. Sleidanus en note avec
inquiétude tous les progrès; il écrit en 1540 au cardinal du Bellay que
Tournon met en place avec l'aide du dominicain Ory une puissante
organisation inquisitoriale, grassement payée par le roi.[106] La nomination

---

[101] R. J. Knecht, op. cit., pp. 483–6, 493–4, 495–500, 508–13.

[102] *Sleidans Briefwechsel*, éd. Hermann Baumgarten (Strasbourg & Londres, 1881).
Maladie du roi, n° 19, p. 38 (27 mars 1545).

[103] Knecht, p. 509.

[104] *Briefwechsel*, p. 40 (4 avril 1545). Voir aussi la lettre n° 22 (13 avril 1545).

[105] Lettre à J. Sturm, n° 32 (29 mai 1545): 'carcinomata illa quae nunc rerum in
Galliis potiuntur et regem gubernant.' Lettre n° 20, p. 40 (4 avril 1545): 'qui
nunc ad flammas et crudelitates instigant, vigent ac vobis infestissimi sunt.' De
même, n° 77 p. 126 (27 avril 1546): 'pestes et carcinomata vestra.'

[106] *Briefwechsel*, p. 23, n° 5 à du Bellay: 'Cardinalis Turnonius monachum Domini-
canum apud se habet. Horris vocatur, quem nosti. Hic factus est generalis

d'Olivier à l'office de Chancelier n'est donc qu'une victoire sans lendemain du parti de la mansuétude sur celui de la rigueur et de la violence. À
cet égard, le supplice d'Étienne Dolet, le 3 août 1546, peut passer pour le
symbole de l'échec que subit la 'philosophie chrétienne' professée par le
Chancelier et ses partisans. D'autres drames vont dans le même sens; le
plus grave est sans doute le massacre des Vaudois du 13 au 23 avril
1545. Olivier, qui n'est alors que garde des sceaux, aurait refusé, selon
Dupré Lasale, qui ne cite pas ses sources, 'd'apposer les sceaux de l'État
aux lettres qui ordonnaient le massacre', allusion à l'arrêt de Mérindol qui
fut repris le 31 janvier 1545.[107] Sleidanus signale encore avec horreur les
condamnations au feu et à la prison des protestants de Meaux en
septembre 1546. Il voit la même politique de répression sauvage en
Belgique.[108] Dès lors, se demande-t-il, à quoi bon un Concile, sinon
pour appuyer, sous la direction de l'Empereur, la politique de répression
mise en œuvre au nom de l'orthodoxie religieuse? À ses yeux, c'est la
violence qui l'emporte et qui sera favorisée par le prochain Concile.[109]

On sait qu'il s'ouvre à Trente le 13 décembre 1545. Les appréhensions
de Sleidanus ne sont pas sans fondement. Le roi envoie au Concile
notamment l'évêque de Clermont, Guillaume Duprat, le fils aîné de son
ancien Chancelier, Antoine Duprat. Comme son père, il est résolument
hostile à la cause évangélique et à la Réforme. Il favorise les compagnons
d'Ignace de Loyola, qu'il installe, quelques années plus tard, à Paris et
dans son diocèse.[110] La quatrième session du Concile, qui a lieu le 8 avril

---

haereticorum inquisitor magno regis stipendio. Adiunctos etiam sub se sex habet
qui nomina innocentium deferunt.'

[107] *Briefwechsel* , p. 49, n° 24 (9 mai 1545): la nouvelle du massacre est arrivée à
Lyon: 'Lugduno hic scriptum est Valdenses in Prouincia summis viribus a rege
oppugnari et vehementer affligi. Non possum affirmare. Hoc est praeludium
fortasse concilii Tridentini.' Nouvelle confirmée dans la lettre suivante du 9 mai
(p. 51, n° 26). Voir Dupré Lasale, I, p. 117. Sur toute l'affaire voir Gabriel
Audisio, *Procès-verbal d'un massacre: les Vaudois du Lubéron (avril 1545)*
(Aix-en-Provence, 1992), Knecht, pp. 513–16, et Marc Venard, *Réforme
protestante, Réforme catholique dans la province d'Avignon au XVIe siècle*
(Paris, 1993), pp. 321–80.

[108] *Briefwechsel*, p. 53, n° 27 (14 mai 1545): persécutions en Belgique; sur les
persécutions à Meaux, le 8 septembre 1546, voir Knecht, p. 510.

[109] Voir ses réflexions amères: *Briefwechsel* , n° 26, p. 51 (9 mai 1545): 'Quis non
uidet qualem illi cogitent ecclesiarum emendationem? Quale concilium?...
Simulant concilium atque interim his praeiudiciis atque suppliciis aperte
denunciant quae sit ipsorum mens atque voluntas.'

[110] Sur lui voir P. Henri Fouqueray, S. J., *Histoire de la Compagnie de Jésus, I Les
Origines et les premières luttes (1528–1575)* (Paris, 1910), pp. 151 sqq:

1546, est singulièrement sévère pour le christianisme savant des humanistes hellénistes et hébraïsants, disciples d'Érasme et de Budé, tels qu'Olivier, ses parents et ses amis; un décret est promulgué sur les écritures canoniques de l'Ancien et du Nouveau Testaments: seule la Vulgate est approuvée, la 'vetus vulgata Latina editio'. Qui plus est, le libre examen est condamné: la lecture de l'Écriture doit être confiée à l'autorité ecclésiastique; surveillance et censure des imprimés sont recommandées.[111] Même si ces décrets ne sont pas près d'être officiellement reçus dans le royaume, ils sont néanmoins mis en œuvre dans les diocèses par des évêques zélés tels que Duprat. On ne peut nier, d'autre part, qu'ils inspirent et secondent une politique de restauration catholique, qui portera ses fruits dès la fin du siècle. En tout cas, à lire Sleidanus, on sent, des deux côtés, un durcissement: certains, dans l'entourage de la duchesse d'Étampes, envisagent une rupture avec Rome, en prenant pour modèle la réforme de Henri VIII, tentation qui apparaît de nouveau avec force dans la crise gallicane des années 1551–2.[112]

* * *

Peut-être n'est-il pas inutile, pour conclure cette étude, de regarder rapidement dans le règne suivant. Plusieurs décisions, avant sa disgrâce de 1551, portent la marque de François Olivier. C'est ainsi qu'après la translation du Concile à Bologne, Henri II envoie, en septembre 1547, l'ambassadeur Claude d'Urfé, accompagné notamment de Michel de l'Hospital et du théologien humaniste et modéré, Claude d'Espence,[113]

Guillaume Duprat, né en 1507, évêque de Clermont le 15 février 1529, mort en octobre 1560. Sur son œuvre voir F. Tournier, 'Monseigneur Guillaume du Prat au Concile de Trente', *Études*, XCVIII (1904), pp. 289–307, 465–84, 622–44.

[111] Mansi, *Sacrorum conciliorum nova et amplissima collectio*, 33 (Paris, 1902), col. 20–3. Duprat arrive à la première session, du 7 janvier 1546 (col. 16). Il y reste jusqu'en mars 1547; cf. F. Tournier, art. cit., p. 295.

[112] *Briefwechsel*, n° 58, p. 108 (30 novemebre 1545). L. Romier, *Les Origines politiques des guerres de religion* (Paris, 1913), I, p. 258: lors du conseil privé du 4 ou 5 août 1551 'l'un des conseillers, peut-être Monluc, soumit à son maître le projet de soustraire complètement l'Église gallicane à l'obédience du pape et de créer, en France, un patriarche qui serait investi de la toute-puissance spirituelle'. Même tentation au début du XVIIe siècle: A. Adam, *Du mysticisme à la révolte: le jansénisme au XVIIe siècle* (Paris, 1968), p. 22: 'Il n'est pas impossible que la mort ait seule empêché Richelieu de faire en France ce que l'Angleterre avait, pour son propre compte, réalisé.'

[113] Dupré Lasale, I, pp. 118, 119 sqq.; L. Romier, I, p. 199.

tous deux amis du Chancelier. À cette époque, le gallicanisme offensif du roi, jaloux de préserver les libertés de l'Église nationale, irrité des abus invétérés de la Curie en matière de fiscalité et de ses ingérences en matière de discipline ecclésiastique, exprime l'esprit unanime de son Conseil, non seulement du connétable de Montmorency et de son neveu le cardinal de Châtillon, mais aussi celui d'Olivier, fidèle à la tradition des légistes du roi.[114] On voit dans un document publié par Romier toute l'influence politique dont il jouit en août 1547 aux yeux du nonce apostolique.[115] Après son départ de la cour, il ne la perd pas entièrement. Dans sa retraite de Leuville, il réunit autour de lui un cercle de familiers et d'admirateurs qui groupe, outre les anciens que nous connaissons, quelques nouveaux venus tels que Joachim du Bellay, Pierre Belon, Antoine Mizauld. On y professe une hostilité toute gallicane à l'égard de Rome et, tout particulièrement, de Jules III;[116] on y est favorable à une politique générale de conciliation avec les 'hérétiques'. Dans ce domaine, le meilleur allié d'Olivier est Michel de l'Hospital. Quand, au lendemain de la mort de Henri II, Charles de Lorraine décide de redonner les sceaux au Chancelier, le 11 juillet 1559, L'Hospital entre au Conseil privé: on reconnaît dans plusieurs réformes la philosophie de l'État que partagent les deux hommes.[117] On peut donc dire que L'Hospital, qui succède à

---

[114] L. Romier, I, pp. 200–1. Voir p. 208: 'Montmorency, le chancelier Olivier et l'Aubespine même enseignent au Très Chrétien l'irrespect à l'égard du pontife.'

[115] I, pp. 56–7, n. 6: 'Au mois d'août 1547, H. Dandino, nonce en France, envoya à la Curie une liste des personnages dont la bienveillance devait être captée par Mich. della Torre, son successeur. Voici ce document, dont nous respectons le classement: Le Roi, La Reine, Le cardinal de Guise, Le connétable, Le duc d'Aumale, Le chancelier. M. de Guise (le père), Mme la Grande Sénéchale (Diane de Poitiers), Le card. de Ferrare, Le card. de Châtillon, La reine de Navarre....'

[116] Les relations de Belon, de Mizauld, et de Turnèbe avec Olivier datent des années de disgrâce. Pour Du Bellay voir le sonnet 162 des *Regrets*: il félicite le Chancelier de s'être retiré de la cour dans sa seigneurie de Leuville. Voir aussi la lettre d'Olivier à Jean de Morel (Leuville, 29 août 1558): Du Bellay, *Œuvres poétiques,* VII, éd. G. Demerson (Paris, 1984), p. 31; Dupré Lasale, II, p. 94. Mais dès 1549, à la fin d'une ode à Antoine Héroët, Du Bellay fait un éloge discret d'Olivier ('Ode XIII', *Œuvres poétiques*, éd. Chamard, III, p. 137, vv. 43–4) et en 1550, dans sa *Musagnœomachie, Œuvres poétiques*, IV, p. 9, vv. 147–8, il répète plus clairement l'éloge. Sur le gallicanisme du poète et son hostilité à Jules III dans les *Regrets*, voir Philip Ford, 'Du Bellay et le sonnet satirique', *Le Sonnet à la Renaissance*, éd. Y. Bellenger (Paris, 1988), pp. 205–14.

[117] Dupré Lasale, II, pp. 137–8.

son ami en 1560, est son disciple le plus fidèle et son meilleur continuateur; sa disgrâce d'octobre 1568 procède des mêmes raisons profondes que celles qui entraînèrent la chute de son aîné.

Mais on doit porter ses regards un peu plus loin, sur les conflits politiques et religieux qui bouleversèrent le royaume et l'État vers la fin du siècle. Dupré Lasale écrit à juste titre au sujet des milieux de juristes des années 1540–50, autour d'Olivier et de L'Hospital: 'On pourrait entrevoir dans les compagnies judiciaires les tendances diverses qui formèrent plus tard les grands partis des ligueurs et des politiques'.[118] On aperçoit en effet dans l'humanisme de François Olivier et de ses amis tous les germes de cette doctrine de l'État et de l'Église qui deviendra, à la fin du règne de Henri III et sous la Ligue, 'le parti des politiques'.

---

[118] Dupré Lasale, I, p. 96.

7

Marot's *Premiere Eglogue de Virgile*: Good, Bad, or Interesting?

Gillian Jondorf

In looking at Marot's translation of Virgil's first Eclogue my interest lies not in Renaissance theories of translation (as examined by scholars such as Glyn P. Norton and Valerie Worth),[1] but in some of the snags and unevennesses of particular renderings, in what seems to have caused difficulty, what has been changed, and finally whether we can trace any connections with Marot's other work.

Marot translated the first Eclogue when he was quite young. We do not know exactly how young, maybe seventeen, maybe nearer twenty, nor do we know why he did it. It was a fairly unusual thing to do, and quite difficult. What help did he have? I assume that the main source of help was the commentary of the fourth-century grammarian and commentator Servius, regularly printed with editions of Virgil,[2] and there is considerable evidence that he used this. (This would be the so-called 'shorter Servius'; the longer one, 'Servius auctus', was not published till 1600.) Chronology would have allowed Marot also to read the additional notes of Josse Bade, available from the beginning of the century, but there is at least one indication that he had no access to these.[3] In re-working his poem after its first appearance he might also take into

---

[1] See Glyn P. Norton, *The Ideology and Language of Translation in Renaissance France and their Humanist Antecedents* (Geneva, Droz, 1984), and Valerie Worth, *Practising Translation in Renaissance France: The Example of Dolet*, Oxford Modern Languages and Literature Monographs (Oxford, Clarendon Press, 1988).

[2] See, for example, Virgil, *Opera* (Venice, Jacobus Rubeus, 1475).

[3] *Buccolicca et Georgica...* [with commentaries of Servius, Mancinellus, and an 'explanatio' by Jodocus Badius Ascensius] (Paris, Jehan Petit, 1500).

account the version of his contemporary Guillaume Michel;[4] evidence of that is inconclusive.

One of the things that attracted me to this poem was the contrary opinions that people have expressed about it. Writing in 1931, Alice Hulubei says: 'dans la première moitié du siècle, presque tous les *traduttori* sont autant de *traditori*.'[5] She goes through some (not all) of Marot's mistakes, mentions his use of 'chevilles', and says that although Marot's translation was admired in the sixteenth century, it 'nous paraît aujourd'hui bien défectueuse' (p. 33). She admits, however, that it is better than that of Guillaume Michel (whom for some reason she calls Michel Guillaume). She also concedes (p. 34) that Marot's version is 'assez harmonieuse et contient peu de verbiage'.

Jean Plattard in 1938 says (inaccurately) that Hulubei 'a relevé toutes les fautes commises par Marot dans sa traduction de la première église'.[6] In fact he points out himself (p. 16) two that Hulubei overlooks: 'servitium' rendered as 'service' instead of 'esclavage', and the 'villae' transformed into 'villes' or 'citez'. He calls Marot a 'faible latineur', but I think he is quite correct when he asserts that this composition is a step towards being a poet, not towards being a scholar, and also that it is not a 'travail d'écolier' since this was not something that schoolboys or students were required to do at the time.

When we come to modern commentators we sometimes find a more positive attitude. Defaux calls the translation 'une incontestable réussite' (p. 414) and with reference to a rendering described by Saulnier as 'fantaisiste' (p. 213 of his 1958 edition of the *Adolescence*) Defaux says staunchly: 'Le latin de Marot me semble ici extrêmement solide' (p. 416).[7]

I should like to take a closer look at some of Marot's mistranslations, and speculate on how they came about. There are some which I think we must admit are plain mistakes, often of construing the syntax. First, there

---

4   *Les Bucoliques de Virgille Maron...*, translated by Guillaume Michel de Tours (Paris, Jean de la Garde, 1516).

5   Alice Hulubei, 'Virgile en France au XVIe siècle' in *Revue du seizième siècle*, XVIII (1931), 1–77. See also the same author's *L'Églogue en France au XVIe siècle. Époque des Valois (1515–1589)* (Paris, Droz, 1938), pp. 209–24.

6   Jean Plattard, *Marot: sa carrière poétique, son œuvre* (Paris, Boivin et Cie, 1938), p. 209 n.

7   See Clément Marot, *Œuvres poétiques. I. L'Adolescence clementine, La Suite de l'Adolescence clementine*, edited by Gérard Defaux, Classiques Garnier (Paris, Bordas, 1990), and Marot, *L'Adolescence clémentine*, edited by V.-L. Saulnier, Bibliothèque de Cluny (Paris, Armand Colin, 1958).

is the misattribution of Virgil's 'spem gregis' (Virgil 15; Marot 29) which seems clearly to refer to the twin kids just lost during or after a difficult birth; Servius and other commentators go into explanations here about how these kids could only have been 'spem gregis' if they were one of each kind, male and female. I do not think this is necessarily the case but at least it shows that they are construing the phrase correctly. Marot however thinks that it refers to the mother, not the babies. This does not seem to me to matter very much. The mother *could* be the 'spes gregis' in that she was expected to produce good young; it is not a mistake that makes nonsense of the text, although it certainly appears careless since 'spem' is plainly an accusative and must be in apposition to the accusative babies, not to the nominative mother.

However, there is perhaps something else going on here. Marot has added some padding here; his line 26 is a 'cheville' and it causes difficulty for the accurate translation of 'spem gregis'. It creates an abundance of young animals, so that the pathos of what Meliboeus is saying has to be shifted. In Virgil, the disaster is that two good kids, which would have been a valuable part of the herd's future, have been lost; and this loss is probably due to the fatigue caused by the trek. In Marot's version, there is no shortage of young animals (see his line 26), but it is disappointing for Meliboeus that what was perhaps his best breeding female, 'spes gregis', has let him down. It is different, but it works. Marot seems to have got himself into an awkward pass where he was obliged to make a further change, once he had added those 'Aigneaulx, et Brebiettes'.

The next point where we may quarrel with Marot is about his misunderstanding of the 'beard' line (Virgil 28); although oddly neither Alice Hulubei nor Jean Plattard seems to have spotted this one. The passage may seem quite straightforward (Tityrus says that his beard was growing white by the time he started thinking seriously about obtaining his freedom) but it has caused some worry among translators and commentators. Servius as far as I can make out understands the Latin but is worried because the allegory seems to be breaking down. Servius identifies Tityrus with Virgil (although he does warn about overdoing this), so here he is unhappy because Virgil wrote the *Bucolics* when he was twenty-eight and not when his beard was getting whiter; therefore, he says, either we must here understand that we are listening not to Virgil speaking of himself, but to 'quemdam rusticum', since anyone can have a beard at twenty-eight but not a white one, or we must read 'candidior' as referring not to the beard but to 'libertas'. Guillaume Michel seems to have read this rather strange gloss in Servius and been confused by it, not surprisingly; in his translation he renders the line as 'when I first had my beard trimmed' ('depuis le temps et l'heure / Que de mon chief la barbe eust tonsure'), ignoring 'candidior'; and in his prose commentary he says this means at the age of twenty-eight. Marot has not understood the Latin either (Marot 61), and also ignores 'candidior', but does at least then make sense of what he has put, because having made Tityrus say that he had a beard by the time love of liberty visited him, he does then, as it were, age Tityrus, by extending the time that elapses before he does anything about it, in line 63: 'Et puis je l'euz assez long temps apres.' Thus he extricates himself from the difficulty that his problem with the Latin got him into.

Next we should look at Marot's erroneous translation of 'nec cura peculi' as if the Latin word had been *pecus* instead of *peculium* (Virgil 32, Marot 69); this has been criticised by several editors and commentators, but it is the passage that Defaux defends as showing 'extrêmement solide' knowledge of Latin. I am not sure that translating a word as though it were another word etymologically related to it is a very convincing demonstration of knowledge; I rather suspect that it is indeed a mistake, but again it works out all right in the end. To clarify that, I should perhaps say a little more about what is going on in this Eclogue. The extent to which some commentators have wanted not only to identify Tityrus with Virgil but indeed to allegorise every figure and item in the poem is laughable — in such an allegorised reading, Amaryllis is Rome, Galatea is Mantua, the fruits hanging on the trees are honours available in Rome, and so on; but the starting point of the Eclogue nevertheless does rest on an identification between Virgil and Tityrus. This poem plainly refers to a passage in Virgil's life when he lost his country property through land-confiscations that began after the battle of Philippi in 42 BC and went on until after the battle of Actium in 31, their purpose being to make land available for the resettlement of veterans from the victorious armies. With the support of powerful friends, Virgil made a successful appeal to Octavian and either got his own land back or was compensated by a grant of land elsewhere. Tityrus in the Eclogue has also had a fortunate outcome from an appeal to Octavian but his position is very different. He is apparently an ageing slave threatened, by the evictions, with losing his one chance of gaining freedom, so he joined a slaves' protest march to Rome (the language of Octavian's reply, addressing the petitioners as 'pueri', makes this clear). The significance of the spend-thrift habits of his first partner, Galatea (not his wife — slaves could not marry), was that he did not save up towards his own emancipation. Rural slaves were allowed to keep some personal profit (*peculium*) from the animals (*pecudes* or *pecora*) that they tended. Now that Tityrus is able to stay on the land, and has a thriftier partner, he will be able to amass the *peculium* and eventually buy his freedom. So Tityrus' financial well-being and ultimate emancipation are indeed very closely connected with the 'bestail' he looks after, and Marot's mistake (and my guess is that it is a mistake) does not make nonsense of the text, far from it. What it does do is remove the traces of the word *peculium*, which is not only quite a technical and perhaps unpoetic term, but one which is particularly bound to the economic and social conditions of first-century AD Rome.

This raises points which I shall come back to, but first I shall mention a few more criticisms by Hulubei which seem to me mistaken for one reason or another. The first is the misreading of 'ingratae urbi' (Virgil 34, Marot 73) as 'à [or 'en'] nostre ingrat village'. There is certainly an error here, but she says Marot has taken the dative for a genitive; I am not sure how she works that out — my guess is that he reads it as a locative, and that this in turn has led to the rather inappropriate translation of 'urbs' as 'village'. Hulubei complains about 'hinc' rendered as if 'hunc' in Virgil 20; but the word is not 'hinc' anyway, but 'huic', and her comment makes no sense to me: Marot translates this quite adequately. 'Submittite tauros' (Virgil 45, Marot 96) Hulubei misquotes as 'submitte', and says that Marot has mistranslated it. Marot's translation does reflect a possible meaning, and it is one which is mentioned by Servius, so although the modern editor, Robert Coleman, considers it the 'least likely' meaning, I think it must be said that this is not a mistake.[8] With respect to 'insueta pabula' (Virgil 49, Marot 103) she gives a wrong line-number and says that Marot's mistranslation of it as 'mauvais pâturage' 'provoque l'obscurité et le non-sens de tout le passage' which is hardly the case, although he plainly has missed something here, and Servius will have been of little use to him because he is in a certain amount of confusion here himself. Then there is the 'frondator' (Virgil 56, Marot 117): here again, Servius authorises Marot's translation of this as 'rossignol' (rather than woodcutter or vine-pruner), because he says there are three meanings, one of which is a bird which lives among the *frondes* (leafy branches or foliage); and Marot's other slight inaccuracies here are consonant with that interpretation (for example rendering 'sub' as if it were 'de' or 'super'). Lastly Hulubei mentions the misattribution of 'tua cura', the doves that Tityrus cares about; the phrase is mistakenly attributed to the

---

8   Virgil, *Eclogues*, edited by Robert Coleman (Cambridge, Cambridge University Press, 1981) (first published 1977).

doves themselves, 'pour te complaire'; again this is a mistake but it does not impede understanding or severely distort meaning.

So far, these errors seem slight and forgivable. Perhaps the most shocking 'error' in Marot's rendering of the first Eclogue is what he does with 'villae'. At the end of the poem Tityrus, who has hitherto been a little smug and cold, invites the unlucky exile Meliboeus to stay the night. He tells him what he can offer him in the way of accommodation and food, and to press the case he says, in the memorable closing lines of the poem:

> et iam summa procul villarum culmina fumant
> maioresque cadunt altis de montibus umbrae.

> (...in the distance the smoke is rising from the rooftops of the farmhouses, and longer shadows are falling from the high peaks.)

Here Marot startles us by translating 'villae' as 'Citez' — 'Puis des Citez les Cheminées fument' (and the first printed version, in the *Adolescence clementine* of 1532, had 'Et puis des villes les cheminees fument', presumably one of the lines he altered to eliminate the *coupe féminine*, once he had learned that that was no longer acceptable). Well, yes, it is an error in that it is certainly not what Virgil meant. And sixteenth-century readers did know what *villa* meant in classical Latin. When the first Latin-French dictionary appears, *villa* will be correctly rendered as 'metairie'. I suppose that what Marot has done here is make what we may consider an unfortunate choice between classical and modern Latin meanings, for in sixteenth-century Latin, *villa* did mean town. Perhaps Marot ought to have known better, but it was probably an easy mistake to make at a time when Latin was still a live language and quite a few Latin words had different meanings in classical contexts and in contemporary usage. Furthermore, Marot may have wanted to bring the 'Citez' or 'villes' into the closing lines of his poem for reasons to be mentioned later. Michel curiously enough makes the same mistake, not in his translation where he translates 'villarum culmina' as 'maisons eslevees' but in his prose commentary where he says laboriously: 'Pour mieulx le soir luy demonstrer les cheminees et fourneaulx qui fument des villes et citez luy demonstre.' You may consider this an elementary mistake, but like most such mistakes it is not completely illogical; Marot and Michel are guilty here not so much of ignorance as of a sort of linguistic ana-chronism. If Marot had consulted Josse Bade's gloss on this passage he would have found a simple, clear, exact definition of 'villarum' as 'domuum in agris constructarum' which would have got him out of trouble. It is from this that I surmise that he did not have access to a Josse Bade edition.

All in all, I think it is true to say that some of Marot's renderings have been wrongly accused of error, and most of the errors which are present are quite slight; either they do not much affect meaning, or Marot has made good the damage by making other, compensatory changes.

To catalogue Marot's mistakes or inaccuracies gives, in any case, a very one-sided impression of this piece, and we ought also to consider his successes. If we can assume that Marot was following Servius in some respects as a guide for the translation of the Eclogue, then it should be mentioned to his credit that there are some passages where he manages better than Servius, as well as better than his contemporary Guillaume Michel. One example of such a passage is Meliboeus' speech beginning 'Fortunate senex' (Virgil 46, Marot 97). Hulubei says Marot has made a mess of this because he has mistranslated 'insueta' as 'mauvais'. I think he has done rather well compared to both Servius and Guillaume Michel, both of whom make perfectly absurd comments on this passage and do not seem to have noticed the concessive clause at all. Meliboeus is saying that even if Tityrus's grazing land is in parts rocky, and in parts marshy, yet he is fortunate in being secure in his occupancy of it. Servius thinks the boundaries of Tityrus's land are being described here, and he seems to be reading 'lacus' for 'lapis', which perhaps explains Marot's introduction of a lake (Marot 101). Michel's translation of this passage is expansive (five lines in Virgil are represented by seventeen and a half lines in Michel) and very loose, completely missing the weighing up of Tityrus's disadvantages and advantages. Marot too is in difficulties here, but at least he puts in a 'quoique' and a 'neantmoins', which suggests that he has some idea of what is going on, although some of his details are inaccurate.

Another respect in which Marot scores over Michel is in something which is quite basic to the task of translating Latin hexameters into French verse. This is hard to achieve line for line, because of the greater concision of Latin (although two twentieth-century versions, by Xavier de Magallon and Paul Valéry, show that it can be done if the alexandrine is chosen rather than the decasyllabics of Marot and Michel). A deca-syllabic French version will inevitably be longer than the Latin, but 'two-lines-for-one' will not quite work either, being too generous a ratio, and will require the use of *chevilles*. There are plenty of these in Marot, and with their help he ends up with a poem about twice as long as Virgil's, 172 lines as against 83. The more expansive Michel has 348 lines, more

than four times as many as the source text and more than twice as many
as Marot. This is partly just amplificatory wordings, partly a tendency to
let the commentary creep in to the translation. Both of these things are
going on, for example, in his rendering of line 82, 'et iam summa procul
villarum culmina fumant' which becomes three lines:

> Regarde sus es maisons eslevees
> Et tu voirras nubileuses fumees
> Qui de la nuyt le somme nous presentent.

Even with a little commentary thrown in, explaining why the smoke is
rising (a sensible gloss, derived from Servius), Marot makes this into
only two lines:

> Puis des Citez les Cheminées fument
> Desjà le feu pour le soupper allument...

When we compare Marot with Michel, we also find that there are
passages where Marot is more successful in rendering Virgil's effects
(and here we may remember Plattard's comment that the Eclogue shows
us Marot practising to be a poet, not a classicist). One example can be
found at the opening. The opening words of Virgil, 'Tityre tu', taken up
three lines later as 'tu Tityre' seem to many commentators to suggest the
sound of Tityrus' 'tenuis avena', his rustic pipe, an effect imitated from
Theocritus. Michel does not do much about this, but Marot creates an
elaborate sound-pattern round 'chant' — 'Chantes Chansons rustiques en
beaulx Chantz' with a following rhyme 'doulx champs' reinforced by
'Chalumeau' and 'Chalumelle', so that the music made by Tityre runs
through the whole opening speech of Melibée. It is a *rhétoriqueur* device,
used with discretion. Similarly he picks up Virgil's alliteration in 'm' in
line 36 (Marot 75), and his humming bees (114–15) with five 'ou'
sounds in two lines are certainly more soporific than Michel's. (Virgil's
bees, in line 55, buzz rather than hum.) Marot does not match all Virgil's
effects. He blurs still further the already rather obscure story of the
Eclogue, and he softens the characterisation of the two women
mentioned in it; Virgil subtly suggests by the use of verbs (30–1) that
these women are quite possessive and bossy; in Marot (64–7) Tityre has
become the grammatical subject and this little vignette of characterisation
has disappeared completely.

It is easy to assume that Marot's mistranslations are accidental, but
perhaps the most interesting are those which seem to be intentional. Why
for example does he translate 'boves' (Virgil line 9) as 'brebis' (Marot

line 15)? When Tityrus says that he used to think that Mantua bore the same relation to Rome as a kid to the mother goat, why does Marot translate 'haedos' (kids, young goats) as 'Agneaulx'? I would suggest that Marot's translation embodies tendencies that account for some of his apparent errors.

The first tendency might be labelled a tendency towards mono-pastoralism. The vocabulary in Virgil points to mixed flocks — cows, sheep, and goats. Marot has not completely eradicated this variety but has certainly developed a bias in favour of sheep. In several passages in the poem, goats or bovines (*boves*) are replaced by sheep. As just mentioned, this happens in Virgil's line 9: 'meas boves' is retained by Michel as 'mes beufz' but in Marot these become 'mes Brebis'. Virgil's reference to goats in line 12–13 is rendered by Michel in goaty terms as 'chievres et cappelles' but Marot has 'Chevrettes / Accompagnées d'Aigneaulx et Brebiettes'. Then look at Marot's rendering of line 14 of Virgil: Virgil does not specify the species of the 'gemellos' but in his text the mother is plainly a goat (see 'capellas' in line 12). Both Michel and Marot here refer to lambs rather than kids. Michel says 'deux aigneaulx', Marot has 'deux gemeaulx Aigneletz'. Tityrus's comparison in line 22, where he says he assumed that Rome was to Mantua as puppies to dogs or kids to mother-goats is somewhat garbled by Michel, but the animals emerge as 'Vaches et veaulx'; Marot once again replaces goats by sheep: 'Mais je faisois semblables à leurs Peres / Les petitz Chiens, et Aigneaulx à leurs meres.' It seems clear that both Michel and Marot are reducing the presence of goats, and Marot even more than Michel. Marot does it again, for instance, when he gives us Meliboeus calling his flock to carry on their trek (Virgil 74, Marot 155). The effect is to shift the ancient Italian mixed flocks and herds into a more northern stock of sheep and cows. Sometimes this leads to slight absurdity as when a goat apparently produces lambs; but in itself the tendency seems to imply a clear intention of making the classical pastoral at home in a more northerly setting. Perhaps the addition of garlic and 'pruneaux' to the meal offered by Tityre at the end of the poem (although probably inspired by the need to add syllables) can also be seen as part of the 'domestication' or naturalisation of the Roman pastoral into French, while another element of French naturalisation is the replacement of the turf hut (Virgil 68) by a thatched cottage (Marot 141).

I suggest that this tendency extends to the removal of other Rome-specific details and technicalities. Jean Plattard complained about 'servitium' (Virgil 40) being translated by Marot as 'service' rather than 'esclavage' (Marot 84). In fact *servitium* can mean service as well as slavery, and although it undoubtedly means slavery in Virgil, Marot's choice of 'service' has the effect of reducing the clash between Roman and French contexts. Rural shepherds in ancient Rome were in slavery, those in early modern Europe were not. A similar effect is promoted by the elimination of the technical term *peculium* and its replacement by 'cure de bestail'. There are other semi-technical and non-pastoral terms which Marot softens or passes over. Thus, 'patriae fines' in line 3 with its emphatic repetition of 'patriam' in line 4 is smoothed down into 'nos Pays'. The word 'limes' in line 53, with strong connotations of legal land-ownership, becomes in Marot 'La grand Closture' which is less strongly legal, and again blurs Virgil's references to a particular moment, and a particular socio-legal system.

Marot also seems to work towards a reduction of the opposition between town and country. Hulubei thinks that Virgil's shepherds 'par leur identité double, étaient à la fois citadins et rustiques, instruits et ignorants'. Maybe. But as 'rustiques', they are part of an opposition between town and country which is fundamental to classical pastoral. Marot does not eliminate this contrast, indeed he hardly can, since the turning-point of Tityrus's fortunes is a trip to Rome. But he does remove one reference to it, and that is when he translates 'urbs', the 'ingrata urbs' to which Tityrus takes his cheeses to market for such poor financial reward, as 'village'. He cannot possibly think 'urbs' means 'village', and he may just be making sense of his own mistake — since he apparently thinks 'ingratae urbi' means in the 'urbs' instead of for it, perhaps this leads him to reduce the city to a village so that Tityrus can plausibly make his cheese there. But it has the effect of removing one moment of the town/country opposition, making the country so to speak self-sufficient, the place of ingratitude as well as of 'beaulx Chantz' and 'doulx champs' and leisure to lie in the shade and pipe or slumber.

This brings me to my last point — Marot's eclogue as a prophetic text. Frank Lestringant speaks of Marot's translation of the Eclogue as an 'autoportrait en partie double — Marot–Tityre et Marot–Mélibée' and says that the Eclogue 'esquisse…pour Marot un programme de vie contradictoire' so that it is 'significative de l'œuvre et du destin de Clément Marot'.[9] Gérard Defaux similarly says: 'On ne peut par ailleurs que souligner la dimension proprement *prophétique* de cette traduction', and he weaves the idea of Marot as both Tityre and Mélibée through the

---

[9]   Marot, *L'Adolescence clémentine. L'Enfer. Déploration de Florimond Robertet. Quatorze Psaumes*, edited by Frank Lestringant, NRF Poésie (Paris, Gallimard, 1987) p. 17.

account of the poet's life with which he introduces his edition. Thus on page clxv: 'Jusqu'à la fin donc, Marot aura en lui un Tityre et un Mélibée, un Tityre qui rêve à la liberté de Mélibée, un Mélibée qui voudrait connaître la sécurité de Tityre.' I think this is a pleasing idea, but it does seem to me that it resides above all in the Virgilian text rather than in anything Marot has done with it. The happy, secure poet-shepherd Tityrus and the sad, dispossessed exile Meliboeus — these are Virgil's invention and not Marot's. If anything is prophetic as regards Marot's life, it must lie in his *choice* of this piece rather than in the details of his rendering.

However, the translation may be prophetic in another way. Perhaps it is prophetic not of his life but of what he (and indeed other, later, French poets) make of classical pastoral. The elimination of specifically Roman or Greek elements will be taken further in later eclogues, without necessarily being eliminated. Characters will have names like Robin, Thenot, Colin instead of Tityre and Melibée (as Ronsard's shepherd in the 'forêt de Gastine' has a girl-friend called Janette). Sheep continue to take over the herds, and they even (as we shall see) take over the domain of simile and comparison. The shepherds in Marot's eclogue on the death of Louise de Savoie keep a sheep dog, which shepherds in Theocritus and Virgil do not. Rather than the countryside being contrasted with the town, the pastoral scene in Marot's later eclogue will stand for the whole republic — Pan is the king, his temple the court; the shepherd mourning Louise recites the grief of the towns and regions of France. The emphasis on *otium* in the Roman pastoral is already weakened in Marot's translation — for example Virgil in line 6 has 'haec otia', Marot translates this in line 10 as 'ce bien icy'. In the eclogue for Louise de Savoie she is shown, in life, teaching young shepherdesses and, drawing on sheep for a moral simile, she warns them specifically that 'oysiveté' (*otium*):

> ...est pire entre jeunes Bergeres
> Qu'entre Brebis ce grand Loup ravissant.

In Marot's hands, pastoral is French, and the pastoral mode embraces the nation; it is a reflection — idealised or distorted — of the world outside (which is perhaps why the *villae* of the countryside become cities), whereas Virgil's pastoral is, in some sense at least, *about* the countryside, and can tolerate a rustic and technical vocabulary that increasingly disappears from modern pastoral until we reach D'Urfé's shepherdesses with their taffeta dresses and complete freedom from sheep.

125

M. Tityre, tu patulae recubans sub tegmine fagi

siluestrem tenui Musam meditaris auena;

nos patriae finis et dulcia linquimus arua.

nos patriam fugimus; tu, Tityre, lentus in umbra

formonsam resonare doces Amaryllida siluas.

T. O Meliboee, deus nobis haec otia fecit.

namque erit ille mihi semper deus, illius aram

saepe tener nostris ab ouilibus imbuet agnus.

ille meas errare boues, ut cernis, et ipsum

ludere quae uellem calamo permisit agresti.   10

M. Non equidem inuideo, miror magis; undique totis

MELIBÉE

Toy, Tityrus, gisant dessoubz l'Ormeau
Large, et espez, d'ung petit Chalumeau
Chantes Chansons rustiques en beaulx Chantz:
Et nous laissons (maulgré nous) les doulx champs,
Et noz Pays. Toy oysif en l'umbrage
Faiz resonner les forestz, qui font rage
De rechanter apres ta Chalemelle
La tienne Amye Amarillis la belle.

TITYRUS

O Melibée, Amy chier, et parfaict,
Ung Dieu fort grand ce bien icy m'a faict.   10
Lequel aussi toujours mon Dieu sera,
Et bien souvent son riche autel aura
Pour sacrifice ung Aigneau le plus tendre,
Qu'en mon Trouppeau pourray choisir, et prendre:
Car il permect mes Brebis venir paistre
(Comme tu voys) en ce beau Lieu champaistre:
Et que je chante en mode pastouralle
Ce, que vouldroy de ma fluste ruralle.

MELIBÉE

Je te prometz, que ta bonne fortune   20
Dedans mon cueur ne met envie aulcune:

usque adeo turbatur agris. en ipse capellas

protinus aeger ago; hanc etiam uix, Tityre, duco.

hic inter densas corulos modo namque gemellos,

spem gregis, a, silice in nuda conixa reliquit.

saepe malum hoc nobis, si mens non laeua fuisset,

de caelo tactas memini praedicere quercus.

sed tamen iste deus qui sit da, Tityre. nobis.

T. Vrbem quam dicunt Romam, Meliboee, putaui

stultus ego huic nostrae similem, quoi saepe solemus   20

pastores ouium teneros depellere fetus.

Mais m'esbays, comme en toutes saisons
Malheur nous suyt en noz Champs, et Maisons.
Ne voys tu point, gentil Berger, helas,
Je tout malade, et privé de soulas,
D'ung lieu loingtain mene cy mes Chevrettes
Accompagnées d'Aigneaulx, et Brebiettes.
Et (qui pis est) à grand labeur je meine
Celle, que voys tant meigre en ceste Plaine,
Laquelle estoit la totalle esperance
De mon Trouppeau. Or n'y ay je asseurance,   30
Car maintenant (je te prometz) elle a
Faict en passant, pres de ces Couldres là,
Qui sont espez, deux gemeaulx Aigneletz,
Qu'elle a laissez (moy contrainct) tous seuletz,
Non dessus l'herbe, ou aulcune Verdure,
Mais tous tremblans dessus la Pierre dure.
   Ha Tityrus (si j'eusse esté bien sage)
Il me souvient, que souvent par presage
Chesnes frappez de la fouldre des Cieulx
Me predisoient ce mal pernicieux.   40
Semblablement la sinistre Corneille
Me disoit bien la fortune pareille.
Mais je te pry, Tityre, compte moy
Qui est ce Dieu, qui t'a mis hors d'esmoy?

TITYRUS

Je sot cuidois, que ce, que l'on dit Romme,
Fust une Ville ainsi petite, comme
Celle de nous: là où maint Aignelet

sic canibus catulos similes, sic matribus haedos

noram, sic paruis componere magna solebam.

uerum haec tantum alias inter caput extulit urbes

quantum lenta solent inter uiburna cupressi.

M. Et quae tanta fuit Romam tibi caussa uidendi?

T. Libertas, quae sera tamen respexit inertem,

candidior postquam tondenti barba cadebat,

respexit tamen et longo post tempore uenit,   30

postquam nos Amaryllis habet, Galatea reliquit.

namque — fatebor enim — dum me Galatea tenebat,

nec spes libertatis erat nec cura peculi.

quamuis multa meis exiret uictima saeptis

Nous retirons, et les Bestes de laict.
Mais je faisois semblables à leurs Peres
Les petiz Chiens, et Aigneaulx à leurs Meres,
Accomparant (d'imprudence surpris)
Chose petite à celle de grand pris:
Car (pour certain) Romme noble, & civile,   50
Lieve son chef par sus toute aultre ville,
Ainsi que sont les grandz, & hautz Cipres
Sur ces Buyssons, que tu voys icy pres.

MELIBÉE

Et quel motif si expres t'a esté
D'aller veoir Romme?

TITYRUS

Amour de Liberté:
Laquelle tard toutesfois me vint veoir: 60
Car ains que vint, barbe pouvois avoir.
Si me veit elle en pitié bien expres,
Et puis, je l'euz assez long temps apres:
C'est assavoir, si tost qu'eus accoinctée
Amarillis, et laissé Galathée.
Certainement je confesse ce poinct,
Que quand j'estoys à Galathée joinct,
Aulcun espoir de Liberté n'avoye,
Et en soucy de Bestail ne vivoye: 70
Voire et combien, que maintesfois je feisse
De mes Trouppeaux à noz Dieux sacrifice,

pinguis et ingratae premeretur caseus urbi,

non umquam grauis aere domum mihi dextra redibat.

M. Mirabar quid maesta deos, Amarylli, uocares,

quoi pendere sua patereris in arbore poma.

Tityrus hinc aberat. ipsae te, Tityre, pinus,

ipsi te fontes, ipsa haec arbusta uocabant.

T. Quid facerem? neque seruitio me exire licebat　　40

nec tam praesentis alibi cognoscere diuos.

hic illum uidi iuuenem, Meliboee, quot annis

bis senos quoi nostra dies altaria fumant,

hic mihi responsum primus dedit ille petenti:

'pascite ut ante boues, pueri, submittite tauros.'

Et nonobstant que force gras fourmage
Se feist toujours à nostre ingrat Village,
Pour tout cela, jamais jour de Sepmaine
Ma Main chez nous ne s'en retournoit pleine.

MELIBÉE

O Amarille: moult je m'esmerveillois
Pourquoy les Dieux d'ung cueur triste appellois:
Et m'estonnois, pour qui d'entre nous hommes
Tu reservoys en l'Arbre tant de Pommes.
Tityre lors n'y estoit (à vray dire)
Mais toutesfois (ô bien heureux Tityre)　　80
Les Pins treshaultz, les Ruisseaulx, qui coulloient,
Et les Buissons adoncques t'appelloient.

TITYRUS

Qu'eusse je faict, sans de chez nous partir?
Je n'eusse peu de Service sortir,
N'ailleurs, que là, n'eusse trouvé des Dieux
Si à propos, ne qui me duissent mieulx.
Là (pour certain) en estat triumphant
(O Melibée) je vey ce jeune Enfant:
Au los de qui nostre Autel par coustume
Douze foys l'An en sacrifice fume.　　90
Certes c'est luy, qui premier respondit
A ma requeste, et en ce poinct me dit:
Allez Enfans, menez paistre voz Boeufz,
Comme devant, je l'entends, et le veulx:

MELIBÉE

Heureux Vieillard sur tous les Pastoureaux,
Doncques tes Champs par ta bonne adventure
Te demourront, et assez de Pasture,
Quoy que le Roc d'herbe soit despoillé,
Et que le Lac de Bourbe tout soillé,
Du Jonc Lymeulx couvre le bon herbage,
Ce neantmoins le maulvais Pasturage
Ne nourrira jamais tes Brebis pleines: 100
Et les Trouppeaux de ces prochaines Plaines
Desormais plus ne te les gasteront,
Quand quelcque mal contagieux auront.
Heureux Vieillard, desormais en ces Prées
Entre Ruisseaux, et fontaines sacrées
A ton plaisir tu te reffreschiras:
Car d'un costé joignant de toy auras
La grand Closture à la Saussaye espesse,
Là où viendront manger la Fleur sans cesse
Mousches à miel, qui de leur bruyt tout doulx   110
Te inciteront à sommeil tous les coups.
De l'autre part, sus ung hault Roc sera
Le Rossignol, qui en l'Air chantera.
Mais ce pendant, la Palombe enrouée,
La Tourte aussi de chasteté louée
Ne laisseront à gemir sans se taire
Sus ung grand Orme: et tout pour te complaire.   120

M. Fortunate senex, ergo tua rura manebunt

et tibi magna satis, quamuis lapis omnia nudus

limosoque palus obducat pascua iunco.

non insueta grauis temptabunt pabula fetas

nec mala uicini pecoris contagia laedent.   50

fortunate senex, hic inter flumina nota

et fontis sacros frigus captabis opacum;

hinc tibi, quae semper, uicino ab limite saepes

Hyblaeis apibus florem depasta salicti

saepe leui somnum suadebit inire susurro;

hinc alta sub rupe canet frondator ad auras,

nec tamen interea raucae, tua cura, palumbes

nec gemere aeria cessabit turtur ab ulmo.

T. Ante leues ergo pascentur in aethere cerui

et freta destituent nudos in litore pisces, 60

ante pererratis amborum finibus exsul

aut Ararim Parthus bibet aut Germania Tigrim,

quam nostro illius labatur pectore uoltus.

M. At nos hinc alii sitientis ibimus Afros,

pars Scythiam et rapidum cretae ueniemus Oaxen

et penitus toto diuissos orbe Britannos.

en umquam patrios longo post tempore finis 70

pauperis et tuguri congestum caespite culmen,

post aliquot, mea regna, uidens mirabor aristas?

impius haec tam culta noualia miles habebit,

TITYRUS

Doncques plustost Cerfz legiers, & cornuz
Vivront en l'Air: et les Poissons tous nudz
Seront laissez de leurs fleuves taris:
Plustost boyront les Parthes Araris
Le fleuve grand: et Tigris Germanie:
Plustost sera ma Personne bannie
En ces deux lieux: et leurs fins, et Limites
Circuiray à journées petites, 130
Ains que celluy, que je t'ay racompté,
Du souvenir de mon cueur soit osté.

MELIBÉE

Helas et nous irons sans demeurée
Vers le Pais d'Affrique l'alterée:
La plus grand part en la froide Scytie
Habiterons: ou irons en Parthie
(Puis qu'en ce point fortune le decrete)
Au fleuve Oaxe impetueux de Crete.
Finablement viendront tous esgarez
Vers les Angloys du Monde separez.
Long temps apres, ou avant que je meure, 140
Verray je point mon Pais, et demeure?
Ma pauvre Loge aussi faicte de Chaulme?
Las s'il advient, qu'en mon petit Royaulme
Revienne encor, je le regarderay,
Et des Ruines fort je m'estonneray.
Las faudra il, qu'un Gendarme impiteux

barbarus has segetes. en quo discordia ciuis

produxit miseros; his nos conseuimus agros!

insere nunc, Meliboee, piros, pone ordine uites.

ite meae, felix quondam pecus, ite capellae.

non ego uos posthac uiridi proiectus in antro

dumosa pendere procul de rupe uidebo;

carmina nulla canam; non me pascente, capellae,

florentem cutisum et salices carpetis amaras.

T. Hic tamen hanc mecum poteras requiescere noctem   80

fronde super uiridi. sunt nobis mitia poma,

castaneae molles et pressi copia lactis,

et iam summa procul uillarum culmina fumant

maioresque cadunt altis de montibus umbrae.

Tienne ce Champ tant culte, et fructueux?
Las faudra il, qu'ung Barbare estrangier
Cueille les Bledz? O en quel grand dangier
Discorde a mis et Pasteurs, et Marchans:
Las, et pour qui avons semé nos Champs?   150
O Melibée, plante Arbres à la Ligne,
Ente Poyriers, mectz en ordre la Vigne:
Helas pour qui? Allez jadis heureuses,
Allez Brebis, maintenant malheureuses.
Apres cecy, en ce grand Creux tout vert,
Là où souvent me couchoys à couvert,
Ne vous verray jamais plus de loing paistre
Vers la Montaigne espineuse, et champaistre:
Plus ne diray Chansons recreatives:
Ny dessoubz moy pauvres Chevres chetives   160
Plus ne paistrez le Treffle florissant,
Ne l'aigre fueille au Saule verdissant.

TITYRUS

Tu pourras bien (et te pry, que le vueilles)
Prendre repos dessus des vertes fueilles
Avecques moy ceste Nuict seullement.
J'ay à souper assez passablement,
Pommes, Pruneaux, tout plein de bon fructage,
Chastaignes, Aulx, avec force Laictage.
Puis des Citez les Cheminées fument,
Desjà le feu pour le soupper allument: 170
Il s'en va nuict, et des haultz Montz descendent
Les Ombres grands, qui parmy l'Air s'espendent.

Fin de la première Eglogue de Vergile.

8

Clément Marot and Humanism

Pauline Smith

Since the rather perfunctory comments I made on aspects of this subject many years ago,[1] much further work on Marot has appeared and, although tantalising gaps in our knowledge remain, I welcome this opportunity to amplify, question and, where necessary, revise suggestions made or conclusions drawn, not only by me but also, in intervening years, by other specialists in the field. I should like to draw attention to two recent and apparently divergent strands of Marot criticism: one which suggests that too much has already been made of Marot's humanism and that it is time to shed more light on his links with his vernacular predecessors,[2] and the other which finds that his humanism is insufficiently known and recognised. In her paper entitled *Marot traducteur d'Érasme*, Marie-Madeleine de la Garanderie began by lamenting the fact that although Marot was a 'poète célèbre', he was also 'un humaniste méconnu'.[3] My purpose is to suggest that these two trends are not irreconcilable or mutually exclusive and to do so, paradoxically or perversely,

---

[1] In *Clément Marot, Poet of the Renaissance* (London, The Athlone Press, 1970), ch. VII. As there, all references to the text of Marot's poems are to the still unsurpassed critical edition in 6 volumes by C. A. Mayer (London, The Athlone Press, 1958–70, vols 1–5, and Geneva, Slatkine, 1980, vol. 6). I have used the following abbreviations in connection with this edition: *Ép.*, *Les Épîtres*, 1958; *OL*, *Œuvres lyriques*, 1964; *OD*, *Œuvres diverses*, 1966; *Épigr.*, *Les Épigrammes*, 1970; *Trad.*, *Les Traductions*, 1980.

[2] See C. Scollen-Jimack, 'Clément Marot: Protestant Humanist or Court Jester?', *Renaissance Studies*, III (1989), 134–46, and A. Williams, *Clément Marot: Figure, Text and Intertext* (Lewiston, E. Mellen, 1990).

[3] M.-M. de La Garanderie, 'Marot traducteur d'Érasme', in *Acta Conventus Neo-Latini Bononiensis* (Binghamton, NY, Medieval Texts & Studies, 1985), 247–57. See also I. D. McFarlane, 'Clément Marot and the World of Neo-Latin Poetry', in *Literature and the Arts in the Reign of Francis I: Essays Presented to C. A. Mayer*, French Forum Monographs, 56 (Lexington, 1985), 103–30, especially the conclusion, pp. 124–5.

by joining forces with Marie-Madeleine de La Garanderie in an attempt to recognise the full extent to which Marot's work displays a conscious and active participation in the humanist agenda. We need not rehearse here in detail the reasons which may explain previous failures to do so. Marot was modest about his own cultural achievements.[4] And we know that some of his contemporaries and immediate successors thought that he had much to be modest about.[5] His relatively limited linguistic compe-tence in the Classical tongues (no Greek or Hebrew and a slowly matur-ing Latinity) and hence his limited direct exposure to the full range of Classical authors then available, helped to fuel the self-serving pro-nouncements of the Pléiade which, taken in conjunction with Boileau's one-eyed vision in the next century, had, as we know, lasting effects. To these factors may be added critics' concern with definition and a desire to restrict the elasticity which the terms humanist and humanism are prone to acquire.[6] I shall attempt to establish Marot's humanist credentials indirectly first of all before considering his activity in three areas traditionally associated with humanism, namely translation, editing, and imitation, since these are the areas in which it assumes its self-appointed responsibility to transmit, preserve, and recreate the past.

Few and fleeting enough are the surviving tributes paid by Marot him-self to the acknowledged humanists of first or second rank of his day: he was not, it seems, unduly concerned to acquire reflected glory. Nevertheless, they demonstrate a common cultural context and aware-ness, an act of association, literally so in the case of the epitaph for Christophe de Longueil since it is one of many such tributes, the majority in Latin, penned at the time. One of the first French humanists, Longueil is commemorated, appropriately enough given that he was a Ciceronian of high repute and a teacher of Étienne Dolet, for his ' beaulx escriptz de stille mesuré' (*OD*, XCI, 10). Dolet himself received a transient com-

---

4   See *Ép.*, XXXVII, 46; ibidem, XXXIX, 35–6; *Trad.*, vii, 19–20; ibidem, XV, I, 165–6.

5   For the context of Boysonné's 'Marotus Latine nescivit' and Pasquier's 'Il ne fut accompagné de bonnes lettres…si n'en était-il si dégarni qui ne les mît souvent en œuvre fort à propos' see P. Villey, 'À propos des sources de deux épîtres de Marot', *Revue d'histoire littéraire de la France*, XXVI (1919), 220–45, especially pp. 238–9; for Scévole de Sainte-Marthe's 'absurdum videatur inter litteratos illum [Marot] collocare cui defuerunt litterae', see J. Plattard, *Marot, sa carrière poétique, son œuvre* (Paris, Boivin, 1938), ch. XIII, p. 206.

6   For a critique of these terms, see M.-M. de La Garanderie, *Christianisme et lettres profanes (1515–1535): Essai sur les mentalités des milieux intellectuels parisiens et sur la pensée de G. Budé* (Paris, Champion, 1976), p. 3.

pliment on his *Commentarii linguae latinae*, a compliment promptly omitted from the very next printing of the *Épigrammes* by S. Gryphius (*Épigr.*, CCIV and note 1). Guillaume Budé is awarded pre-eminence in learning above all contemporaries (*OL*, IX, 119–20), a note of cultural patriotism colouring judgement here since the compliment reduces Erasmus, applauded elsewhere almost in passing (*Épigr.*, CCLXXX, 3–4) to the status of an also-ran. In some ways the most interesting of these tributes, certainly from the literary historical viewpoint, is the convoluted compliment to Benedetto Tagliacarne (Theocrenus) in *Rondeau* XV. It combines Horatian cliché and Ovidian echoes, mythological periphrasis and allusion to the Argus–Mercury episode in *Metamorphoses*, Book I (which Marot was currently translating), a triple comparison inspired by the same source and, as a final flourish, antonymic word play. This rondeau suggests a personal relationship from the outset ('Plus profitable est de t'escouter lire'), probably struck up at court since the Italian exile was appointed tutor to the children of François Ier in 1524. It applauds, possibly even attempts to reflect, his 'langue ornée & nompareille' and his 'parler [qui] les endormis esveille' for the pleasure and instruction it affords (*OD*, XV, 1, 4, 14). Altogether more cryptic is the passing reference from exile in 1535 to another Italian humanist, Celio Calcagnini 'Celius de qui tant on aprent' (*Ép.*, XXXVII, 41), disappointingly cryptic in view of what it might have revealed to us about so many facets of Marot's evolution at the time in Ferrara. But more of that later.

More to the point, however, as McFarlane has shown[7] after making judicious allowance for elements of convention and flattery, are the tributes paid to Marot himself in growing numbers throughout his published career by the leading humanist scholars and neo-Latin poets in France (not to mention those from abroad): Nicolas Bérault, acclaimed as a teacher of literature in Paris before becoming the first holder of the Chair of Greek at the Collège des Lecteurs Royaux, Geofroy Tory, humanist, translator, editor and printer, Étienne Dolet, even more distinguished in all these capacities and, chief among the poets, Salmon Macrin, Nicolas Bourbon, Jean Visagier — the list is illustrative rather than comprehensive — eager to applaud Marot's achievements, to recognise him for one of their own, to accord him the status of national poet, 'Maro gallicus ille' writes Dolet,[8] on a par in his time with Virgil in Ancient Rome, paying tribute thereby to Marot's mastery of his craft and his learning which combined to produce, in the words of Visagier, 'docta

---

[7]   In 'Clément Marot and the World of Neo-Latin Poetry', art. cit.
[8]   Quoted by McFarlane, ibidem, p. 123.

carmina, docta manu'.[9] The most striking of all these tributes is contained in the second of two liminary poems by Salmon Macrin published in the *Suite de l'Adolescence clementine* whose significance can only be fully appreciated when read in conjunction with the Horatian subtext to which Soubeille has drawn attention:

> Si Graecis Maro litteris vacasset,
> magno par potuisset esse Homero.
> Esset si Latias secutus artes
> Clemens Francigenum decus Marotus,
> aequaret dubio procul Maronem;
> sed primas Maro maluit Latino
> quam sermone pares habere Graeco.
> Et noster patrio Marotus ore
> princeps maluit esse, quam Latinae
> in linguae eloquio pares habere,
> huic ut Gallia debeat, quod ipsi
> Hellas Meonidae, Ausones Maroni.[10]

While the by now obligatory Maro–Marotus comparison is abundantly exploited throughout the twelve-line poem, it is notable that Macrin accords to Marot the status of *princeps* ('Et noster patrio Marotus ore / princeps maluit esse...'), precisely the term which Horace had used in *Epistles* I. 19 to describe his own pleasure and pride in being the first to introduce into Latin verse, while preserving his own originality and language, the spirit and rhythms of Archilochus and the lyrical songs of Alcaeus. This is no mean tribute to Marot for the leading role he had taken in French poetry at the time. (Horace had spoken of himself walking on untrodden ground and as a leader ruling the swarm, words which Ronsard would later appropriate to himself.)[11] My reading of this tribute however differs in emphasis from that of Soubeille. He sees it as primarily linguistic, an 'hommage rendu au français et aveu qu'un néo-latin peut égaler, mais non dépasser les Anciens'; and he continues: 'loin de mépriser le français, de condamner son utilisation en littérature, Macrin lui reconnaît donc une supériorité.'[12] This is certainly one

---

[9] Ibidem, p. 115.

[10] G. Soubeille, 'Amitiés de Salmon Macrin parmi les poètes de langue vernaculaire', in *Neo-Latin and the Vernacular in Renaissance France*, edited by G. Castor and T. Cave (Oxford, 1984), 98–112, especially p. 101.

[11] Horace, *Epistles* I. 19. 21–3. Ronsard, 'Au lecteur', *Les Quatre Premiers Livres des Odes* quoted these lines on his own behalf, see *Œuvres complètes*, edited by P. Laumonier, 20 vols (Paris, STFM, 1924), I, 45.

[12] Soubeille, art. cit., p. 102.

legitimate reading, but it seems to me to relegate another, namely the acknowledgement by the overt comparison with Virgil and the implied comparison with Horace that Marot's role as a poetic innovator in his own language paralleled theirs in Latin. Indeed, the facts tend to reinforce this interpretation, for at the time when Macrin composed his tribute, Marot had written the first French eclogue, embodying material from Theocritus and Bion, and an epithalamium partially inspired by Catullus.[13]

Marot's activity as a translator occupied him at various times throughout his career, yet it is an activity which has been largely neglected by critics until recently.[14] One cannot but agree therefore with Marie-Madeleine de La Garanderie's remark that 'l'œuvre érudite de Clément Marot représente un vaste secteur mal éclairé et qu'il importerait d'explorer et d'apprécier'.[15] However, the subject is not without its problems, in the case of Marot's Psalm translations in a rather acute form, since the question of the base texts and intermediaries to which the poet might have had recourse is still not decisively resolved and may never be so.[16] There is thus no sure basis on which to evaluate his own work. However, with a relatively well-established text such as Ovid's *Metamorphoses*, the problem recedes somewhat, while recent discoveries have revealed with a fair degree of certainty the edition of the Greek text, Latin translation, and Latin paraphrase of Musaeus's *Hero and Leander*, which Marot translated before the end of 1540.[17] Taken in conjunction with the recent impetus given to translation studies, there are grounds for hoping that further progress may be made in the study of Marot's translations. Of one thing I am certain: it is no longer possible to dismiss Marot's efforts in this field as a matter of fashion. In any case, to do so begs far more questions than it answers. The importance of translation to the humanist agenda is conveyed in countless prefaces.[18] One preface which, although

---

[13] *OL*, LXXXVII, pp. 321–37 and LXXXV, pp. 309–13 for sources.

[14] For a complete bibliography of the subject up to 1983 see H. P. Clive, *Clément Marot: An Annotated Bibliography*, Research Bibliographies and Checklists, 40 (London, Grant and Cutler, 1983), pp. 131–43; for subsequent items, see the annual bibliographies of O. Klapp or the *MLA*.

[15] M.-M. de La Garanderie, art. cit., p. 247.

[16] See C. A. Mayer, *Clément Marot* (Paris, Nizet, 1972), pp. 461–2; Defaux, ed., Clément Marot, *Œuvres poétiques*, II (Paris, Garnier, 1994), pp. 1201–13, especially pp. 1207–8.

[17] Defaux, ibidem, II, 1196–7 on the copy of the Paris, C. Wechel, 1538 edition held in the Bibliothèque municipale de Toulouse.

[18] For discussion and analysis of some translators' prefaces at the time see G. P. Norton, *The Ideology and Language of Translation in Renaissance France* (Geneva, Droz, 1984).

not dealing with translation as such, helps to explain why, prior to 1549, the translation of poetry was so highly regarded, is particularly pertinent to our present enquiry since it dates from the beginning of the period of Marot's career as a translator and was written by Nicolas Bérault who was to supply liminary verse for Marot's *Adolescence clementine*. Writing in the introduction to a course on Politian's *Rusticus* he had given at the Collège de Tréguier in Paris in 1513, Bérault describes the role of interpreter, that is commentator and teacher of poetry, in neo-Platonic terms as a link in the magnetic chain of poetic inspiration extending from heaven to earth. If, by extension, the exegetic or paraphrastic translator is part of this chain, then it is difficult to imagine a more powerful legitimisation in humanist eyes of the translator's role.[19] The status of translation among poets and learned readers is abundantly reconfirmed shortly after Marot's death by the chronicler of his achievements, Thomas Sebillet. In his *Art poétique*, he applauds translation as a phenomenon not of impoverishment but of enrichment since the 'pure et

---

[19] *Angeli Politiani Sylva, cui titulus est Rusticus, cum docta elegantissimaque Nicolai Beraldi interpretatione* (1518?; BL 837. h. 1), f. D3[r]: 'Poetarum interpretes & ipsi divino afflati furore, mysteria enarrant poetici...Et (quemadmodum apud Platonem disputat Socrates) Musae poetas agitant instinctu divino. Poetae eodem suo furore interpretes accendunt ac extimulant. Sicut itaque à Musis, id est, à coelo ipso divinus ille spiritus primum emanat ad poetas, ita à poetis ad interpretes, atque ab his ad alios exit ac transfunditur...Et sicut Herculeo lapidi non tantum insita est arcana illa vis annulorum ferreorum ad se trahenda, sed et ipse vim quoque suam annulis infundit. Ita Musae poetas, poetae suos interpretes, atque hi deinceps alios coelesti furore corripiunt.' For a full discussion of this preface and Bérault's lofty conception of the translator's mission in non-poetic texts as well see M.-M. de La Garanderie, *Christianisme et lettres profanes*, op. cit., pp. 55–74; see also art. cit., p. 248.

What needs to be stressed, however, is the very early date at which Ficinian neo-Platonic ideas of poetic inspiration penetrate educated Parisian society via Politian and Bérault, some three decades before they resurface in the vernacular in the entourage of Marguerite de Navarre, according to A. Lefranc, 'Le Platonisme et la littérature française', in *Grands écrivains de la Renaissance française* (Paris, 1914), vol. 2, and M. Jeanneret, 'Marot traducteur des *Psaumes* entre le néoplatonisme et la Réforme', in *Bibliothèque d'Humanisme et Renaissance*, XXVII (1965), 629–43. Norton, op. cit., p. 148, comments on the conflation of translation and poetry as the century progresses with reference to Marot's statement in the preface to his *Metamorphoses*, book I, that 'je me suis pensé trop entreprendre de vouloir *transmuer* [my italics] celluy qui les autres transmue. Et apres j'ay contrepensé que double louange peult venir de transmuer ung transmueur' (*Trad.*, VII, 56–60). A recent and abundantly documented discussion of Politian's role as an intermediary source in the early transmission to France of neo-Ficinian ideas on the divine inspiration of poetry, which was unfortunately not available to me when this paper was submitted, is to be found in J. Lecointe, *L'Idéal et la différence*, Travaux d'Humanisme et Renaissance, 275 (Geneva, Droz, 1993), ch. 2, especially pp. 289–304, 314–38.

argentine invention des poetes' becomes in the process 'dorée et enrichie de notre langue'. The same notion reappears and is reinforced in the analogy of buried treasure, excavated with enormous effort and toil before being made available to all.[20] Both these writers in their own way touch upon the vulgarising function of the *interpres* (whether as commentator or translator) which is very much to the fore in Marot's own prefaces or dedications, particularly that of *Metamorphoses*, Book I and in the epistles preceding the Psalm translations which have a proselytising dimension as well. To the King, Marot explains:

> Bien est il vray (comme encores se veoit)
> Que la rigueur du long temps les avoit
> Renduz obscurs & durs d'intelligence.
> Mais tout ainsi qu'avecques diligence
> Sont esclarcis par bons espritz rusez
> Les escripteaulx des vieulx fragmentz usez,
> Ainsi (ô roy) par les divins espritz
> Qui ont soubz toy Hebrieu langaige appris
> Nous sont jectez les Pseaulmes en lumiere
> Clairs & au sens de la forme premiere,
> Dont, apres eulx, si peu que faire sçay,
> T'en ay traduict par maniere d'essay
> Trente sans plus en ton noble langaige.
>
> (*Trad.*, XV, 155–67).

Similarly, in an epigram to Antoine Macault (*Epigr.*, CCLXXX), Marot acknowledges the translator's role in the chain of transmission of 'bon sçavoir' from the Greek of Plutarch to the Latin of Erasmus's *Apophthegmata*, now made accessible to the French.

Marot's dedicatory preface to his translation of *Metamorphoses*, Book I reveals a work undertaken at first sight in a spirit of self-interest no different, apparently, from that of many of his Rhétoriqueur predecessors. Ambitious to make his mark and to enter the King's service thereby, he needed a work of sufficient distinction to reflect his future patron's: 'à Prince de hault Esprit haultes choses affierent' (*Trad.*, VII, 14–15). Obviously, therefore, given the obligatory humility *topos*, not one of his own invention. But there is much more to this preface. It reveals a Renaissance rather than a medieval sensibility, capable of sound aesthetic judgements of his Latin predecessors, notwithstanding the assumed modesty in the phrase 'si peu que je y comprins' (ibid., 19–20),

---

[20] T. Sebillet, *Art poetique francoys*, edited by F. Gaiffe (Paris, STFM, 1910), ch. XIV, p. 188.

judgements of the formal beauty, rich diversity, and narrative cohesion of the *Metamorphoses* which have stood the test of time. It reveals a poet with a mission, not to moralise Ovid as his predecessors had, but to make this treasure house of mythological lore accessible to a wider public with little or no Latin, to inculcate in the reader a sense of difference 'entre les Anciens & les Modernes' (ibid., 40), to provide a source book of information and inspiration for poets writing in French, and for painters too, and finally, in acknowledgement of the King's cultural policies, to embellish the French language by translation of a classic of Antiquity. In other words, Marot is actively participating in the venture by which the King 'en France en leur entier ramaines / Tous les beaulx artz et sciences rommaines' (*Epigr.*, CLXXIX, 3–4). At what level did Marot intend to undertake his translation? In spite of his protestations of limited competence, Marot's aim was to reproduce as faithfully as possible the style of the original to those who would otherwise have no means of appreciating it: 'deliberay…de tout mon pouvoir suyvre & contrefaire la veine du noble Poete Ovide pour mieulx faire entendre & sçavoir à ceulx qui n'ont la langue Latine de quelle sorte il escrivoit' (*Trad.*, 35–9), no mean task! It was in somewhat of the same spirit and with the same determination that he approached the Psalm translations, the earliest of which, Psalm VI, is roughly contemporaneous with parts of the translation of *Metamorphoses*, I and is announced in some versions as being 'au plus pres de la verité Ebraicque' (*Trad.*, 333), a formula which echoes that used by Bucer and Campensis.[21]

How well did Marot acquit himself as a translator of Ovid? In the absence as yet of any complete study of the work, we are fortunate to have the views of a near contemporary of Marot and one moreover by no means ill-disposed to him or the school of poetry he represented. Barthélemy Aneau needs no introduction. A more than accomplished Latinist and teacher, principal in fact of the new Collège de la Trinité in Lyons,[22] he published in 1556 a French version of Books I–III of the *Metamorphoses*, the first two of which were Marot's and the third his own. This edition, to which Ghislaine Amielle has drawn attention, deserves to be better known:[23] first, because the text offers some variants

---

21 Bucer, 'ad ebraicam veritatem' and Campensis, 'ex veritate hebraica', quoted by Defaux, *Œuvres poétiques de Marot*, II, 1207.

22 We still lack a complete study of this important and in some ways enigmatic figure, but see the series of articles by J. Gerig, 'Barthélemy Aneau, a Study of Humanism', *Romanic Review*, 1910–13.

23 *Trois premiers livres de la Métamorphose d'Ovide* (Lyon, M. Bonhomme, 1556). See G. Amielle, *Les Traductions françaises des Métamorphoses d'Ovide*

not noted elsewhere; secondly, the volume is enriched by a substantial preface which not only conveys Aneau's judgement on Marot's translation but also detailed comments on the emendations which Aneau felt himself called upon to make to his predecessor's work, very helpfully as far as the modern researcher is concerned in the form of interlinear alternatives. Some of the suggested corrections are of marginal interest, for instance the routine replacement of the relative *dont* by *d'où* or *que* as the sense demands. Others may seem merely pernickety, as in the substitution of 'muées' for 'changées' where Ovid's prologue has 'mutastis' (l. 2).[24] There is no difference in general sense but the correction is closer etymologically to the original. But neither translator, Marot or Aneau, seeks to reproduce the verbal echo of Ovid's first two lines, 'mutatas'/'mutastis', which underlines the theme of the entire poem. Not for either poet apparently the stylistic refinements of equivalent effect. Neither attempts the verbal patterning of line 141:

iamque nocens ferrum ferroque nocentius aurum

but of the two, Aneau's emendation is more accurate and effective as he achieves some compensation by splitting 'mal faisant' to achieve a rather strained alliteration at the end of the line.[25] But this is perhaps somewhat incidental to our main purpose.

Aneau's revisions and more detailed comments demonstrate three major concerns: with accuracy, defined as fidelity to the sense of the original rather than literalness (a principle endorsed by Dolet in his *La Maniere de bien traduire d'une langue en aultre*),[26] with clarity and, finally, with appropriateness at the level of style. Under the first heading, two examples will suffice. Aneau objected to Marot's reference to 'Le clair Phebus à la barbe dorée' (*Trad.*, VIII, 43) on the grounds that Phoebus 'est tousjours descript par les Poëtes & à longz cheveux, & sans barbe. Parquoy j'ay mis à Perruque dorée. Vela exemple de motz improprement traduictz, & des vers trop esloignez de la vraye sentence de l'auteur'.[27] Also included under that same stricture is Marot's translation of *Metamorphoses* II. 43: 'Clymene veros...edidit ortus' by 'Clymene a produit / Vray, naturel & legitime fruict ' (*Trad.*, VIII, 83–4). There are

---

(Paris, J. Touzot, 1989), pp. 140–57, and on Aneau's style of translation generally, see Norton, op. cit., pp. 113–20.

24 Aneau-Ovide, op. cit., p. 2.

25 Ibidem, p. 18 (line 278 in Marot's translation).

26 É. Dolet, *La Maniere de bien traduire d'une langue en aultre* (Lyon, É. Dolet, 1540); this is the third of five basic principles outlined here.

27 Aneau–Ovide, f. C2r.

two problems here: the sense of the verb: it has two meanings but not, as
Aneau points out, in this particular context; and secondly, the juxtaposition of the adjectives 'naturel & legitime':

> le translateur a entendu *Edidit* pour generation où c'est declaration, & *Veros
> ortus* pour la personne, où c'est l'origine d'icelle…Ainsi *Edidit veros ortus*
> n'est à dire a produict vray fruict mais a declairé vraye naissance & origine.
> D'advantage, en ces deux motz, naturel & legitime, y a repugnance selon les
> Jurisconsultz, & faulseté en disant legitime celluy qui estoit Bastard.
> Lesquelles choses regardées, m'a semblé plus pres de la parolle Latine, &
> plus propre au sens de ainsi le rendre
> > Et de vraye naissance
> > Clymene t'a donné la cognoissance.[28]

It has to be said though that Aneau's own suggestions are not always
acceptable: he rejects Marot's translation of 'turbine' (*Metamorphoses* I.
336), describing the shape of the Triton's conch shell, by 'tourbillon'
(*Trad.*, VII, 662) in favour of the more fishy 'turbot',[29] although the
charitable may be disposed to regard this as a 'typo' rather than a howler!

Aneau is on firmer ground where he indicates examples of obscurity
and incoherence. That time should not efface the memory of his exploit
(the reference is to Apollo slaying the Python in *Metamorphoses* I. 445),
becomes in Marot:

> Et puis, afin que vieil temps advenir
> Ne sceust du faict la memoire ternir
>
> (*Trad.*, VII, 875–6)

producing in the first line, because of its compression of thought, a
contradiction in terms which exposes the translator to the charge of writing nonsense: 'de ces vers, on n'en sauroit aucun sens extraire.'[30] Aneau
himself takes four lines to resolve the confusion which Marot has created
in two.[31]

Decorum, or the lack of it, is something which exercises Aneau greatly
and whereas in his view Ovid scrupulously maintained it, the same
cannot unfortunately be said for Marot whom he regards as 'plus prenant

28 Ibidem, ff. C^v–C2^r.
29 Ibidem, p. 49: 'Qu'un tourbillon' emended to 'Comme un turbot'.
30 Ibidem, f. C2^v.
31 Ibidem, p. 56: 'Et puys affin que la longueur du temps / Qui adviendroit aux
    siecles succedens / Ne peut tollir, ou mettre hors de memoire / D'un si hault faict
    la renommée, & gloire.'

garde à remplir son vers qu'à cela suyvre'.[32] The two instances picked up both feature Jupiter of whom Aneau has a distinctly un-Lucianic view. Not surprisingly, therefore, he objects on the grounds of *bienséance* to a translation which has the god appear more like 'un homme forcené ou une femme furieuse':

> ...des haulz cieulx Juppiter
> Crie, gemyt, se prend à despiter
>
> (*Trad.*, 319–20)

The problem lies with Marot's translation of 'ingemit' (*Metamorphoses* I. 164), not given its true value which is 'intus gemit', 'donnant à entendre un viril gemissement, bas, taisible, & à part soy'.[33] Similarly, a second outpouring of divine wrath, rendered by Marot thus:

> Puis tout despit devant tous il desbouche
> En tel' façon son indignée bouche
>
> (ibidem,VII, 354–4)

has Aneau spluttering: 'Desboucher sa bouche est du tout impropre, & Despit appartient à un villain non à Jupiter auquel convient indignation Royalle'.[34] On occasion, the verse technician merges with the pedagogue in Aneau to attack 'apostrophe' (by which he means syncopation, as in the example above) and improper rhymes as in 'cruelz' and 'tuez'.[35]

Aneau suggests fewer revisions to Marot's later translation of *Metamorphoses* Book II, which may conceivably reinforce the impression promoted by Marot himself and generally accepted by modern scholarship of his increasing competence in Latin (*Ép.*, XXXVII, 46). Nevertheless, Aneau's overall judgement of his translation in linguistic terms is relatively severe, although balanced by his acknowledgement of the stylistic problems posed by the Latin poets for any French translator:

Clement Marot de sa propre & naturelle invention, vene, & elocution Françoise escrivoit tresheureusement, & tres facilement: Ainsi estant en estrange translation, de langue à luy non assez entendue traduisoit-il durement, & mesme les Poëtes Latins, qui sont assez scabreux, artificielz, & figurez de schemes qui a pene se peuvent rendre en François.[36]

---

[32] Ibidem, f. C3r.

[33] Ibidem, f. C3v.

[34] Ibidem, ff. C3v–C4r.

[35] Ibidem, f. C3r.

[36] Ibidem, ff. C4v–C5r. Note the earliest attestation of *schemes* in this sense, predating that attributed to Ronsard (1586) by thirty years.

There is, however, no place in Aneau's commentary for an examination of how far other more literary aspects of Marot's translation, its narrative momentum, variations in pace, heightened dramatic effects, sometimes underlined by skilful use of enjambement, matched those achieved by Ovid himself, after making due allowance for the different linguistic and metrical conventions within which they each worked. Surprisingly, perhaps, given the potentially even greater problems posed by the Psalms, Aneau rates Marot's performance in this area far more highly, and even provides a valuable clue of his own to a possible intermediary source when he writes: 'Quant aux Pseaumes de David, veritablement il les a mieux entenduz, & à son plaisir à la suycte de Campense, paraphrasez bien doucement plustost que translatez.'[37] Johannes Campensis was the Hebrew scholar from Louvain whose Latin Psalms (translation and paraphrase) had already found their way into Coverdale's English version as well as into French.[38]

It may seem at first sight perverse, as I indicated it would, to include in a discussion of Marot's commitment to the humanist agenda the subject of textual editing when it follows from what has already been established that he had neither the linguistic competence nor the erudition to attempt the editorial tasks which Valla, Erasmus, and others performed to restore to the texts of Classical Antiquity and the Christian tradition greater authenticity. But there is no doubt that in his edition of the poetry of Villon, Marot fully shared humanist concerns with both the restoration and transmission of authentic texts while at the same time redirecting these concerns to a far less remote and vernacular past where his own expertise could not be called into question. Accordingly, and at the King's behest, 'qui fustes seul cause de l'entreprise' (*Épigr.*, CCLXXV, 8) he applied as far as possible the best practices of humanist methodology to the national cultural patrimony as others had to the heritage of Classical Antiquity. Recent scholarship is divided on the question of how far the manuscript tradition of Villon was available to, and exploited by, Marot.[39] He himself lists his sources as 'les vieulx imprimez' which he

---

37 Ibidem, f. C5[r].

38 See *A Paraphrase upon all the Psalms of David from the Latin of Johannes Campensis*, published anonymously in 1534 but reasonably attributable to Coverdale (see *Cambridge History of the Bible*, III, 148). Gryphius printed Campensis' Latin paraphrases several times in the 1530s (for details see Baudrier), and Dolet a French version in 1542.

39 See M. Speer, 'The Editorial Tradition of Villon's *Testament*: From Marot to Rychner and Henry', in *Romance Philology*, XXXI (1977), 344 sqq., especially p. 346, and M. Lazard, 'Clément Marot éditeur et lecteur de Villon', in *CAIEF*, XXXII (1980), 7–20.

judges rightly to be less corrupt than '[les] nouvelles [impressions]', supplemented and clarified by an oral tradition preserved in the memories of '[les] bons vieillardz' (among whom I would place Guillaume Cretin as much as Jean Marot), and in the last resort his own instinctive judgement.[40] His revised text was not modified until the eighteenth century and not really superseded until the nineteenth, which is some measure of its success. What is outstanding is Marot's commitment to the integrity of Villon's text, his determination not to modernise under the guise of revision, to leave untouched 'l'antiquité de son parler...sa façon de rimer...ses meslées & longues parentheses...la quantité de ses sillabes...ses couppes, tant feminines que masculines', even though not recommending such features. So scrupulous in fact is his concern for the authentic Villon that he makes no claim to definitive authority for his revisions and asterisks those lines which he has had to restore in their entirety 'au plus pres (selon mon possible) de l'intencion de l'autheur', so that those who knew them in their original state may delete 'les nouveaulx pour faire place aux vieulx'. There are in addition instructive parallels to be drawn between the Villon preface and the dedication to Marot's translation of Book I of Ovid's *Metamorphoses*. The newly revised and more accessible Villon, accompanied by philological notes to facilitate comprehension, is recommended no less than the French version of Ovid as a source of inspiration to be exploited by the new generation of French poets:

> qu'ilz cueillent ses sentences comme belles fleurs, qu'ilz contemplent l'esprit qu'il avoit, que de luy apreignent à proprement d'escrire, & qu'ilz contrefacent sa veine, mesmement celle dont il use en ses Ballades, qui est vrayment belle & heroique.

Not advice that would commend itself to the Pléiade poets.

We have already had occasion to comment on Salmon Macrin's tribute to Marot for having introduced into the vernacular the poetic genres of Classical Antiquity. He did much more of course. The logical culmination of Marot's participation in the humanist agenda from translation

---

40 *Les Œuvres de Françoys Villon de Paris, reveues & remises en leur entier par Clement Marot, valet de chambre du roy* (Paris, G. du Pré, 1533). All quotations from the preface are from this edition. Cretin's knowledge of Villon's poetry is apparent in his own works. See the edition by K. Chesney (Paris, Firmin-Didot, s. d.), Introduction, p. xxiv. In addition, both Marot (*Ép.*, XLV, 44 and 49) and Cretin, ed. cit., XLVII, especially l. 5 and l. 36, make humorous metaphorical use of real tennis terms, one of which may be traced back to Villon, where it is described as a first usage. See A. Henry, 'Quelques réflexions d'un "coéditeur" des œuvres françaises de Villon', *CAIEF*, XXXII (1980), p. 29, n. 8.

onwards is the practice of imitation in all its manifestations (thematic and stylistic as well as formal) and subtle gradations. Never reluctant to act upon his own advice, to provide example as well as precept, Marot creatively wove parts of his own youthful translation of Virgil's first eclogue into the eclogue of his own poetic maturity, *Eglogue* III. *Eglogue de Marot au Roy, soubz les noms de Pan & Robin* (*OL*, LXXXIX), using first the *locus amoenus* (*Trad.*, I, 107–20) to evoke the delights of pastoral living enhanced by generosity from on high (*OL*, LXXXIX, 89– 102) and secondly, much adapted, the impossibility *topos* (*Trad.*, I, 121– 30) to assure the King that he could never be anything but eternally grateful (*OL*, ibidem, 252–6). This is imitation at one remove; there are more direct imitations from both Classical and French sources in a poem which represents a sustained and on the whole successful exercise in *contaminatio*.[41]

Marot's second and last eclogues (II and IV), both inspired by the same Virgilian source, the celebrated fourth eclogue, offer an interesting opportunity for the comparative study of two different imitations of a single source and identical pretext, the (anticipated) birth of a child. Very rare are the textual borrowings made by Marot from the Latin source in the *Avant-Naissance* (*OL*, LXXXVIII). On the other hand, he has adapted the structure and movement of the original to his own purpose, he has clearly seen and grasped the poetic possibilities presented by Virgil's use of the Sybil's prophecy of a coming Golden Age which, without any overt reference, he has transposed to accommodate the advent of Renaissance and Reformation in sixteenth-century France. In addition, Virgil's modified optimism, with its reminder of the Age of Iron, exemplified by 'sceleris uestigia nostri' and subsequently by 'uestigia fraudis' and 'altera bella' (IV, 13, 31, 35) provides Marot with an opportunity to launch into anti-Catholic invective, first against the theologians of the Sorbonne:

> Vien hardiment, car ayant plus grant aage
> Tu trouveras encores davantage:
> Tu trouveras la guerre commencée
> Contre ignorance et sa tourbe incensée

> (*OL*, ibidem, 21–4)

and secondly against the priesthood and the Papacy:

> Viens escouter verité revellée,

---

[41] For details of these sources, see *OL*, LXXXIX, notes, pp. 342–53.

Qui tant de jours nous a esté cellée!
Viens escouter, pour ames rejoir,
Ce que caphards veullent garder d'oyr!
Viens voir, viens veoir la beste sans raison,
Grand ennemy de ta noble maison,
Viens tost la veoir à tout sa triple creste,
Non cheute encor, mais de tomber bien preste!

(ibidem, 51–8)

Prophecy and polemic are thus skilfully combined. Not surprisingly, given the tradition of Messianic readings of Virgil's fourth eclogue, and the sympathies of Renée de Ferrare, biblical echoes are never far away. For various reasons, circumstantial and personal (Henri II and Catherine de Médicis were certainly not of the same persuasion as Renée) as well as aesthetic, Marot could not repeat this transformation in his later eclogue celebrating the birth of the dauphin's son. His imitation on this occasion is much closer, more specific, underpinned by erudition and commentaries. This does not of course make it a better poem, although Du Bellay thought it did, and paid it a condescending compliment. [42] But it does demonstrate a difficulty which Du Bellay, for polemical reasons, refused to face, the difficulty of distinguishing, in certain sections of this poem, between translation and imitation. After an allusive introduction, Marot's fourth eclogue flaunts its source. Adaptation is largely confined to omission or change of names, of locations, of deities, persons, plants, to suit the time and place. Pastoral details are closely followed, the prophecy is blandly encomiastic:

Et si l'on voit soubz Henry quelque reste
De la malice aujourd'huy manifeste,
Elle sera si foible & si estaincte
Que plus de rien la terre n'aura craincte

(*OL.*, XC, 27–30)

The opportunity for invective is not pursued but transformed on second appearance to a confident prediction of heroism in the national tradition:

Ce neantmoins des fraudes qui sont ores
Quelque relique on pourra veoir encores.
La terre encor du Soc on verra fendre,
Villes & Bourgs de murailles deffendre,

---

[42] J. Du Bellay, *Deffence et illustration de la langue françoise*, edited by H. Chamard (Paris, STFM, 1948), p. 228: 'un des meilleurs petiz ouvrages.'

147

Conduyre en Mer les navires volans:
Et aura France encores des Rolands.

(ibidem, 59–64)

In both these eclogues, Marot's literary humanism, his creation by translation, imitation and adaptation, provided an object lesson in extending
the range of anticipatory lyricism in French occasional poetry.

Ovid was the literary companion of Marot's exile, far more so than the
exilic Psalms. M. A. Screech has speculated on the reasons which led
Marot to 'elaborate his exile poetically in term's of Ovid's *Tristia*' and
suggests that the humanist Celio Calcagnini was the crucial influence.
This is not implausible given the poet's reference to the scholar. Screech
has pursued his enquiries in Calcagnini's posthumous and voluminous
Opera aliquot (1544) but without so far as I know discovering anything
helpful.[43] I myself have made selective and fruitless forays in this direction. Marot's own reference is so vaguely expressed that we do not know
exactly what he learnt — although we know that his Latin apparently
improved — nor in what circumstances, public or private, but his request
to the King to receive his wages in Ferrara is linked to this tuition:

Vueilles permettre (en despit d'eulx) mes gaiges
Passer les montz et jusque icy venir,
Pour à l'estude ung temps m'entretenir
Soubz Celius, de qui tant on aprent.

(*Ep.*, XXXVII, 38–41)

It requires some audacity for a man in Marot's position, condemned in
his absence for grave heresy, forced into exile, to represent this involuntary exile as a form of sabbatical leave, but how far do these lines represent Marot the person, rather than the poetic persona, like Ovid but with
more spirit, whiling away the tedious months of exile in study or, since
the two may not be mutually exclusive, when does one begin to shade
into the other?[44] For a variety of reasons, it seems to me, both Screech
and I may both be looking in the wrong place. Is it likely, after all, that
Calcagnini would have committed much if anything to paper, even in

---

43 The quotation is from Screech, 'Clément Marot and the Face in the Gospel', in
   Pre-Pléiade Poetry, edited by J. C. Nash, French Forum Monographs, 56
   (Lexington, KY, 1985), p. 74. See also 'Celio Calcagnini and Rabelaisian
   Sympathy', in *Castor and Cave*, op. cit., p. 46, n. 5. Calcagnini's *Opera* appeared
   under the Froben imprint, Basel, 1544.
44 See the paper by Hugo Tucker, 'Clément Marot, Ferrara, and the Paradoxes of
   Exile' in this volume for the strategies pursued by Marot.

unpublished form, about Marot, a notorious Lutheran and persistent thorn in the flesh of his, Calcagnini's, patron, Ercole d'Este, to whom he had incidentally bequeathed all his autograph manuscripts and who in 1544 supervised their publication?[45] Do we have a record of the courses (texts and authors) taught by Calcagnini at the Accademia di Ferrara which Defaux, without a shred of evidence, assumes Marot attended?[46] Some documents relating to students attending the Studio di Ferrara at the relevant time (Marot's name is not among them) have been published,[47] but many more unexplored documents of possible interest are to be found in the Archivio di Stato in Modena, to which city the Biblioteca estense was transferred. Would Marot, in any case, familiar as he already was with many of Ovid's works (the *Metamorphoses*, the *Heroides*, the *Amores* among them) have needed to wait until 1535 for knowledge of the *Tristia* when we know that the Aldine text, accompanied by Merula's commentary, was published no fewer than three times in France (in Paris and Lyon) by the 1520s?[48] In this connection, it may be useful to note that Marot, in his *Dieu Gard...à la Court de France*, both acknowledged his debt to Ovid and distanced himself from the writer in lines which offer a commentary on his own imitation. A commentary which in essence echoes Merula's appraisal of Ovid's work as, among other things, 'plenum affectibus et miseratione', powerful and persuasive in its evocation of, and appeal to, the emotions,[49] while Marot, in turning a compliment to François Ier for ending his exile, has this to say:

> Non que je vueille (Ovide) me vanter
> D'avoir myeulx sceu que ta Muse chanter.
> Trop plus que moy tu as de vehemence,
> Pour esmouvoir à mercy et clemence.

---

[45] For the historical, political, and religious background to Marot's stay in Ferrara, see Mayer, *Clément Marot*, op. cit., pp. 313–33. For details concerning the publication of Calcagnini's manuscripts, see the preface to the *Opera aliquot*.

[46] Franceschini's *Nuovi documenti relativi ai docenti dello studio di Ferrara nel secolo XVI*, Deputazione provinciale ferrarese di storia patria, Serie monumenti, vol. VI, 1970, is not as helpful as its title might suggest. It lists payments and dates thereof, but gives no precise indications of curricula.

[47] See F. Borsetti, *Historia almi ferrariae gymnasii: in duas partes divisa* (Ferrara, 1735).

[48] See A. Moss, *Ovid in Renaissance France: A Survey of the Latin Editions of Ovid and Commentaries Printed in France before 1600*, Warburg Institute Surveys, VIII (London, The Warburg Institute, 1982), pp. 19, 69, 70, and 71 (for later editions without commentary).

[49] In *P. Ovidii Nasonis Tristium libri* (1526; BL 79. a. 5), Preface (no foliation or pagination).

Mais assez bon persuadeur me tien,
Ayant un prince humain plus que le tien...
Ruisseaux de pleurs sur ton papier jectoys
En escrivant, sans espoir de retour.

(*OL*, LXXVIII, 49–54, 58–9)

Whatever the influence, apart from force of circumstances, which encouraged Marot's exploitation of Ovid's poetry of exile, and without wishing to repeat in detail what I and others have said elsewhere, I have no doubt that in the realm of personal poetry, it acted as a stimulus to variety of expression: to the concrete notation through imagery and metaphor of psychological insights and states of feeling, to the development of the rhetoric of comparison and argument, to the discreet use of mythological symbolism in the figures of Ulysses, Icarus and Daedalus, to the reflective or vibrant use of *sententiae*, culminating in the rightly admired epistle LVI, *A ung sien Amy 1543,* Marot's *De contemptu rerum fortuitarum,* but infinitely more memorable than Budé's.[50] Marot certainly set a precedent. One which was not ignored.

Leaving aside its combative function, Marot's humanism is of the vulgarising and creative kind, not only participating in the cultural moment to which it belongs, but helping to shape it too. Eclectic in nature rather than exclusive, it happily embraces indigenous, classical, biblical, and neo-Latin sources. It will elevate Villon to the status of a classic with the same enthusiasm that it affords Ovid. Its aim is to promote, by restoration in the widest sense, and by recreation, the development of French poetry. In this it was more than modestly successful.

---

[50] Budé's work, in prose, never attains the vibrancy of Marot's epistle in its elaboration of shared commonplaces such as the imperishability of things of the spirit, the vicissitudes of fortune and of court life. For a full listing of editions, starting in 1521, and a discussion of the work, see D. McNeil, *Guillaume Budé and Humanism in the Reign of Francis I* (Geneva, Droz, 1975), pp. 59 and 134.

9

Les Œuvres de Clément Marot:
Questions bibliographiques

Jeanne Veyrin-Forrer

En souvenir de Brigitte Moreau,
qui savait mieux que personne
découvrir l'imprimeur anonyme.

En raison de la complexité manifeste de son histoire éditoriale, la première publication collective des *Oeuures* de Clément Marot, en 1538, re-
quiert tout spécialement l'investigation bibliographique. Celle-ci permet-
elle d'expliquer objectivement la double parution, durant la même année,
de volumes portant tantôt le nom d'Étienne Dolet, tantôt celui de
Gryphius, et contenant des textes souvent identiques, parfois différents?

Il faut préalablement remonter deux ans en arrière, au moment où la
mort inopinée du dauphin François, le 10 août 1536, vient de mobiliser à
Lyon une vingtaine de poètes conviés à édifier son tombeau poétique. La
place qu'y occupent, en tête des pièces imprimées, trois compositions
latines d'Étienne Dolet et un avis au lecteur, daté du 13 novembre 1536,
attribuable au même auteur, indiquent suffisamment que l'humaniste
orléanais a joué le rôle principal dans la réunion des textes et que c'est lui
qui en a confié l'édition à François Juste, l'imprimeur-libraire renommé
de la rue Mercière. Ce *Recueil de vers latins et vulgaires sur le trespas de
Monsieur le Daulphin* comprend à la fin du deuxième cahier (b7) une
épitaphe en 24 vers français, signée de Clément Marot, qui revenait à
peine de son exil transalpin.[1] Occasion de rencontre, peut-être, entre
Dolet et Marot avant le fameux banquet parisien de février 1537, offert
par Dolet à ses amis. Contacts probables, également, entre Clément
Marot et François Juste qui, depuis février 1533, multiplie à Lyon les
éditions du poète, parfois à partir de manuscrits originaux.

---

[1] (Lyon, F. Juste, 1536, id. nov). Voir: V.-L. Saulnier, 'La Mort du dauphin
François', *Bibliothèque d'Humanisme et Renaissance*, VI (1945), 72–89;
C. Longeon, *Bibliographie des Œuvres d'Étienne Dolet* (Genève, 1980), n° 2.

Un an et demi plus tard, le 6 mars 1538, à Moulins, Étienne Dolet obtient du roi, pour ses travaux personnels et d'édition, un privilège général d'exclusivité, valable pour dix ans. Il se voit alors confier, par Mellin de Saint-Gelais, la traduction que celui-ci venait de réviser du *Cortegiano* de Baldassare Castiglione. Ne possédant pas encore d'atelier typographique, Dolet s'empresse de transporter son privilège sur François Juste, qui reconnaît en 'Monsieur maistre Estienne Dolet pour certain en litterature, eloquence et scavoir une des precipues lumiere [*sic*] de France'.[2]

Mais c'est avec l'imprimeur-libraire Sébastien Gryphius ou Gryphe, l'un des meilleurs de la cité rhodanienne, que Dolet entretient les relations de travail les plus suivies. Gryphius, qui l'a accueilli libéralement lors de son arrivée à Lyon, en 1534, imprime depuis lors la plupart des écrits de Dolet qui, à son tour, l'assiste dans ses travaux d'édition.

En février 1538, Gryphius vient d'imprimer le deuxième tome des *Commentarii linguae latinae* d'Étienne Dolet.[3] Peut-être est-ce le moment où s'amorce entre eux le projet d'une association pour la publication des *Œuures* de Clément Marot en un volume in-octavo. Le poète, présent à Lyon cette année-là, a décidé en effet de réunir l'ensemble de ses œuvres, auparavant séparées, qu'il pourra ainsi revoir et corriger. L'idée semble lui en avoir été suggérée par Étienne Dolet, fort de son privilège et de sa collaboration fructueuse avec Gryphius. Il est certainement prévu de laisser une structure indépendante (titre, signatures, foliotation) à chacune des quatre parties: *L'adolescence Clementine*, *La suite de L'adolescence*, *Deux liures d'Epigrammes*, *Le premier liure de la Metamorphose d'Ouide*, et d'imprimer le tout avec un petit caractère gothique fort prisé des Lyonnais.

Mais une fois l'impression achevée, l'entreprise se heurte visiblement à des difficultés, puisque les *Oeuures*, publiées après le 31 janvier 1538, se présentent en définitive sous deux formes et deux adresses différentes:

Les Oeuures de | CLEMENT MAROT | DE CAHORS VA- | let de chambre du | Roy. |…A Lyon: au Logis de Monsieur Dolet. | M. D. XXXVIII. | Avec priuilege pour dix ans. | 8°.[4]

---

2 Longeon, op. cit., n° 29.
3 H. Baudrier, *Bibliographie lyonnaise* (Paris, 1964), VIII, p. 111; Longeon, n° 11.
4 Paris, BN, Rés. Ye. 1457–1460; Wolfenbüttel, H.A.B. 116. Poet. C. A. Mayer, *Bibliographie des éditions de Clément Marot publiées au XVIe siècle* (Genève, 1975), n° 70; Longeon, n° 33.

Les Oeuures de | CLEMENT MA- | ROT VALET DE | chambre du | roy. |
...On les uend a Lyon chez | Gryphius. | 8°.[5]

Il est clair que Gryphius ne revendique aucun partage du privilège,
signe manifeste d'une rupture. Parmi les neuf ou dix exemplaires
recensés, deux seulement portent le nom d'Étienne Dolet. Tous les autres
sont au nom de Gryphius. En dépit d'un même nombre de cahiers et de
feuillets (30 cahiers comportant au total 244 feuillets), il existe, on le sait,
de nombreuses différences entre ces exemplaires, que celles-ci soient
textuelles ou typographiques. Pour tenter d'en rendre compte valable-
ment, il est nécessaire de les mettre en relation avec la structure matérielle
des cahiers et les étapes de leur fabrication. Ce sont les points sur lesquels
je voudrais attirer l'attention, tout en sachant que ces constats ne peuvent
pas faire toute la lumière sur une situation qui, à tant d'égards, dut avoir
des implications psychologiques.

Les Caractères

L'imprimeur des *Oeuures* n'a pas donné son nom, et une observation
qui a déjà été faite à ce sujet doit être rappelée ici: il ne peut s'agir, ni
d'Étienne Dolet qui ne possédait pas encore d'atelier typographique à
cette date, ni de Sébastien Gryphius qui, pendant toute sa carrière, a
exclusivement utilisé des caractères italiques et romains dans ses très
nombreuses éditions (plus de cinquante, par exemple, en 1538). Où donc
chercher cet imprimeur, sinon parmi ceux qui, à Lyon, avaient déjà
travaillé pour Marot? Il est intéressant de constater, en effet, que la petite
gothique bâtarde qui a servi pour l'édition collective des *Oeuures*
(69 mm pour vingt lignes) est la même que celle qu'on peut voir dans
une douzaine d'éditions du poète, publiées séparément par François Juste
depuis février 1533.[6] Juste s'était ainsi donné, plus ou moins licitement,

---

5   Paris, BN, Rés. Ye. 1462–1464; Rothschild, VI E. bis (19); Lyon, BM;
     Carpentras, N. 312; Chantilly, Musée Condé, III. B. 31; Cologne, Bibl. Bodmer;
     Genève (anc. coll. Barbier; anc. coll. Droz); Cambridge (Mass.), Houghton. Voir:
     É. Picot, *Catalogue des livres composant la collection de M. le baron de
     Rothschild* (Paris, 1884) I, n° 605; Baudrier VIII, pp. 36–8.
6   Éditions publiées par François Juste:
     — LADOLE | SCENCE | CLE- | MENTINE. 23 février 1533. 12° long.
     Mayer 13 (Picot 597)
     — Ladolescence Clementine. 12 juillet 1533. 12° long. Mayer 14 bis
     — LADOLE= | SCENCE CLE | MENTINE. 12 décembre 1534. 12° long.
     Mayer 24 (Picot 600)

le quasi-monopole des éditions lyonnaises de Clément Marot, qui ne semble pas, de son côté, s'être jamais opposé aux initiatives de son imprimeur-libraire.

Outre cette petite gothique, le matériel de Juste comprend un alphabet de capitales romaines d'un corps supérieur et d'une graisse plus forte, dites lettres de deux-points. Ces dernières, destinées à marquer des *incipit*, occupent en théorie la place de deux lignes de texte. Certaines d'entre elles présentent des anomalies provenant des matrices défectueuses dans lesquelles elles ont été fondues et qui n'ont pas été éliminées pour autant. Ces lettres 'anormales' se trouvent ainsi individualisées parmi leurs homologues. On détecte notamment une lettre 'L' dont l'empattement supérieur droit est altéré et apparaît comme tronqué, ou bien une des lettres 'M' dont la hampe droite, plus courte que la gauche, donne au caractère un aspect boiteux, un autre 'M' dont la hampe gauche présente une ondulation disgracieuse, un 'N', privé d'empattement à l'angle supérieur gauche, etc. De tels défauts se remarquent dans la plupart des éditions imprimées par François Juste. Parmi celles de Marot, on peut citer *Ladolescence Clementine* du 12 décembre 1534, dans laquelle le 'L' défectueux est utilisé au moins à quatre reprises (soit aux feuillets C4^v (28^v), E8^r (56^r), G3^r (75^r) G10^v (82^r)), et le 'N' une fois, au feuillet D3^v (39^v). Il en est de même pour *La Suyte* de 1534, avec les deux lettres 'L' et 'N' des feuillets D3^v (39^v), D7^v (43^v) et E7^v (55^v).

Il serait fastidieux de dresser une liste exhaustive de ces occurrences dans les éditions de Clément Marot données par François Juste, mais la répétition, aux mêmes emplacements, des lettres de deux-points défectueuses 'L' et 'N' a permis de constater que *Ladolescence Clementine* du 6

— LA SVYTE | DE LADOLESCEN- | CE CLEMENTINE. 1534. 12° long. Mayer 25 (Picot 600)

— LE PREMIER | LIVRE DE LA ME | TAMORPHOSE D'OVIDE. 1534. 12° long. Mayer 26 (Picot 602)

— LADOLE= | SCENCE CLE | MENTINE. 6 février 1535. 12° long. Mayer 31 (Picot 602)

— LA SVYTE | DE LADOLESCEN= | ce Clementine.... 1535. 12° long. Mayer 34

— LE PREMIER | LIVRE DE LA ME | tamorphose d'ouide.... 1536. 12° long. Mayer 35

— L'ADOLESCEN- | CLEMĒTINE aultremẽt, | Les Œuures de Clement Marot...Auec le | residu despuis faict. 1536. 16°. Mayer 48 (Vente Lignerolles, n° 896)

— La Suite | de L'Adolescence Clementine, | reueue. 1537. 16°. Mayer 61 (Vente Lignerolles, n° 896)

— Le pre- | mier Liure | de la Metamorphose | d'Ouide. 1537. 16°. Mayer 62 (Vente Lignerolles, n° 896)

— Les Oeuures de Clement Marot. 1538. 16°. (Vente La Vallière, 1767, n° 2813)

février 1535 réutilisait, curieusement, les cahiers D et K de l'édition du 12 décembre 1534.

En dehors des éditions de Marot, et pour retenir le même exemple, la lettre de deux-points défectueuse 'L' se rencontre fréquemment dans les impressions de François Juste, notamment en 1534, dans la *Pantagrueline Prognostication pour Lan M. D. XXXV* (A6[r])[7] et dans *Lhistoire de Thucydide Athenien...translatee...par feu Messire Claude de Seyssel* (39[r]), édition qui comprend un dizain de Marot au lecteur (fig. 2).[8] Elle se voit aussi, en 1535, dans les *Oeuures* de Guillaume Coquillart (37[v]),[9] en 1536, dans les *Omnium gentium mores* de Boemus (p. 298),[10] et encore en 1539, dans *Les tragedies...de Seneque, traduites par Pierre Grosnet* (D1[v]).[11] Des observations similaires pourraient être faites à partir d'autres lettres défectueuses.

Il est remarquable que l'édition collective des *Oeuures* de Clément Marot, parue en 1538 dans le format in-octavo,[12] soit imprimée avec deux fontes identiques à celles de François Juste, la gothique du texte, et la série romaine des lettres de deux-points. Celle-ci y présente les mêmes défauts, en particulier cette lettre 'L', à l'empattement tronqué, repérable sur huit pages de tous les exemplaires, dont quatre dans *L'adolescence* (26[r], 50[v], 59[r], 76[r]), une dans la *Suite* (27[v]), deux dans les *Epigrammes* (4[v], 25[v]), une dans la *Metamorphose d'Ouide* (5[v]). Il faut y ajouter, pour les *Epigrammes*, trois occurrences particulières aux exemplaires Dolet (10[r], 14[v], 20[v]). La conclusion semble s'imposer: François Juste est l'imprimeur de l'édition de 1538. Mais on peut alors s'étonner de voir, l'année suivante, les mêmes caractères, anomalies comprises, dans les mains d'un autre imprimeur lyonnais, Jean Barbou, qui en imprime, précisément pour François Juste, une nouvelle édition des *Oeuures* de Clément Marot, cette fois dans le format in-seize.[13]

---

[7] S. Rawles et M. A. Screech, *A New Rabelais Bibliography* (Genève, 1987), n° 18.

[8] Thucydide, *Lhistoire de la guerre qui fut entre les Peloponesiens et Atheniens translatee...par Claude de Seyssel*, 4°, e6[r] (39[r]), u1[r] (153[r]). Voir: Y. de La Perrière, *Supplément provisoire à la Bibliographie lyonnaise du Président Baudrier. Fascicule I* (Paris, 1967), n° 35; Mayer, n° 237.

[9] G. Coquillart, *Les Oeuures* (Lyon, F. Juste), 1535. 8°. La Perrière, n° 36.

[10] J. Boemus, *Omnium gentium mores* (Lyon, F. Juste), 1536. 8°. La Perrière, n° 47.

[11] Sénèque, *Les tragedies*. Trad. F. Grosnet (Lyon, pour F. Juste), 1539. La Perrière, n° 15.

[12] Voir pp. 152–3 et nn. 4 et 5.

[13] Paris, BN, Rés. Ye 1478; Smith-Lesouëf, Rés. 188; Rothschild, II.5.60; Mayer, n° 76. Voir P. Ducourtioux, *Les Barbou, imprimeurs à Lyon, Limoges, Paris* (Limoges, 1896), n° 27; Baudrier V, pp. 6–18; XII, p. 95; Picot, n° 607.

Peut-on en conclure, avec Gérard Defaux, que Jean Barbou est aussi l'imprimeur de l'édition de 1538?[14] La réponse est autre. Il faut rappeler ici que le Lyonnais François Juste, qui exerce depuis dix ans rue Mercière, en face du couvent des frères prêcheurs, nommé Notre-Dame de Confort, détient à la suite de son père, Aymon, la fonderie de caractères la plus importante de Lyon, auprès de laquelle ses confrères viennent naturellement s'approvisionner. Quant à Jean Barbou, Normand d'origine, il n'est alors qu'au début d'une carrière relativement brève, entièrement consacrée au service des libraires de la ville où il a élu domicile, les frères Frellon en tête. Il ne donne pas d'adresse, et l'on sait seulement qu'il demeure dans la même maison que l'imprimeur François Fradin, 'grant rue', c'est-à-dire rue Mercière, près de Notre-Dame de Confort, à quelques pas, donc, de François Juste. À l'exception de *Decretales*, imprimées pour Hugues de La Porte en gothiques de forme (ou *textura*), et peut-être d'un *Breviarum Romanum*, il emploie essentiellement des caractères romains et italiques.[15] Il est extrêmement probable que François Juste lui fournit les deux fontes[16] destinées à l'impression des *Oeuures* de Clément Marot dont il lui passe commande à la fin de 1538 ou au début de 1539.

La liste des éditions de François Juste, établie par Yvonne de La Perrière, montre d'ailleurs que les années 1536 et 1537 sont très chargées pour celui-ci, avec vingt éditions chacune, et que les chiffres tombent brusquement à quatre en 1538, pour ne remonter qu'à huit en 1539. Il semble donc que Juste ait des raisons de ralentir son activité, au moment où il entreprend cette édition de Clément Marot en petit format que, pour la première fois, il n'imprime pas lui-même.

Les caractères typographiques qui ont servi, en 1538, puis en 1539, à imprimer ces éditions de Clément Marot, ont manifestement été fondus dans les mêmes matrices: leurs similitudes et leurs défauts mêmes en témoignent. Cependant, les lettrines, très individualisées, qui ornent chacune d'entre elles indiquent que la composition et l'impression ont été effectuées dans des ateliers différents: fonds blancs ou criblés, représentations animales ou végétales en 1538, fonds striés et images de doctes et

---

[14] G. Defaux, 'Clément Marot et ses éditions lyonnaises: Étienne Dolet, Sébastien Gryphius, et François Juste', in *Intellectual Life in Renaissance Lyon: Proceedings of the Cambridge Lyon Colloquium, 14–16 April 1991*, (Cambridge, 1993), p. 93, n. 19, pp. 108–9. Texte repris dans *Clément Marot. Œuvres poétiques complètes: Édition critique établie, présentée et annotée avec variantes par Gérard Defaux*, vol. II (Paris, 1993), pp. lxii–lxvi.

[15] La Perrière, op. cit., p. 85.

[16] Sur Jean Barbou, voir n. 13.

de livres, chez Barbou, en 1539.[17] Par ailleurs, les lettrines qui apparaissent dans les *Oeuures* de 1538, soit sous le nom de Dolet, soit sous celui de Gryphius, ont pu, grâce à de nombreuses comparaisons, être identifiées avec certitude comme propriété de François Juste. À la différence, en effet, des caractères typographiques, fondus et promis à la multiplication, le matériel ornemental, gravé sur bois, n'est pas destiné à une large circulation et reste, par principe, entre les mains de celui qui l'a commandé ou qui l'a reçu légitimement. Celui-ci peut éventuellement le prêter à l'un ou à plusieurs de ses associés, mais il en demeure propriétaire. Convenablement authentifié, ce matériel autorise des attributions crédibles.

Les Lettrines de François Juste

Parmi les huit lettrines gravées sur bois qui décorent les *Oeuures* de Clément Marot, publiées en 1538, il en est au moins sept que l'on retrouve dans d'autres éditions imprimées par François Juste et par son successeur, Pierre de Tours. Celles-ci appartiennent à trois alphabets dont les deux plus grands présentent une unité de style (voir tableau I):

I. *Alphabet ombré sur fond blanc, à trois filets d'encadrement (34 x 34)*

La grande lettrine L à l'oiseau crêté et à long bec, qui apparaît au début de *L'adolescence Clementine*, en tête d'une épître de Marot (a2[r]) (fig. 3), avait déjà été utilisée par François Juste en 1537, au moment où il imprimait les *Ordonnances des Foyres de Lyon, de Brie et de Champaigne* (feuillets 23[v], 29[r], 34[v], 36[v], 48[v]).[18] On la retrouve dans *Le Triumphe de...Dame Verolle*, portant au titre la mention: 'On les vend par Francoys Iuste', et à la fin: 'Imprime nouvellement par Francoys Iuste le XII du moys de Septembre Lan mil cinq cens XXXIX' (fig. 4),[19] et dans les *Ordonnances sur le faict de la Iustice*, publiées vers la même date, à l'adresse de Thibault Payen et de François Juste (a6[r]).[20]

---

17 Trois lettrines de Jean Barbou se voient aux feuillets 5[r], 7[r], 10[v], de l'édition in-16 des *Oeuures* de Clément Marot, imprimées par lui pour François Juste en 1539. Ces lettrines sont très différentes de celles qui ornent l'édition in-8° de 1538. La consultation de nombreux ouvrages sortant de l'atelier de Jean Barbou, ainsi que les reproductions incluses dans l'ouvrage de Ducourtioux, cité plus haut, montrent l'unité et le style très particulier de son matériel décoratif.

18 La Perrière, n° 75.

19 La Perrière, n° 94.

20 Baudrier, IV, p. 212; XII, p. 178; La Perrière, n° 42.

Une lettrine T, montrant deux oiseaux affrontés, de même style, orne le début de 'La Premiere Eglogue des Bucoliques de Virgile'.

II. *Alphabet ombré sur fond blanc, à trois filets d'encadrement (26 x 26)*

Ce modèle intermédiaire, à décor floral, est représenté dans les *Oeuures* de Marot par les trois lettrines A, E, et I. La lettrine A, qui offre en outre deux cornes d'abondance, placée au feuillet A3^r de la *Metamorphose d'Ouide*, est la dernière du livre (fig. 5).[21] On pouvait la voir, quelques mois plus tôt, dans l'édition du *Courtisan*, donnée par Étienne Dolet, et imprimée à sa demande par François Juste, qui y faisait l'éloge de Dolet cité plus haut (fig. 6). Ainsi, la lettrine n'avait guère quitté l'atelier. Les deux autres lettrines sont utilisées pour *L'adolescence Clementine*. Le E annonce l'épître 'A Messire Nicolas de Neufuille...' (B1^r) (fig. 8–9), le I, l'épître 'a ung grand nombre de frères...' (a5^r). Ces trois lettres se retrouvent dans les *Ordonnances* de 1539 (A3^r et A3^v, A5^r) (fig. 7).[22] Dans les exemplaires des *Oeuvres* imprimés pour Gryphius, la lettrine I, différente, qui représente un enfant et un cerf, appartient à son matériel.[23]

III. *Alphabet blanc sur fond criblé, à un filet d'encadrement (15 x 15)*

Deux lettrines du petit alphabet, I (fig. 10) et Q, se voient dans *La Suite de L'adolescence* (A3^r et B8^r), la troisième, L, dans *Le Premier Liure de la Metamorphose d'Ouide* (A2^r). En raison du petit format et de la fréquence de l'article défini en français, ces lettres se rencontrent fréquemment dans les impressions de François Juste et de son successeur, Pierre de Tours. On peut citer, dès 1532, *Des mots dorez*, traduit de Sénèque (fig. 11),[24] puis en 1537, *La familiere institution pour les legionnaires*,[25] en 1542, *Pantagruel* et *Gargantua*.[26] Les trois lettrines sont toutes visibles dans *Le Courtisan* de 1538.

---

[21] Voir n. 3. Lettrine reproduite dans l'ouvrage cité n. 7, p. 152, d'après les *Grands Annales...du grand Gargantua et Pantagruel...*, imprimés en 1542 par Pierre de Tours, gendre et successeur de François Juste (qu'il ne faut pas confondre avec Pierre de Sainte-Lucie, successeur de Claude Nourry).

[22] Voir n. 20.

[23] Lettrine fréquemment employée par Gryphius. Un exemple dans N. Bourbon, *Nugarum libri VIII*, 1538, feuillet a3^r. Baudrier, VIII, pp. 118–19.

[24] La Perrière, n° 93.

[25] La Perrière, n° 50.

[26] Rawles et Screech, op. cit., n° 12 et n° 23.

Autour de la fabrication

Des motifs qui ont amené Étienne Dolet et Sébastien Gryphius à publier séparément et diversement les *Oeuures* de Clément Marot, entreprises en commun en 1538, nous ne pouvons guère connaître que ce qui nous est montré par les livres eux-mêmes. Il faut donc tenter d'interroger les trente cahiers qui en contiennent les quatre parties et qui, comme on a essayé de l'établir, sortent de l'atelier de François Juste. On soupçonne que dans cette histoire, apparemment houleuse, l'imprimeur aura préféré garder l'anonymat.

Dans le tableau II sont indiqués, à gauche, la collation des cahiers, leur nombre, et celui des feuillets (indications valables pour tous les exemplaires), à droite, ceux dans lesquels on observe des différences matérielles et textuelles entre les exemplaires imprimés au nom de Gryphius et ceux qui portent le nom de Dolet, soit dix cahiers entiers ou partiels sur les trente que comportent les *Oeuures*. Ces différences, introduites par des cartons (cahiers ou feuillets de substitution), sont plus nombreuses, on peut le voir, dans *L'adolescence Clementine* et dans les *Deux liures d'Epigrammes* que dans les autres parties (voir tableau II).

Dans l'ensemble, cependant, les éléments communs ici restent de loin majoritaires, avec vingt cahiers entiers qui n'ont pas été modifiés par des cartons. Ceux-ci procèdent des mêmes opérations de composition et d'impression. Les défauts mêmes des caractères typographiques et de l'impression sont garants de cette simultanéité des opérations. Ainsi dans *L'adolescence Clementine* au feuillet d2^r (26^r), 'Oraison contemplative', l'utilisation, au même emplacement, de cette lettre de deux-points défectueuse, L, dont il a été parlé. Ainsi également, aux feuillets f4^r (44^r) et h4^r (60^r), la trace indésirable de grosses lettres employées comme garnitures pour serrer la composition dans le chassis de la forme. Ainsi enfin, au feuillet k8^r (80^r) l'empreinte accidentelle de trois caractères couchés dans la forme. Ces traits sont communs à tous les exemplaires. On peut en déduire qu'au moment où les compositeurs de l'imprimerie travaillaient sur ces textes et où les pressiers tiraient les feuilles correspondantes, les lots de feuilles imprimées étaient identiques pour les deux destinataires et qu'il n'était pas prévu d'établir de distinctions entre eux.

Cependant, comme dans la plupart des travaux d'imprimerie de l'époque, des corrections ont été introduites au cours du travail d'impression, sources de variantes qui ne proviennent pas de cartons. S'il n'a pas été possible d'établir tous les rapprochements nécessaires à un examen systématique, le cahier b de *L'adolescence Clementine*, contenant, presque entier, le texte du 'Temple de Cupido', a pu être spécialement étudié à partir de cinq exemplaires, dont les deux connus au nom de Dolet, et trois à celui de Gryphius. Cette comparaison a permis de constater qu'il ne se trouvait pas de variantes sur l'une des formes de composition passées sous la presse, la forme intérieure (inner forme), mais qu'au contraire, la forme extérieure (outer forme) présentait trois états successifs, le premier dans l'un des exemplaires Dolet (BN, Imprimés), le second dans l'autre exemplaire Dolet connu (Wolfenbüttel), présentant, sauf erreur, 45 corrections par rapport au précédent (fig. 8), le troisième dans tous les exemplaires Gryphius examinés (BN, Imprimés; BN, Rothschild; Lyon, BM) (fig. 9). Ici, ce sont 39 corrections qui ont été ajoutées aux précé-dentes. Cette comparaison permet de voir dans quel ordre les feuilles sont passées sous la presse.

Les corrections concernent essentiellement la ponctuation et la substitution de capitales pour certains noms personnifiés, comme Monde, Terre, Chantre, et Beau parler, ou mis en valeur comme Princes, Oeuures. Une variante plus intéressante concerne, au feuillet B3^r (11^r), le vers 14 qui se lisait 'Le grant Dieu Pan, de par ses pastoureaux' chez Dolet, devenu '…avec ses pastoureaux' chez Gryphius. Au feuillet b6^v (14^v), les deux derniers vers ont subi deux corrections successives:

Mais il eut de la Soulcie:
Vela qui me trouble le sens.

(Dolet, BN)

Mais y il eut de la Soulcie:
Vela qui me trouble le sens.

(Dolet, Wolfenbüttel)

Mais il y eut de la Soulcie:
Voila qui me trouble le sens.

(Gryphius)

Les cahiers c et d de *L'adolescence* portent aussi la trace de 'correc-tions sous presse', effectuées sur la forme extérieure: l'addition insolite et fautive 'Fueil XXii' au feuillet c8^v (24^v) et celle, appropriée, du sous-titre 'EPISTRES' au feuillet d4^v (28^v).[27]

---

[27] Sur les corrections sous presse, ou introduites au cours de l'impression, et les 'états' ainsi engendrés sur un côté de la feuille imprimée, voir F. Bowers, *Principles of Bibliographical Description* (New York, 1962), pp. 42 sqq. Je remercie vivement le Dr Martin Boghardt de m'avoir envoyé des reproductions du cahier b de l'exemplaire Dolet de Wolfenbüttel et d'avoir lui-même procédé à des comparaisons sur 'collating machine' avec des reproductions de l'exemplaire

Cartons

Les corrections introduites au moyen de cartons offrent ici un intérêt particulier, parce qu'elles portent la marque d'une intervention personnelle et énergique de Clément Marot lui-même. Ce ne peut être que sur son injonction, en effet, que Gryphius, remplaçant désormais Dolet comme éditeur en titre, a été chargé de transmettre à Juste de nouvelles directives concernant l'ouvrage, à peine terminé. Il s'agit de corriger des leçons fautives, de restituer des passages omis, et même d'éliminer toute trace de collaboration avec Dolet. Il faut donc reprendre les exemplaires disponibles, procéder aux suppressions requises et à l'insertion des cartons permettant de notifier les erreurs ou de restituer des textes amendés. Cette opération va en réalité concerner dix cahiers des *Oeuures* de 1538, dont trois intégralement, et entraîner, en définitive, la recomposition de quarante feuillets, soit le sixième de l'ensemble.

Le premier cahier, a, de *L'adolescence Clementine*, entièrement changé, porte naturellement au premier feuillet recto un nouveau titre au nom de Gryphius, le verso étant rempli par une liste d'errata. Ce cahier est témoin d'un grand brassage opéré dans la distribution des pièces liminaires par Clément Marot, qui supprime toute allusion à Étienne Dolet, en particulier les vers dont celui-ci avait honoré son livre, et transforme en partie l'épître qu'il avait dédiée lui-même à Dolet, le 31 juillet 1538, et dont il gratifie, avec ironie et à la même date, 'ceulx qui par cy-devant ont imprimé ses Oeuures'. Au milieu des remaniements, Juste n'oublie pas de réinsérer ses grandes lettrines décorées d'oiseaux, aux emplacements mêmes qu'ils occupaient précédemment, mais il doit remplacer son I floral par un autre I, appartenant au matériel de Gryphius.[28]

Pour les trois autres parties, les substitutions d'adresse sont effectuées au moyen d'un double feuillet formant paire dans le cahier, le premier et le dernier. Comme précédemment, ce premier feuillet porte au recto le nouveau titre et au verso une liste d'errata.

La première intervention sur le texte poétique lui-même est limitée matériellement au demi-cahier intérieur, i, de *L'adolescence Clementine*. Au recto du troisième feuillet, i3 (67), il s'agit seulement de changer le titre du rondeau intitulé 'De compter sa Fortune', dédié maintenant 'A madame de Bazauges'. Mais, au verso, il s'impose de restituer un vers

---

parisien. Nos observations ont été concordantes. Les exemplaires Gryphius correspondent bien ici à un nouvel 'état' et non à une 'recomposition'.
28 Voir p. 158 et n. 23.

du 'Rondeau par contradictions', dont l'omission laissait précisément pendante la contradiction:

Me tourmentant de ce, qui me contente,
Me contentant de ce qui me tourmente:

Il est plus important encore de rétablir, au feuillet i3ᵛ (68ᵛ), la leçon authentique du refrain intéressant le rondeau 'De la Conception Nostre Dame', que toutes les éditions antérieures donnaient sous la forme 'Comme Nature', et que Dolet, apparemment sous sa seule autorité, a transformé en 'Contre Nature'. Cette altération, particulièrement grave dans le contexte religieux de l'époque, a dû être très mal ressentie par Marot.

Au feuillet i6ʳ (70ʳ), à la troisième strophe du rondeau ayant pour refrain 'Soubz Esperance', le verbe 'percevoir' vient heureusement remplacer les mots 'par ce voir', que répétait, pour ainsi dire, la finale du vers suivant 'se veoir'.

Pour la *Suite de L'adolescence*, même au prix d'un resserrement peu harmonieux de la composition, il est indispensable de réintroduire, au feuillet L4ᵛ (84ᵛ) des 'Chants divers', un huitain omis au 'Chant de May':

Quant vous verrez rire les cieulx,
Et la terre en sa floriture,
Quant vous verrez deuant vos yeux
Les eaux lui bailler nourriture,
Sur peine de grant forfaicture,
Et destre larron & menteur
N'en louez nulle creature
Louez le nom du createur.

De même que pour le feuillet de titre, afin d'éviter toute obligation de montage et de collage, le changement s'opère par substitution de feuillets devant faire paire dans le cahier.

Au cahier suivant, M, du 'Cymetiere', deux nouveaux feuillets 'conjoints' doivent remplacer les feuillets M3 et M6 (91 et 94) du 'Cheual de Vuyart', afin de permettre le changement du vers 'Escume bauant' en 'Escumeur bauant', la restitution du vers omis 'Mon ame finir', et enfin la modification des quatre vers finaux qui deviennent:

Mon los bruit et fame:
Car iadis plus cher

Mayma cheuaucher
Que fille ne femme.

En recomposant le texte du feuillet M6^v (94^v), dans les 'Oraisons', le compositeur omet malencontreusement un mot de l'avant-dernier vers de l'*Ave Maria*, qui se lit: 'Car le fruict, qui est ton ventre', faute qui échappera à l'œil du correcteur.

Les *Epigrammes* sont la partie des *Oeuures* de 1538 la plus largement modifiée par des cartons. Deux cahiers entiers sont recomposés, ainsi qu'à l'instar de la *Suite de L'adolescence*, le premier et le dernier feuillet du premier cahier. Il s'agit là d'un ensemble de dix-huit feuillets cartonnés sur les vingt-quatre que comprennent les *Epigrammes*. Les changements opérés à travers les textes et les dédicaces ont été attentivement étudiés par Gérard Defaux.

Les deux cartons concernant *Le premier liure de la Metamorphose d'Ouide* ont chacun un seul but: le premier, de substituer, comme précédemment, le nom de Gryphius à celui de Dolet, et d'introduire les errata, le deuxième, d'éliminer la marque de Dolet à la fin du livre.

Les Errata

Le carton entier et les trois cartons partiels que Gryphius a fait placer en tête des quatre parties des *Oeuures* de Clément Marot contiennent, chacun, au 'verso de la nouvelle page de titre, une liste de 'Faultes d'imprimerie' que l'éditeur invite à corriger 'sur la marge auec la plume'. Ces listes forment, en quelque sorte, le complément des textes de substitution introduits par les cartons. La première liste, au verso du titre général, est précédée, sur la même page, de douze vers sans titre, qui reprennent ceux que Marot adressait 'A SON LIVRE' dans l'émission Dolet. Une variante y a été introduite, avec le premier mot 'Oster' remplaçant celui de 'Racler'.

Les corrections indiquées sont au nombre total de cinquante-quatre, réparties à travers vingt-et-un cahiers. Curieusement, la graphie des mots relevés ne respecte pas toujours celle du texte lui-même. Tantôt, par ailleurs, les renvois sont faits au feuillet et à la page (première partie de *L'adolescence Clementine* jusqu'au feuillet 44; deuxième partie de la *Suite*, à compter du feuillet 58; *Metamorphose d'Ouide*). Tantôt, ces renvois se bornent à indiquer le numéro d'ordre de la pièce (deuxième partie de *L'adolescence*; première partie de la *Suite*). Encore ce schéma souffre-t-il des exceptions. Pour les *Epigrammes*, la référence est seule-

ment donnée à l'*incipit*. Enfin, le numéro d'ordre du vers n'est mentionné que pour la première partie de la *Suite* et pour la *Metamorphose
d'Ouide*.

Quelques exemples d'errata

N.B. Chaque citation se terminant, d'une manière générale, par deux
points, et chaque correction par un point, il est manifeste que la
ponctuation n'a pas été prise en considération dans ces listes.

L'adolescence Clementine

'Le temple de Cupido'	dangereux plus que traitz: dangereux plus que tres.	11^v
'Epistres'	En ce hault lieu: En ce chault lieu.	42^r
	tu dys estre alloué: tu doys estre alloué.	45 (=65)^r
'Chansons'	A eu un filz au ciel voué: A ung filz du ciel aduoué.	86^r

La Suite de L'adolescence

'Elegies'	Ou si ne faulx: Ou si ie faulx.	25^r
	fors en suyuant: fors en fuyant.	28^r
	Est-il doulceur: Est il douleur.	33^r
	de douleur accomply: de doulceur accomply.	42^v
'Chants diuers'	croy qu'en ceste aliance: quoy qu'en ceste aliance.	79^v

| 'Cymetiere' | Les verms se pastent:
Les vers s'apastent. | 92^v |

Epigrammes

| 'Premier Liure' | toutes les fleurs perissent:
toutes tes fleurs _____. | 3^v |

| 'Le Second Liure' | car ma Bouche:
car ma Boete. | 26^v |

Premier liure de la Metamorphose d'Ouide

'Premier Livre'	tenir le nom Rommain: ternir le nom Rommain.	9^r
	Les Cieulx qui paroissent: Les lieux qui paroissent.	13^r
	en donnant la blessé: en dormant l'a blessé.	24^v

L'Édition de 1539

L'histoire de la publication, en 1538, des *Oeuures* de Clément Marot trouve sa prolongation dans l'édition commandée par François Juste à Jean Barbou, qui l'imprime donc en 1539, avec les mêmes caractères, mais avec son propre fonds de lettres ornées.

Cette fois, un format plus réduit est adopté, celui de l'in-seize dont Juste avait déjà, depuis deux ans, fait usage pour les œuvres séparées du poète. Selon une mention donnée par le catalogue de la vente La Vallière de 1767, ce format serait également celui d'une édition des *Oeuures* de Clément Marot publiée par François Juste en 1538. Malheureusement, aucun exemplaire n'en est aujourd'hui connu. À travers — on non — cette édition intermédiaire, les *Oeuures* de 1539 sont très proches de celle de l'année précédente, mais elles n'offrent plus maintenant de divisions matérielles entre les parties. Signatures et foliotation sont donc continues. Barbou y a-t-il bien incorporé les corrections signalées dans l'émission Gryphius de l'année précédente? Pour les treize de *L'adolescence*, intégralement. Pour les autres parties, avec une fidélité moindre: sept sur quinze pour la *Suite*, sept sur neuf pour les *Epigrammes*, neuf sur treize pour *Le premier Liure de la Metamorphose d'Ouide*. Par ailleurs, Barbou doit lui-même introduire une liste de cinq errata à la fin de son impression. Rectifiant de simples coquilles, ceux-ci ne reprennent pas les corrections omises.

Imprimeur apprécié d'une dizaine de libraires lyonnais, pour lesquels il se sert de son fonds de lettres italiques et romaines, Jean Barbou semble n'avoir jamais travaillé pour François Juste en d'autres occasions que celle du Marot de 1539, et n'en avoir jamais utilisé les caractères, ni auparavant, ni pendant les trois années suivantes, les dernières de sa carrière. Ces raisons, jointes aux preuves fournies par le matériel décoratif, permettent d'attribuer, sans erreur, à François Juste le mérite d'avoir imprimé la première édition collective connue de Clément Marot, sous la conduite d'Étienne Dolet, puis sous celle de Gryphius. Mérite, certes, pour celui qui, pendant cinq ans et plus, avait édité Marot publiquement, et sans intermédiaire.

Le Privilège

Le privilège accordé par François Ier à Clément Marot lui-même — et non à l'un de ses libraires — pose un problème. Cette 'Declaration sur l'impression des oeuures de Marot' fait défense à tout libraire ou imprimeur d'imprimer ou de faire imprimer quelque œuvre de Marot que ce soit, ou d'auteur publié par lui, si elle n'a pas été revue par lui-même, et si une copie ou un exemplaire signé de sa main, et accompagné de sa permission, n'a pas été remis au roi. Ce privilège est étendu aux juridictions provinciales. Aucune limitation de temps n'est indiquée.[29]

Ph. A. Becker qui a fait transcrire ce document en 1914 d'après un formulaire de chancellerie,[30] et C. A. Mayer qui l'a suivi,[31] ont pensé que ce texte s'appliquait à l'édition de 1538. La question est à reprendre à la suite de l'étude consacrée par Hélène Michaud en 1972 aux formulaires de grande chancellerie.[32]

Comme l'a montré Hélène Michaud, la compilation de ce recueil de 189 modèles de lettres patentes a été effectuée par un commis pour le compte de Du Lys, Sr de Choullot-Chichamp, entre 1560 et 1570. Les

---

[29] Paris, BN, MS fr. 18111, ff. 57r–59r.

[30] Ph. A. Becker, 'Das Druckprivileg für Marots Werke von 1538', *Zeitschrift für französische Sprache und Literatur*, XLVII (1914), 224–9.

[31] C. A. Mayer, *Clément Marot* (Paris, 1972), pp. 427–30.

[32] H. Michaud, *Les Formulaires de grande chancellerie, 1500–1800* (Paris, 1972), pp. 4, 112–20. Voir aussi: H. Michaud, *La Grande Chancellerie et les écritures royales au XVIe siècle* (Paris, 1967).

mentions de signature et d'enregistrement manquent. 'L'inscription suit un ordre chronologique, mais la compilation, écrit Hélène Michaud, est sensiblement postérieure à l'établissement des lettres dont le texte est reproduit.' Étant donné cet intervalle de temps entre originaux et copies, on peut penser que le scribe — toujours le même au long des pages du recueil — 'a compulsé un ou plusieurs registres d'enregistrement....Les premières lettres se rattachent aux dernières années du règne, en particulier aux années 1543–1544.' C'est probablement le cas de la lettre patente concernant Marot, quatorzième du formulaire, qui suit de peu la copie d'un document daté du 3 novembre 1543.

À cette époque, Clément Marot n'était plus en France. Mais a-t-il fait allusion à ce parchemin dans l'épigramme adressée 'A ung sien amy', après son départ de Genève, au début de 1544?

> Ce neantmoins par mont & par campaigne,
> Le mien esprit me suyt et m'accompaigne:
> Malgré fascheux i'en iouys & en use,
> Abandonné iamais ne m'a la Muse,
> Aulcun n'a sceu auoir puissance là,
> Le Roy portoit mon bon droict en cela.[33]

---

[33] *Epigrammes de Clément Marot faictz à l'imitation de Martial*, Poitiers, Jean et Enguilbert de Marnef, 1547, 27 septembre. 8°. La citation se trouve au feuillet d1[r] (49[r]). L'épigramme porte en marge: 1543. Privilège royal accordé aux libraires pour cinq ans, le 13 novembre 1545. Arsenal 8° B.L. 8732 Rés. Voir C. Marot, *Œuvres poétiques*. Éd. G. Defaux, éd. cit., vol. II, pp. 703–5 et 1288–91.

TABLEAU I

Lettrines des Œuvres in-8°, 1538

	DOLET	GRYPHIUS	
L'adolescence			
	a2: L (grande)	x	*id.*
	a5: I (moyenne)	x	I (différente, Gryphius)
	a6: T (grande)	x	*id.*
	b1: E (moyenne)		*id.*
Suite			
	A3: I (petite)		*id.*
	B8: Q (petite)		*id.*
Metamorphose			
	A2: L (petite)		*id.*
	A3: A (moyenne)		*id.*

Formats:	grandes:	34 x 34
	moyennes:	26 x 26
	petites:	15 x 15

x = lettrine utilisée sur un cahier cartonné

TABLEAU II

Les Œuvres de Clément Marot, 1538

	IMPRESSION ORIGINALE			CARTONS (GRYPHIUS)		
	cahiers	n. de cahiers	n. de f.	cahiers entiers	parties de cahiers	n. de f.
L'adolescence Clementine	$a–k^8\ l^{10}$ (1–90)	11	90	a^8 (1–8)		8
					$i^3–i^6$ (67–70)	4
La suite de L'adolescence	$A–M^8$ (1–96)	12	96		A1, A8 (1, 8)	2
					L4–L5 (84–85)	2
					M3, M6 (91, 94)	2
Deux liures d'Epigrammes	$Aa–Dd^8$ (1–32)	4	32		Aa1, Aa8 (1, 8)	2
				Bb^8 (9–16)		8
				Cc^8 (17–24)		8
Le premier liure de la Metamorphose d'Ouide	$A–B^8\ C^{10}$ (1–26)	3	26		A1, A8 (1, 8)	2
					C1, C10 (17, 26)	2
Totaux		30	244	3	7	40

(La graphie des titres reproduit celle qui apparaît sur le premier feuillet recto du titre général. Les chiffres entre parenthèses se réfèrent aux feuillets chiffrés.)

On remarque que le dernier cahier de *L'adolescence Clementine*, l, de même que le dernier cahier, C, de la *Metamorphose d'Ouide*, comportent anormalement dix feuillets. Les quatre pages excédentaires de chacun de ces cahiers ont donc dû être imposées dans le châssis, selon l'un des schémas d'imposition par demi-feuille. Dans les exemplaires Gryphius, le premier et le dernier feuillet du cahier, C, correspondent à des cartons.

admonnestrent que deuuez auoir souuenãce du
serment que Boz peres leur ont faict. Car quãt
a eulx ilz nentendoit point dy riẽs innouer. La
quelle response entendue par les Plateens de
liberrent nabandonner point les Atheniens,
ains de resister aulx ennemys quãt bien ilz deu
uroient Beoir deuant leurs yeulx Busser a gas
ster tous les Biens quilz auoient aulx champs,
q souffrir tous les aultres maulx que on leur
pourroit faire. Et non pourtant ne Boulurent
plus renuoyer leurs messaigiers deuers les
Peloponesiens, ains leur firent
respõse, quil ne leur estoit possible faire ce quilz
leur auoient requis.

☙ La protestation de Archidamus
contre les Plateens.

Lors Archidamus Bint deuant la mu
raille q protesta contre eulx en telle ma
niere. Nous dieux q saincts qui gardez
la cite q la terre des Plateens, Nous appelle
a tesmoing cõme ceulx cy sont les premiers qui
rompent leur serment, q que loultraige ne Biẽt
par nostre faulte, ie Nous Benons Bostilement
en leur terre, en laquelle noz ancestres Nous
ayans faicts leurs Bieux q sacrifices eurent la
Bictoire cõtre les Medes, moyennant Bostre
ayde q faueur. Et que ce que nous frons do
res, en auant contre eulx, ce sera a leur tort nõ
point aux nostre, pourtant que quelques remõ
strances q enhortemẽs raisonnables que leur
ayons sceu faire, nauons riens peu proffiter,
ne les retirer a la raison. Par quoy Bueillez
permettre que ceulx qui ont les premieres fault
loultraige, en peinent la peine a ceulx qui
se preparent pour les punir iustement se puis
sent faire. ☙ Apres quil eust faict ceste protestie
q requeste aux dieux il permist a ses gens bar
ines quilz commençassent la guerre. Et pre
mierement des arbres qui furent incontinent
couppes, fit enclose la Bille de grosses Barrieres
q de paulx, affin que nul nen peult sortir ne y
entrer. Apres commencerent a dresser Bne te
tue q donue, esperans en peu de temps lachetuer, Beu le grant nombre de gens qui aydoit a
louurraige, q par ce moyen de prendre la Bille.

☙ La somme de la donue.

Et la somme dicelle donue estoit telle. Car
premierement ilz faisoient des rameaux
des arbre, des clayes en somme de panier
q les mettoient des deulx coustes de la donue

attachees q soustenues de paulx pour retenir
la terre q aultre matiere q lon mettoit dedans,
q apres iectoit pierres, Boys, terre, q toute aul
tre chose que pouoit seruir a la replir. Auquel
ouurraige continuerent, lxx. iours continuelz
sans cesser de besoigner nuyct ne iour. Car
quant les Bngs sen partoient pour aller man
ger ou dormir, les aultres y Benoient chascun
a son tour. Et pour solliciter q faire auancer
ledict ouurraige, furent deputes les Lacedemo
niens qui auoient soubz leur charge les soul
dars mercennaires, q auecques eulx les ducs
q chiefs de toutes les cites. Quant ceulx de la
Bille Birent ceste donue mõter q haulser, cõmẽ
cerent a sõdroict dicelle au dedans de leur mu
raille, faire Bng aultre mur de pierres q de Bri
ques. Lesquelles ilz prenoient des prochaines
maisons quilz abbatirent pour ce faire, q pour
se soustenir entremessoient des pieces de Boys,
q au debois sarmerent de cuirs, affin que en
ouurant ilz ne Bissent blecez, q aussi que si on
iectoit du feu, il ne peut prendre au Boys, en ma
niere que Bng coustel q baultre louurraige mõ
toit soul. Et neantmoins ceulx de sa Bille pour
retarder louurraige des ennemys, saduiserent
dune telle habilite. Cest quilz percerent la mu
raille a Bng endroit de sa donue. Auquel les en
nemys auoient dessus soubxte Bng aultre par
partie de Boys q de terre q Benoit ioindre iusques
a la muraille pour Benir a couuert iusques au
pied dicelle muraille. Apres q sa donue eust este
acheuee, q par cestuy trou quilz auoient faict, se
tiroient par dessoubz la terre que les aultres le
estoient dessus. Dont apres que les Lacede
moniens sapperceurent, firent force paniers q
les remplissoient de terre molle q moiste, puis
la iecterent au lieu de celle que on en auoit ti
ree, en maniere que on ne la pouoit plus aisee
ment tirer, aussi quant les Plateens Birent se
reniethe ne sy amuserent plus en cestuy endroit,
ains firent de grans mine a conduyctz dedãs
terre par dessoubz la muraille, qui astoient re
sponde iusques a la donue, par lesquelles mi
nes ils retiroit sans cesse la terre de la donue,
q se firent longuement que les ennemys
sen apperceussent, combien quilz fussent tous
esbahys de Beoir que leur donue ne se haulsoit
gueres, pour la merueilleuse quantite de terre
quilz iectoient dedans, q que elle sabaissoit ne
sondoit au mylieu. Toutesfoys les citoyens

CLEMENT MAROT

A CEVLX QVI PAR CY
DEVANT ONT IMPRI
ME SES OEV-
VRES.

E ſçais, que vous m'aurez faict, vous auſtres, qui par cy deuãt auez imprimé mes Oeuures, eſt ſi grand, et ſi ouſtrageux, qu'il a touché mon honneur, & mis en danger ma perſonne : car par auare conuoitiſe de vendre plus chers, et pluſtoſt, ce qui ſe vendoit aſſez, auez adiouſté à icelles miennes oeuures pluſieurs aultres, qui ne ſont rien; dont ſes Unes ſont froidement, & de mauuaiſe grace compoſees, mettant ſur moy l'ignorance d'aultruy : et les aultres toutes pleines de ſcandale, & [ſ]ediſion: de ſorte qu'il n'a tenu a Dieu, que durant mon abſence, ſes imprimeurs de Verſun n'apyt gardé la ſtaſce, & moy, de iamais plus nous entreueoir. mais ſa grace de Dieu par ſa bonté du Roy (comme ſçauez) y a pourueu. Certes i'oſe bien ſans mentir (ſouffrez qu'il le die) que de tous ces miens labeurs le proffit vous proche; que de tous ces miens labeurs le proffit vous en retourne. I'ay planté les arbres, Vous en cueillez les fruicts. I'ay fraiñé ſa chaſrue, Vous en ſerrez la moiſ- ſon: et a moy n'en reuient qu'un peu d'eſtime entre les hommes; laquel encor vous me Uouſez eſtaindre, m'at- tribuant oeuures ſottes, & ſcandaleuſes. Ie ne ſçay comment appeller cela, ſinon ingratitude, que ie ne puis auoir deſſeruie; ſi ce n'eſt par ſa faulte, que ie ſçais.

a ij

Oſter le Veulx (appuyé ſur ſey) mon Liure
Veu tant de ſcriptz, qui par d'aultres ſont faicts,
Diſ ſu, c'eſt faict: tout ce qui eſt deſiure:
Deſchargez-ſay d'un trouble, à preſent fait.
Si ils ſont eſcriptz (d'un ſouffure) imparfaicts,
Ce Veulx fu faire en ſeurs faulſes reprendre:
Si ils ſere ſont bien, ou mieulx, que ie ne fais,
Pourquoy Veulx fu ſur leur gloire entreprendre?
Vous euſiez (mon Liure) en Unes Vers pourras prendre
Vie apres moy, pour ſemais, ou long temps.
Mes Oeuures donc content te deuient rendre
Pourpres, ô Roys ſi'en tiennent bien contents.

Aucunes faulſes d'impuimerie en ſado[l]ſcence qu'on
pourra cotrigr ſur ſa marge aueccas ſa pluſme. __
Au fueillet vpi, ſeconde page, y a, dangereuy, pluſque
traicts, i, ſaur't, plus que tres.
Au f. vvpi, ſecõde page y a, au ſac de pa cur, y a ſauſt
— Au bui de pauur.
Au f. vſii, premiere page, y a, en ce ſault ſicut y ſaulſt,
en ce ſhaulſt ſeru.
Au fueillet meſme, ſeconde page, y a, ſinon de dieu: &
y ſauſt, ie ſuis de dieu.
Au f. lip prem page, y a, Qui ſa côgnoiſſe en ſa Voye:
a y ſault, Qui ſla cognoiſſe ne ſa Voye.
Au f. vvii, vvii page, y a, ſu dye eſtre aſſouſ : & y ſault,
ſu dope eſtre aſſouſe.
En preuuſiimc Rondeau, y a, q, aultremēt faſchēt: & y
ſault, mais aultremēt faſchet. Et la meſmes, au dernier Vers y aquaſte ne ſe: & y ſault, que ne ſe.
Au der. Rondeau, y a, ſoue du parc: & y ſault, hors du
par. Et apres le derñ. Vers ſault renſer, En ſiſerte.
En la gooſe chanſon, y a, & un ſng fils au cief Vouſ: &
y ſault. A ſng fils du cief aſſouue.
En la ſe. chanſon, y a, Ne ſçay combien ſa faire : & y
ſault, ſa Baine.

Fig. 3

Fig. 4

Le Triumphe de

TRESHAVLTE ET
puiffante Dame Verolle,
Royne du Puy
d'Amours,

El mal qui eft commun
entre plufieurs eft moins
amer & plus tollerable,
que quand vng feul en
peult faire plaincte, &
lamenter: Et bien eft dit ce
prouerbe, La confolati-
on des miferables eft da-
uoir de pareils miferables pour compaignons.
Chafcun fcait les calamitez & deftructions in
A iiij

Fig. 4

Fig. 5

Hault.iiii.

**LINTENTION
DV POETE**

Ayant defir d'efcrire vng hault
ouurage
Da diuement incité le courage
A reciter maintes chofes formées
En autres corps tous nouueaulx
tranffoumées.
Dieu fouuerains, qui tout faire
fcaues,
Puis qu'en ce point eftanges les aues,
Donnes faueur à moy commencement,
Et defruples mes propos doulcement,
A commencer depuys le premier naiftre
Du monde rond, jufque au temps de mon eftre.

Chaos mué en quatre Elemens.

A Dant la Mer, la Terre, & le grand Deurre
Du Ciel freffaulx, qui toutes chofes cœuvre,
N'y auoit en tout ce monde enorme
Tant feullement de Nature vne forme,
Dicte & baos, vng monceau amaffe
Gros, grans, lourds, nullement compaffe,
Bref, ce n'eftoit qu'vne pefanteur bife
Sans aucun Art, vne Maffe immobile:
Ou gifoient les femence enclofes,
Difcordes font prochuictes toutes chofes,
Qui lors eftoient enfemble mal coupplées,
Eft vne en l'aultre en grand diffcords troublées,
Buſcun Sofeil encores au bas Monde
Reffargiffoit lumiere claire, & munde:
La Lune auffi ne fe renouuelloit,
Et rammener fes Cornes ne fouloit
B iij

Fig. 5

A REVEREND ET ILLV‑
STRE SEIGNEVR MI‑
CHEL DE SILVA
EVESQVE DE
VISEE.

Pres que le seigneur Guy‑
debault de Monseltre, Duc
D'Vrbin fut passé de ceste
vie, Ie auecques aulcuns
aultres gentilz hommes,
qui lauoient seruy, demou
ray au seruice du duc Fran
cois Marie de la Rouere
son heritier, & successeur es estatz qu'il te‑
noit. Et comme en mon entendement fut en‑
core fresche l'odeur des vertuz du duc Guy‑
debault, & la satisfaction que r'auoye en ce‑
luy temps sentu de l'amiable compaignie de
tant dexcellentes personnes, qui lors se trou‑

a iᵇ

Fig. 6

¶ Le temple de Cupido.

¶ A Messire Nicolas de Neufuille, Cheualier, Seigneur de Villeroy, Clerc. Marot. ↄ.

En reuolant ses escriptz de ma ieu-
nesse, pour les remettre plus clers,
que deuant, en lumiere, si m'est en-
tré en memoire que estant encore
page, ça, a toy, tresbonoré Seigneur,
le composay par ton commande-
met sa queste ie trouuay au meilleur en-
queste ie trouuay au meilleur en-
Soit du temple de Cupido, en se Bisiant, comme l'age
fors se requeroit. Et est bien raison donques, que sour-
ure soit a toy bessée, a toy qui la commandas, a toy mon
premier maistre, a cestuy seul, sbors mis les Princes
qui iamais ie seruy. Soit donques consacré ce petit liure a ta puissance, noble Seigneur de Neufuille, assin
qu'en recompense de certain seruice que Marot a Brsu
auecques toy en ceste Bie, tu Biures ta Bas apres sa mort
auecques luy, tant que ses œuures durront. De
Lyon ce quinzisme iour de May. 1538.

Fig. 9

¶ Le temple de Cupido.

¶ A Messire Nicolas de Neufuille, Cheualier, Seigneur de Villeroy, Clerc. Marot. ↄ.

En reuolant ses escriptz de ma ieu-
nesse, pour les remettre plus clers,
que deuant, en lumiere, si m'est en-
tré en memoire que estant encore
page, ça, a toy, tresbonoré Seigneur,
le composay par ton commande-
met sa queste ie trouuay au meilleur en-
queste ie trouuay au meilleur en-
Soit du temple de Cupido, en se Bisiant, comme l'age
fors se requeroit. Et est bien raison donques, que sour-
ure soit a toy bessée, a toy qui la commandas, a toy mon
premier maistre, a cestuy seul, sbors mis les Princes
qui iamais ie seruy. Soit donques consacré ce petit liure a ta puissance, noble Seigneur de Neufuille, assin
qu'en recompense de certain seruice que Marot a Brsu
auecques toy en ceste Bie, tu Biures ta Bas apres sa mort
auecques luy, tant que ses œuures durront. De
Lyon ce quinzisme iour de May. 1538.

b

Fig. 8

Les iuges ou leurs lieutenãs feront
ceulx messiers, les proces ce iusques
articlé.

En interrogatoires seront diligemmẽt
faictz & repetez. art. i. c. extra.

Q uoy se gratificatif &
blictõ sur les gens lais
& les iugereatz sar te
gens de glisse. at. iiii.
Imitation si soyt trou
ue la matiere disposé a proces ordinaire. art. c. i.

Il ne sera requis saict applie
clef maisons, auant que sui
extdue.

Fig. 7

DEPLORATION SVR LE
trespas de Messire Floimon8
Robertet,

F. iiii.iii.

Abis ma plume en beit son bol estendre
En gre d'amour, q d'ung bas fille, q t8ke
Distiller dict, que foubois mettre en c8ait:
Mais ung regret de tous costes trenchãt
Luy fait laisser ceste boulce coustume,
Pour la tremper en ancre d'amertume.
Ainsi le fauft, q quand ne se faußoit,
Mon cueur (belac) encore se boußoit:
Et quand mon cueur ne se boußoit encores,
Dudtre son dueil contraint y seroit ores
Par faiguison d'une mort quise point:
Que vis ce mort? D'une mort n'esse point?
Aine d'une amour: car quand chaseun mourroit
Sans Diaye amour, plainbre qu ne se pourroit:
Boise quand ba Mort a faict son masßice,
Amour abone Bie de son office,
Raillant porter auß Diaye Ampe te dueil,
Mon point Ung dueil de faintes farmes d'oeil,
Mon point Ung dueil de Diap noir annuel,
Mais Ung dueil tainct d'ennuy perpetuel:
Mon point Ung dueil, qui besoig apparoist,
Deß la qui au cueur (sans apparence) croist,
Deß la de dueil, qui d'Baineu ma ioye:
Me sonne ennuy: c'est ce qui me procure,
Que couleur blanche a l'oeil me soit obscurs,
Et que tour clere me semble noire nupct:
De tel façon, que ce, qui tant me nuyst,
Corrompt du tout le maif be ma Muse,
Lequel se soy ne Deult que ie m'amuse,
A composer en triste Tragedie:

B iii

Fig. 10

Benque
Sensuyt le Bnuesme chapitre
des mots bons cõtenus en ce li
ure qui se comméce par M,
Des meurs.

E8 plus notable m. urs
q sont Bit assez a auoir
a cha8al sont: effet flibral
q Diay Difant. le libéral ne
peult mal Buurer, le Diay Difant ne
peult estre deßonnor. Loutes bõp
ses peuvent estre adreßees soubz maul
uaise meurs, quil est de bõne meurs
et est de bõne e seurs Buurer si est ayme
des hommes: q qui est de maultaises
meurs. il a tout le cõtraire. Le remaul
uaises meurs baincut la destruit sõt ses
œurres cõme saincteur. e du bõs bas
soes destruit la bouleur du miel.

Tu merite de malice q deme8tage.
Ai8e soy de sa compaignie
ung mescur en toutes besoi
gne, soyt grãbes ou petites
Malice ne peut bauner sa

Fig. 11

10

Clément Marot, Ferrara, and the Paradoxes of Exile

George Hugo Tucker

I. The Cultivation of Exile: Marot and Italy (1535–6)

> Si de celuy le tumbeau veux scavoir
> Qui de Maro avoit plus que le nom,
> Il te convient tous les lieux aller voir
> Ou France a mis le but de son renom.
>
> (Du Bellay, 'Epitaphe de Clement Marot' [1544])[1]

In this paper I shall take my cue from Joachim Du Bellay's early epitaph on Clément Marot. In the spirit of its advice I shall be concerned not so much with the 'cult', or cultivation, of humanism under François Ier within the boundaries of France itself, as with placing a French humanist writer of exile and court poet of that age, such as Marot, within the wider context abroad of Italy and Italian humanism. This will necessarily impinge upon the Franco-Italian court in Ferrara of François's sister-in-law Renée de France, wife of duke Ercole II d'Este — where, after the 'affaire des placards' of 1534, Marot sought and obtained refuge for a year and some months during his first exile from France and François Ier's

---

[1] Taken from *Vers lyriques* (Paris, 1549); see J. Du Bellay, *Œuvres poétiques*, edited by H. Chamard [œuvres françaises] and Geneviève Demerson [œuvres latines], 8 vols, STFM (Paris, Droz/Didier/Nizet, 1908–85), III (*Recueils lyriques*, vol. I; Paris, Droz, 1912), p. 54. This epitaph's hyperbolic identification of Marot's tomb with the geographical extent of his posthumous renown throughout the world is a variation upon the more usual conceit contrasting the two (as narrowly small and widely extensive) in Jacopo Sannazaro's 'Epitaphio di Cesare' (Sannazaro, *Le rime* ([Venice?], P. Alex. Pag. Benacensis, [c. 1535–40?]), terza parte, s. I (*Spargi di palme, Lauri, & Mirti, foglie...*), f. 49[r]), quoted in full and discussed in G. H. Tucker, *The Poet's Odyssey: Joachim Du Bellay and the* Antiquitez de Rome (Oxford, Clarendon Press, 1990), p. 84.

favour.[2] My purpose will be to situate Marot's Franco-Italian cultivation of exile within a larger humanistic and literary tradition, if only to under-stand better the interplay of existential and literary strategies of identity that it gives rise to. Moreover, the Ferrara of the 1530s and 1540s is an ideal focal point for such broader contextualisation. In particular, it pro-vides a link with the converse example of an Italian 'exile' in France, Ortensio Landi (or Lando; *c.* 1512–*c.* 1555?), and his no less significant treatment of the paradoxes of exile towards the close of François Ier's reign.[3] This is a legacy, in short, whose cultivation would be passed on,

---

2   On the 'affaire' and Marot's resultant exile, see, notably, P. M. Smith, *Clément Marot: Poet of the Renaissance* (University of London, Athlone Press, 1970), pp. 16–30, 111–24, and C. Marot, *Œuvres complètes — I. Les Épîtres*, edited by C. A. Mayer (Paris, Nizet, 1977), pp. 188–253 [notes on *Épîtres*, XXXIV–XLVII]; cf. also, more recently: C. Béné, 'Exil et création littéraire chez Marot', in *Exil et littérature*, edited by J. Mounier (Grenoble, Centre de recherche sur l'édition, 1986), pp. 245–9; G. R. Elton (ed.), *The New Cambridge Modern History — Volume II, Second Edition: The Reformation 1520–1559* (Cambridge, Cambridge University Press, 1990), pp. 249–50; C. Marot, *Œuvres poétiques complètes — I: L'Adolescence clementine, La Suite de l'Adolescence clementine*, edited by G. Defaux, Classiques Garnier (Paris, Bordas, 1990), pp. cxix–cxlvii; A. Prosperi, 'L'eresia in città e a corte', in *La Corte di Ferrara & il suo mecenatismo 1441–1558: The Court of Ferrara and its Patronage. Atti del convegno internazionale Copenhagen maggio 1987*, edited by M. Pade, L. Waage Petersen, & D. Quarta, Renæssance studier MUSEUM TUSCULANUM 4 & Istituto di Studi Rinascimentali Ferrara saggi (Copenhagen, Museum Tusculanum & Modena, Ferrara/Edizioni Panini, Forum for Renæssancestudier Københavns Universiteit, 1990), 267–81 (pp. 273–4); M. L. King, *Women of the Renaissance*, Women in Culture and Society (Chicago and London, Chicago University Press, 1991), pp. 141–2; and R. J. Knecht, *Renaissance Warrior and Patron: The Reign of Francis I* (Cambridge, Cambridge University Press, 1994), pp. 466–7.

3   On Landi/Lando, see above all P. F. Grendler, *Critics of the Italian World [1530–1560]: Anton Francesco Doni, Nicolò Franco & Ortensio Lando* (Madison, Milwaukee and London, University of Wisconsin Press, 1969). See also C. H. Rose, *Alonso Núñez de Reinoso: The Lament of a Sixteenth-Century Exile* (Rutherford, Madison, and Teaneck, Fairleigh Dickinson University Press, 1971), pp. 50–2, 54, 56–8; and, most recently, C. Heesakkers, 'From Italian Prose to Latin Poetry: Jacob Eyndius's *Ioci Funebres*', in *La Satire humaniste: Actes du Colloque international des 31 mars, 1er et 2 avril 1993*, edited by R. De Smet, Université Libre de Bruxelles — Travaux de l'Institut Interuniversitaire pour l'étude de la Renaissance et de l'Humanisme, XI (Brussels, Peeters Press, 1994), 189–222 (pp. 199, 201, 207).

in the following age of Henri II, to that other literary example of exile between France and Italy, Joachim Du Bellay.[4]

* * *

Recent critics of Marot such as Charles Béné and Gérard Defaux have commonly stressed the positive, enabling nature of Marot's period in Ferrara (*c.* April 1535 to *c.* June 1536) under the protection of the sympathetic Renée de France: not just as the author there of the 'blason du beau tétin', and so the inspirer, with the duchess's complicity, of the famous *concours* of *blasons* 'du corps féminin',[5] but also as a religious poet finding a new voice. If, for Béné:

> C'est un nouveau Marot qu'engendre l'exil. Le 'gentil poète' fait place au créateur d'une poésie engagée dans le mouvement humaniste de renouvelle-ment religieux...[6]

so likewise for Defaux:

> C'est du séjour à Ferrare que datent ses épîtres les plus hardies et les plus religieuses, celles où se découvre un Marot plus que jamais décidé à louer le nom de l'Éternel et à servir sa Parole.[7]

Indeed, as Defaux has also noted in introducing his recent edition of Marot (pp. cxxxv–cxxxvii), nowhere is the juxtaposition of these two 'discours' — of these two poetic identities — so strikingly evident as in Marot's *épître* from Ferrara of November 1535 'Au Roy nouvellement sorty de maladie', where the poet's witty prediction to the French King of

---

4 On Du Bellay's period in Rome, see Tucker, *The Poet's Odyssey*, and idem, 'Writing in Exile: Joachim Du Bellay, Rome and Renaissance France', in *Travel Fact and Travel Fiction: Studies on Fiction, Literary Tradition, Scholarly Discovery and Observation in Travel Writing*, edited by Z. W. R. M. von Martels, Brill's Studies in Intellectual History, 55 (Leiden, Brill, 1994), 120–39; E. MacPhail, *The Voyage to Rome in French Renaissance Literature*, Stanford French and Italian Studies, 68 (Saratoga, CA, ANMA Libri, 1990), pp. 38–94.

5 A vogue, of which one example, the 'Blason du corps' (*Ma plume* [*est*] *lente et ma main paresseuse...*) first published in the subsequent *Blasons anatomiques des parties du corps féminin* (Lyon, 1536), has been attributed to François Ier himself by J. E. Kane (ed.) in his François Ier, *Œuvres poétiques*, La Renaissance Française — Éditions et monographies, 2 (Geneva, Slatkine, 1984), pp. 334–6.

6 Béné, 'Exil et création', art. cit., p. 246.

7 Defaux, 'Introduction', in Marot, *Œuvres poétiques complètes, I,* ed. cit., p. cxxix.

his, Marot's, increased humanist accomplishment and usefulness to him
at Ferrara (belying the common perception of exile as an evil) — as long,
of course, as he be allowed to continue to receive there his royal pension
— suddenly yields (apparently) to an impassioned protestation of faith:

> Tu trouveras ceste langue italique
> Passablement dessus la mienne entée,
> Et la latine en moy plus augmentée,
> Si que l'exil, qu'ilz pensent si nuysant,
> M'aura rendu plus apte & plus duysant
> A te servir myeulx à ta fantasie,
> Non seullement en l'art de poesie,
> Ains en affaire, en temps de paix ou guerre,
> Soit pres de toy, soit en estrange terre.
>   Je ne suis pas si laid comme ilz me font;
> Myré me suis au cler ruysseau profont
> De verité, et à ce qu'il me semble,
> A Turc ne Juif en rien je ne ressemble.
> Je suis chrestien, pour tel me veulx offrir,
> Voire plus prest à peine & mort souffrir
> Pour mon vray Dieu et pour mon Roy, j'en jure,
> Q'eulx une simple et bien petite injure;...[8]

Yet it is also true that behind this juxtaposition of genial, positive thinking
about the opportunities of exile, on the one hand, with the alienated,
indignant irony of an outcast, on the other hand — and behind the traditional opposition of poetic *otium* with public *negotium*, whose introduction here by Marot seems (*pace* Defaux) to serve as a transitional element
between the two — lie two opposed conceptions of exile, actually alluded
to in Marot's text: the 'exil...nuysant' — exile as an evil — of common
perception ('qu'ilz pensent') and of the elegiac tradition, but also its other
(equally traditional) side, exile as a hidden blessing, as an enabling occasion for Stoic virtue.

This 'paradox' of exile, Stoic versus elegiac, positive versus negative
— or rather, the subtly orchestrated interpenetration of the two — will
later inform the poetic productions of Joachim Du Bellay's *séjour romain* (1553–7). In Marot's Ferrara, and in this *épître* of his, it may similarly unite what have seemed to be discrete, even jarring, modes of exiliar
address to the King. Earlier in the same poem the exiled Marot had
apparently hinted at François's timely support (l. 14: 'Le fort appuy

---

8   Marot, 'Au Roy nouvellement sorty de maladie', *Épîtres*, XXXVII. 44–60, ed.
    Mayer.

contre fortune amere') of Renée's French (not simply pro-Reformist) entourage in the Ferrarese court against the increasing hostility (for political
and religious reasons) of duke Ercole II.[9] If this is so, behind the witty
praise of the benefits of Ferrara as an exiliar space for the poet in relation
to his king may lurk the more serious, less private, consideration of political tension between France and Ferrara as well as cultural emulation.[10]
Implicit may even be a pro-French critique of that same exiliar space, and
a sense of cultural alienation and xenophobic hostility — such as, indeed,
Marot will subsequently make great play of just before leaving Ferrara
and then whilst in Venice (*Épîtres*, XL-XLII, XLIV, ed. cit. Mayer).[11]

It is perhaps appropriate, then, that in the second, contrasting part of the
Ferrara epistle just quoted, Marot's bitter, ironic denial of resembling a
Turk or a Jew, which functions as a protestation of his worth as a good
Christian and French subject, should also appear to imply resentment
against exile in Ferrara as an unjust punishment. Yet for all that, paradoxically, it may still be more positive than negative; it also seems to double
as a deft counter-swipe, on behalf of the duchess's pro-Reformist faction,
at Ercole's economically expedient (and no less politico-religiously sensi-
tive) cultivation of an important Iberian-Jewish community of Marrano
merchants in Ferrara, for the purpose of tapping the lucrative Adriatic
trade route to Constantinople. Yet this defensive–offensive reproach,
which seems thus to valorise Marot's position positively as spokesman
for the French faction in Ferrrara, and not just as a lamentable exile there,
might even be understood, ironically, to allude to François Ier's own
expedient cultivation of the Ottoman Empire against the Imperial forces
of Charles V.[12] If so, Marot seems to be having his exile both ways —

---

[9]   According to Mayer, ed. cit., ad loc.

[10] See Smith, *Clément Marot*, pp. 22–4, on Ercole II's increasing embarrassment in
      this period at the French presence in Ferrara, his increasing persecution of his
      wife's Reformist entourage under papal pressure, and his meeting with Charles V
      in autumn 1535 with a view to an alliance at the expense of France. See also
      Knecht, *Renaissance Warrior*, pp. 329–30, on cardinal Jean Du Bellay's visit to
      Ferrara in early summer 1535 on the way to Rome in an attempt to patch up the
      quarrel between the duke and duchess of Ferrara at a time when François Ier was
      preparing for war with Charles V and had sought an alliance with the Ottoman
      Empire.

[11] As has been noted by Defaux, 'Introduction', Marot, ed. cit., p. cxliii, who
      interprets Marot's presentation of alienation as an 'histoire inventée', however,
      and so seems to underestimate its importance in the wider political context.

[12] See Elton, *The Reformation*, pp. 577–9; Knecht, *Renaissance Warrior*, pp. 295–
      6, 329.

that is, as a liberating space for self definition, whether for or against home, whether for or against Ferrara.

It is perhaps significant also that the poet who on arrival had appropriately hailed Renée's Ferrara as a 'pays plantureux, / Fertile en biens, en dame bienheureux' (*Épîtres*, XXXIV. 1–2, ed. Mayer), should reserve the alternative, supremely literary card of intertextual self-association with the elegiac, exiled Ovid of the *Tristia* and *Epistolae ex Ponto* (in further self-association with the figure of Ulysses), for the two great *épîtres*, 'Au Roy' (XLIV) and 'A la Royne de Navarre' (XLVI), subsequently written from Venice in the summer of 1536, precisely when — as Pauline Smith and Defaux (following Mayer) have noted — the question of his being able to return safely to France no longer seems to have been so much at issue in the wake of François Ier's general amnesty of 31 May 1536 to those involved or implicated in the 'affaire des placards'.[13]

This has prompted Gérard Defaux to explain Marot's pre-Bellayan adoption of the exiliar voice of Ovid thus:

> Marot…ne fait même plus confiance à son propre discours pour exprimer ses angoisses et ses doutes, ses craintes et son espoir. L'expression du moi intime est devenue littéraire.[14]

Yet this interpretation risks recalling the well-worn opposition between sincere, spontaneous self-expression and self-conscious literarity that, significantly enough, has bedevilled critical appraisal of Du Bellay's subsequent exile poetry, by identifying overt intertextual practice with poetic crisis and failure (ingenuously taking the poet at his word) — to the point even of contrasting Du Bellay's *Regrets* as relatively spontaneus and direct (despite evident literary allusions to Ovid, Tibullus, Horace, and Persius) with the Classical convolutions and 'emphase' of his *Antiquitez de Rome*. It may just be, rather, that Marot is cleverly preparing his return to France (of which he is already confident) by playing a highly flattering, intertextual game — one disingenuously investing his addressee François Ier with the role of a new Augustus who has the potential to outdo the old Augustus by allowing his poet (unlike Ovid) back from exile. If so, Marot incidentally thus makes Venice, by witty implication, the Tomis of the Adriatic in opposition to the Rome of humanist France, and he makes François himself more a Roman

---

13   Smith, *Clément Marot*, p. 28; Defaux, 'Introduction', Marot ed. cit., pp. cxliv–cxlvi.

14   Defaux, 'Introduction', ed. cit., p. cxliv.

Emperor than Charles V (his erstwhile rival for the imperial title and his longstanding opponent for dominance in Italy.)[15]

Indeed, literary allusiveness is pursued to further ends in these Ovidian elegiac epistles, where Marot, in the wake of Horace, and like Du Bellay later, makes no bones about conceding the dubious nature of travel and the traveller:[16]

> Oultre le mal que je sens, treshault Prince,
> De plus ne veoir la gallique province
> Et d'estre icy par exil oppressé,
> Je doubte et crains que, moy aiant laissé
> L'air de Ferrare, il ne te soit advis
> Que j'ay les sens d'inconstance ravis,
> Et qu'en ton cueur n'entre une impression
> Que de vaguer je fais profession,
> Sans en ung lieu povoir long temps durer,
> Ne la doulceur de mon aise endurer,...[17]

— just as Marot, again anticipating the ironies of Du Bellay (*Regrets*, XXXI), alludes significantly to that equally dubious archetypal traveller and exile, the curious, wise, yet foolhardy, impious and unfortunate Ulysses, who had been evoked by the exiled Ovid himself:[18]

> Ulixes sage, au moins estimé tel,
> Fit bien jadis refuz d'estre immortel
> Pour retourner en sa maison petite,
> Et du regret de mort se disoit quitte

---

[15] See Elton, *The Reformation*, pp. 232, 344, 378–9. Compare in this volume Stephen Bamforth on humanist celebration of François Ier in the image of Augustus.

[16] See G. H. Tucker, 'Ulysses and Jason: a Problem of Allusion in Sonnet XXXI of *Les Regrets*', *French Studies*, XXXVI (1982), 385–96.

[17] Marot, 'Au Roy', *Épîtres*, XLIV. 1–10, ed. Mayer. Compare Horace, *Epistles* I. 11 and *Odes* II. 16.

[18] Ovid, *Epistolae ex Ponto*, I. 3. 33–4; cf. Du Bellay, *Regrets* XXXI. See, notably, W. B. Stanford, *The Ulysses Theme: A Study in the Adaptability of a Traditional Hero* (Oxford, 1963: 2nd edn), especially Chapter 14, on the 'Janus-like' figure of Dante's Ulysses; and G. Defaux, *Le Curieux, le glorieux et la sagesse du monde dans la première moitié du XVIe siècle: l'exemple de Panurge (Ulysse, Démosthène, Empédocle)*, French Forum Monographs, 34 (Lexington, KY, French Forum, 1982), 23–68 (Defaux laying emphasis on the sceptical force of Marot's qualification: 'Ulixes sage, *au moins estimé tel*'); G. H. Tucker, 'Joachim Du Bellay, poète français et néo-latin, entre l'exil et la patrie', in *Op. cit.: Revue de littératures française et comparée*, III (1994), 57–63.

Si l'air eust pu de son pays humer
Et veu de loing son vilage fumer![19]

This strategy of duplicity in relation to travel — as something potentially reprehensible and foolish, as well as something that has been self-
evidently educative and enabling — mirrors the similar duplicity we have
noted on Marot's part in relation to the idea of exile itself: his having it
both ways at once, paying lip-service to exile as an evil, whilst experienc-
ing it as a blessing, generative of writing and of the forging of a new
poetic and intellectual identity in 'fertile' Ferrara. It is precisely this larger
sort of intellectual Nicodemism on Marot's part (to use Calvin's coinage)
that we now need to place in its Italian, humanist context.[20]

Where better, then, to begin such an investigation than with Petrarch,
for whom 'Exile was a central and abiding preoccupation...as it would
be for that cultural epoch, the Renaissance, that he seems to initiate' (A.
Bartlett Giamatti, *Exile and Change*, p. 12).[21]

II. The Legacy of Petrarch, and the Humanist Tradition of Exile

As the late Bartlett Giamatti also noted (*Exile and Change*, pp. 12–17),
Petrarch's letters poignantly emphasise his origins 'in exile, at Arezzo'
(*Senilium rerum libri*, XVIII, 1 'Posteritati'). They make him out to be
more an exile than even Odysseus himself, because 'begotten in exile'
and 'born in exile' (*Familiarium rerum libri*, I. 1. 22, 'Ad Socratem
suum'). Indeed, they even wearily characterise his mode of being, in
hindsight, as one of pathological restlessness and compulsive motion
(worthy of Horace's foolish traveller): 'incapable of standing still, not so
much out of a desire to see what I have already seen a thousand times, as
in an attempt, as with sick people, to relieve the tediousness by changing
position' ('Posteritati').[22] Yet such observations, intuitions, and interpret-

---

19 Marot, 'A la Royne de Navarre', *Épîtres*, XLVI. 157–62, ed. Mayer.

20 On Calvin's strictures upon those he termed 'Nicodemites' after John 19. 39 (still
    outwardly practising a Catholicism that they secretly reject), see Elton, *The
    Reformation*, pp. 305–6.

21 A. Bartlett Giamatti, *Exile and Change in Renaissance Literature* (New Haven
    and London, Yale University Press, 1984).

22 Reference is to *Epistole di Francesco Petrarca*, edited and translated by U. Dotti,
    Classici Italiani XII, 2 (Turin, UTET, 1978), pp. 970–89 (pp. 876–7, 888–9;
    using my own translation), and to Petrarch, *Le familiari: Libri I–IV*, edited and
    translated by U. Dotti, Pubblicazioni dell'Università di Urbino — serie di lettere e
    filosofia, XXIX (Urbino, Argalìa, 1970), pp. 72–97 (pp. 82–3). The translation of

ations of self on Petrarch's part also raise questions for him about the proper external and internal conditions for, and precise definition of, exile — a phenomenon, according to him, not to be confused simply with 'travel', and a product more of a state of mind than of mere geographical dislocation in space. Such a view — or rather, a 'groping for a definition' (Bartlett Giamatti, *Exile and Change*, p. 16) — takes issue from the start with traditional etymological definitions whereby exile might simply denote either a physical 'leaping out' (from *exilio*) or — to use Servius' definition (on *Aeneid*, III. 11), and later Isidore's (*Etymologiae*, 5. 27. 28) — a geographical movement 'outside the land' (*extra solum*).[23] Rather:

> It is necessary that force and pain of some kind intervene in order to have a real exile. If you accept this, you will then understand whether you are an exile or a traveler resides in you. If you depart sad and dejected you will know without doubt that you are an exile; but if…willingly and with the same appearance and state of mind that you had at home, you obeyed the order to depart, then you are a traveler and not an exile.…Similarly in death, which is very similar to exile, it is not so much the harshness of the thing itself as the anxiety and distortion of opinion that is painful.[24]

Here, by subtle gradations, Petrarch's argument distinguishing between the traveller ('peregrinus') and the exile slips from the necessary factor of external compulsion to the even more essential element of inner attitude, only to be applied by analogy to the larger questions of the human condition and death itself. Indeed, later for Petrarch not only will the living world itself become the indifferent locus either of home or exile, depending on one's metaphysical and physical outlook, but also exile itself, again implicitly equated with death, will be counted a blessed release:

> Every corner of the world is a homeland to a man, nor is there exile anywhere except that created by impatience; when the spirit begins to desire heaven, it is

---

the latter is taken (here as elsewhere), from Petrarch, *Rerum familiarium libri*, translated by A. S. Bernardo, 3 vols (Albany, NY, State University of New York Press, 1975–85), I, 3–14 (p. 8).

23 On the Isidorean etymology and the related Italian vernacular term 'fuoruscito' (which would have been familiar to Petrarch from his parents' 'banishment' to Arezzo), see R. Starn, *Contrary Commonwealth: The Theme of Exile in Medieval and Renaissance Italy* (Berkeley, Los Angeles, and London, University of California Press, 1982), pp. 1–2.

24 Petrarch, *Familiarium rerum libri*, II. 3. 1–3 (using the term *peregrinus* for 'traveller'); tr. A. S. Bernardo, I, 70.

in exile everywhere until it reaches where it longs to be; the wise man takes his belongings with him wherever he goes, unafraid of shipwreck, fire, or theft. What is called poverty is actually solace against anxieties and dangers, what is called exile is escape from countless cares; for the good, death is the end of toil and the beginning of a truly happy repose.[25]

Petrarch's stoicising, consolatory reflections on exile are in fact part of a long line of such works, which included (most notably) Seneca's *Ad Helviam de consolatione* and Plutarch's essay on exile, περὶ φυγῆς (*Moralia*, 599A–607F). It would extend later to the famous (but never published) anti-Medicean dialogue, the 'Commentationes Florentinae de exilio' (*c.* 1434) of the exiled Francesco Filelfo (1398–1491),[26] and culminate, in the sixteenth century, in the influential, pro-Medicean, Ciceronian exile dialogue of Petrus Alcyonius (1487–1527?), the *Medices Legatus de exsilio* (Venice, 1522) — to be found later among the books that accompanied Joachim Du Bellay to Rome and back in a travelling-chest belonging to his patron, cardinal Jean Du Bellay.[27]

All these texts, in whose wake Marot also was writing, tended to reject the 'lament of exile' (such as found in Euripides' *Phoenissae* or in Ovid's *Tristia* and *Epistolae ex Ponto*), advocating Stoic fortitude instead, refuting the common notion of exile as an evil, even examining its advantages, and problematising the very notion of a fixed, pre-determined *patria* itself as misleading (the whole world being a potential *patria* for the virtuous man). Sometimes (as in the cases, notably, of Plutarch or of Filelfo), they would add the Platonic consideration that the whole of human existence is anyway a form of 'exile' from an ideal heavenly 'patria'. To quote (in Amyot's French) the close of Plutarch's essay, with its resonances of Plato and its allusion to Empedocles:

Ce n'est pas de luy seul [Empedocles], mais de nous tous apres luy, qu'il nous declare tous en ce monde passagers, estrangers & bannis: car...la generation de l'ame qui vient d'ailleurs icy bas, il la desguise du plus gracieux nom qu'il peut, l'appellant un bannissement & relegation hors de son païs, mais à la verité elle vague & erre, chassee par les divines loix & statuts, iusques à ce qu'elle vienne à estre attachee à un corps, ne plus ne moins que l'ouystre à quelque roc en une Isle fort battue des vents & des vndes de la mer tout à l'entour, pource qu'elle ne se recorde, ny se souvient point de quel

---

25 *Familiarium rerum libri*, XXI, 9; tr. Bernardo, III, 182.
26 MS Firenze Bibl. Naz. II. II. 70.
27 See G. H. Tucker, 'Exile Exiled: Petrus Alcyonius (1487–1527?) in a Travelling-Chest', *Journal of the Institute of Romance Studies* [University of London], II (1993), 83–103 (pp. 91, 101–2).

honneur, & de quelle beatitude elle est transferee...pour avoir changé la
demeure du ciel & de la lune à la terre, & à la vie terrestre....[28]

This alternative, 'truer', perspective of exile on earth itself (from
heaven) would also characterise humanist Christian and neo-Platonic
allegorisation of Homer's *Odyssey*. In the period of Marot's exile poetry,
for example, we may find it in Guillaume Budé's *De transitu Hellenismi
ad Christianismum* (1535)[29] — just as later we shall find it, as Philip
Ford has noted, in surviving manuscript notes taken down from a lecture
given by the Pléiade's mentor, Jean Dorat:

> The 'patria' is heaven whence in the beginning souls are sent into their bodies;
> felicity is denoted by harsh Ithaca. For we indeed come in the end to a state of
> beatitude, but along a harsh, narrow, and steep path through many labours,
> torments, and miseries. He calls irksome straying [*error*] a voyage [*cursus*]
> or travelling [*peregrinatio*], which men in this world must accomplish in
> order to come in the end to the heavenly 'patria'. [30]

Here, by contrast with Amyot's Plutarch quoted above, the 'harsh' island
in question, Ithaca, now represents the process of homecoming and death
(not exile) — indeed, as the happy last stage of the harsh, yet purposeful,
journey or pilgrimage of life back to the 'patria' of heaven, in a movement of restitution, not just aimless 'straying'. The earthly *viator* that is
man in exile is in fact not just any 'wayfarer'. Rather, like Petrarch's own
putative 'traveller', he is a *peregrinus* — that is, a 'foreigner' temporarily
journeying through alien lands for a purpose. Indeed, for Plutarch too, as
we have seen, 'we are all' (indistinguishably) 'migrants here [in this
world], foreigners and exiles'.[31] *Homo viator* is in fact a *peregrinus*, and

---

[28] Plutarch, 'Du bannissement, ou de l'exil.' *Œuvres morales*; translated by Amyot
(Paris, 1572) ff. 129ᵛ–130ʳ [= *Moralia* 607F].

[29] See Defaux, *Le Curieux*, p. 62; cf. idem, 'Introduction', Marot, ed. cit. p. cxxxiii.

[30] MS Milan, Biblioteca Ambrosiana A 184, ff. 2–21 (f. 5ᵛ). My translation of the
Latin text first quoted and discussed in relation to the anonymous *Moralis
interpretatio errorum Ulyssis Homerici*, Latin translation by C. Gesner
(Hagenau, 1531), by P. J. Ford, 'Conrad Gesner et le fabuleux manteau',
Bibliothèque d'Humanisme et Renaissance, XLVII (1985), 305–20 (p. 317); cf.
Tucker, The *Poet's Odyssey*, p. 50 (nn. 154–5).

[31] *Moralia* 607D: 'πάντας ἀποδείκνυσι μετάναστας ἐνταῦθα καὶ ξένους καὶ
φυγάδας ἡμᾶς ὄντας' (from the passage already cited and closely rendered by
Amyot as 'il nous declare tous en ce monde passagers, estrangers, & bannis').

the spirit of a *peregrinus* is by definition (as Petrarch would concur) 'in exile everywhere until it reaches where it longs to be.'[32]

Petrarch's idea of exile, then, though derived in part from a Stoic tradition privileging individual mental attitude over external circumstance (and common opinion), falls within the orbit not just of a Platonic critique of the material world, but also of the broader tradition of 'man the traveller''s engagement upon what might be termed the 'Pilgrimage of Life'.[33] Within this metaphysical perspective, the attempt to distinguish sharply between mere 'travel' or displacement and 'exile' would seem pointless; the one would be a direct expression, an actual manifestation, of the other. Witness later the wandering existence (under both François Ier and Henri II) of the French Hebrew scholar and mystic, Guillaume Postel (1510–81), for whom 'the concept of journey was both a metaphysical and a physical reality' (M. L. Kuntz).[34] However, the very way in which Petrarch does attempt to make such a distinction not withstanding is highly significant. It suggests rather the dynamic inner freedom of the individual human being within his own interpretative space before the external, set parameters of the human condition. The actual 'journey' is in fact an affective, intellectual, and artistic one of ceaseless self-questioning and self-(re-)definition (in relation to these parameters) in the truly exiliar space of one's own being and of one's writing, which, in all its fluidity, might alone constitute, paradoxically (but ever provisionally), a true *patria*.

Later, in the 1540s and 1550s, it will be this fundamental perception that will stand between the dynamic odyssey of artistic self-definition on the part of a Marot, or of a Joachim Du Bellay,[35] on the one hand, and,

---

[32] cf. also Hugh of St Victor (1096–*c.* 1141): 'The man who finds his homeland sweet is still a tender beginner; he to whom every soil is as his native one is already strong; but he is perfect to whom the entire world is as a foreign land...' (*The Didascalion: A Medieval Guide to the Arts*, translated by Jerome Taylor (New York, Columbia University Press, 1961), p. 101). For this information I am grateful to Dr Andrew Brown of King's College, Cambridge.

[33] cf. G. B. Ladner, '*Homo Viator*: Mediaeval Ideas on Alienation and Order', *Speculum: A Journal of Mediaeval Studies*, XLII, 2 (1967), 233–59, and (more generally) S. C. Chew, *The Pilgrimage of Life* (New Haven and London, Yale University Press, 1962).

[34] M. L. Kuntz, 'Journey as *Restitutio* in the Thought of Guillaume Postel (1510–1581)', *History of European Ideas*, I (1981), 315–29.

[35] With regard to Du Bellay, cf. J. C. Persels, 'Charting Poetic Identity in Exile: Entering Du Bellay's *Regrets*', *Romance Notes*, XXVIII (1988), 195–202 (p. 195): 'Du Bellay as cartographer maps out spatial, temporal, and creative relations of the self to that which is absented from self. Explorations of the

on the other hand, static, formulaic works such as the *Peregrinatio humana* (Paris, Gilles de Gourmont, 1509) written in his youth by that other 'Renaissance warrior and patron' of François Ier's reign, Guillaume Du Bellay (1491–1542).[36]

III. Ortensio Landi (c. 1512–c. 1555?), Ferrara, and the Paradoxes of Exile: The Comings and Goings of a 'Poly(u)topian'

> 'For exile,' he [Cicero] says, 'is not a punishment, but a refuge and harbour from punishment.' [37]

The dynamic process of artistic self-definition, at once existential and literary, is a journey of restlessness and ceaseless motion through the equally itinerant space of exile itself — a space which, along with the connected notions of *patria* and the self, is continuously redefined in the course of that very motion. The movement may be understood to be one of ceaseless imaginative oscillation between, on the one hand, a pre-determined (and thus ultimately discredited) *patria* of origins, putative arrival elsewhere or return, and, on the other hand, an alternative, fluid *patria* of desire itself (whether prospective or retrospective), whose fulfilment must ever be postponed. [38] Hence too, perhaps, Marot's tardy,

---

representations of such relations, understood broadly in the concepts of exile or distance, on literal and figurative planes, will possibly provide a view of the self-definition process for a poet working in and on the Renaissance consciousness of a literary heritage.'

36 A 'Pilgrimage of Human Life' centring largely around the motif (best known from Xenophon's *Memorabilia* II. 1. 21 sqq.) of the Herculean 'choice of the ways' between the path of pleasure and the path of virtue, on which, see E. Panofsky, *Hercules am Scheidewege und andere antike Bildstoffe in der neueren Kunst* (Leipzig and Berlin, B. G. Teubner, 1930). Seven years after publishing G. Du Bellay's *Peregrinatio humana*, the printer Gilles de Gourmont would bring out an edition of More's *Utopia* (after 1 November 1516); see M. A. Screech, *Erasmus: Ecstasy and The Praise of Folly*, (Harmondsworth, Penguin Books, 1988; 2nd edn), p. 2.

37 Guillaume Budé, *In Pandectas* (altera editio; Paris, Badius, 1526), f. 35^r quoting Cicero *Pro Caecina* XXXIV. 100. My translation of the Latin text: 'Nam exilium (inquit) non supplicium: sed perfugium portusque supplicii.' More particularly *supplicium* may denote capital punishment.

38 More broadly, such continual 'postponement' (on the part of the errant, desiring subject) may also be understood to be a significant feature of Renaissance philosophical fictions of the 'quest for knowledge' cast in the form of romance; on which, see the excellent study of N. Kenny, *The Palace of Secrets: Béroalde*

fictional adoption of the Ovidian voice and stance from Venice in 1536, as if re-entry to France and the concomitant poetic fulfilment that should go with it were an ever-receding possibility, displaced in fact by the fictional, exiliar writing itself.

The exiliar space of this inner oscillation between given or chosen points of reference and an indeterminate void inviting exploration, constitutes, then, an enabling, dynamic space for self-definition and writing. It corresponds also to that privileged space of freedom and choice for the exercise of virtue, adumbrated in stoicising works on the topic of exile such as Petrus Alcyonius' Ciceronian dialogue *Medices legatus*. It may further be understood to be the early-modern, literary, and existential counterpart of the earlier Roman juridic notion of a *libertas exilii* — that is, of a positive notion of exile as a vehicle of freedom: a notion, according to which, exile is not so much a punishment as a dignified space of asylum, a refuge for the citizen from punishment (in particular, punishment by death), further affording him the possibility of adopting a new civic community or of eventually returning to the old one (under changed circumstances).[39] For the Renaissance, the distinction had been famously illustrated by the example of Cicero's self-exile (and subsequent triumphal return to Rome) as a consequence of his legally questionable suppression, when consul, of the Catiline conspiracy. It had also been made, just as famously, in Cicero's own writings (*Pro Caecina* XXXIV. 100) — as was readily noted, for example, by Guillaume Budé in his juridic commentary upon the *Digests* of Justinian (quoted in the epigraph immediately above).

Moreover, the *topos* of exile, both juridic and literary, was itself in fact a 'place' of oscillation, a dialogic space, between positive and negative interpretations of exile either as a privileged vehicle for freedom or as a means of punishment, either as a place or state of liberation and joy, or as one of confinement and suffering. (An oscillation which we have already seen suggested by Marot's Ferrara *épître* of late 1535, 'Au Roy

---

de Verville and Renaissance Conceptions of Knowledge* (Oxford, Clarendon Press, 1991), pp. 191–203 ('Searching in Circles'), discussing *L'Histoire veritable, ou Le Voyage des princes fortunez* (Paris, P. Chevalier, 1610) of Béroalde de Verville (b. 1556), in comparison notably with the latter's French interpretation — *Le Tableau des riches inventions...dans le Songe de Poliphile* (Paris, M. Guillemot, 1600) — of Francesco Colonna's *Hypnerotomachia Poliphili* (Venice, Aldus Manutius, 1499), Rabelais's *Quart Livre* and Montaigne's *Essais*.

[39] See G. Crifò, *Ricerche sull''Exilium' nel periodo repubblicano* (Milan, A. Giuffrè, 1961), pp. 50–70.

nouvellement sorty de maladie', with its ironic qualification of 'l'exil nuysant'.) In the 1540s, exile would serve as a topic of dialogic discussion *par excellence* for the itinerant outsider and inveterate exile, the humorous Milanese writer and satirist, Ortensio Landi (or Lando), as a vehicle for his own oscillatory process of textual self-definition. Furthermore, this would now be not only between these opposing views of exile, but also against them and against Italian society. Indeed, the very place of publication of Landi's various Latin and Italian writings was itself subject to oscillation (mainly between Venice and Lyon), just as Landi's notorious Italian vernacular *Paradossi* of 1543 were also to enjoy parallel diffusion in French as well (from 1553 onwards) in the translation of Charles Estienne.[40] In short, they constituted an Italo-French exiliar legacy from the age of François Ier to the new reign of Henri II.

* * *

Landi's life was one marked by 'restless travel and intellectual discontent', earning him, through ironic antiphrasis, the academic name 'Tranquillus' from his induction into Alberto Lollio's Accademia degli Elevati at Ferrara in 1540.[41] In this respect a parallel could be made with that other restless discontent and dialogic Italian author on exile, whom we have already noted: the inveterate misfit and exile in the Republic of Letters, Petrus Alcyonius, of reputedly 'hybrid' civic origins, whose stormy life and character were belied by the storm-calming, nobler connotations of his adoptive humanist name, 'Halcyon'. For Alcyonius the writing of a Ciceronian exile dialogue in the early 1520s, for all its lofty Stoic theorising, had been in fact an ambitiously desperate bid for acceptance into Roman humanist circles.[42] Landi knew Alcyonius' writing, for he alluded to the latter's prowess as a Ciceronian stylist in his first published work — the ironically juxtaposed anti- and pro-Ciceronian dialogues *Cicero relegatus & Cicero revocatus* (Venice, 1534; Lyon 1534: f. 22[v]). Yet, unlike Alcyonius' text on exile, Landi's twin dia-

---

[40] See V.-L. Saulnier, 'Proverbe et paradoxe du XVe au XVIe siècle: Un aspect majeur de l'antithèse: Moyen Age–Renaissance', in *Pensée humaniste et tradition chrétienne aux XVe et XVIe siècles*, edited by H. Bédarida, Publications de la Société d'Études Italiennes — Éditions Contemporaines (Paris, Boivin, 1950), 87–104 (pp. 91, 93–5, 98, 100); as well as Grendler, *Critics of the Italian World*, pp. 20–38, 222–39.

[41] See Grendler, *Critics*, pp. 20, 28.

[42] See Tucker, 'Exile Exiled', pp. 87, 97, 100–103.

logues satirised, and so took their distance from, the whole vexed question of Cicero's merits or demerits as a stylistic model in Latin, in the form of two far-fetched and contradictory fictional debates. [43]

Landi's satire upon the Ciceronian debate is in fact interwoven with a parody of the very topic of Alcyonius' splendidly Ciceronian exile dialogue, whose polarities (positive and negative views of exile) serve the Italian satirist's purpose indifferently (and thus humorously): first, as part of the textual evidence against Cicero (his fictional detractors conjuring up his supposedly contradictory evaluations of exile);[44] secondly, as the means of punishment — exile being regarded as an ironically appropriate 'evil' to inflict upon Cicero (understood now as the man rather than as the text), who had known exile, but also as the means of exoneration, because both Cicero (read, his text) and exile itself are shown eventually, in the supposed 'practice' of Landi's fiction, to be vehicles of virtue and edification. Moreover, if exile is the dominant metaphor of Landi's satire, it also equates, at another level, with the elusive author's intellectual stance of detachment from either side of the Ciceronian and the exiliar debates. Even the two fictional initiators of the whole quarrel — the naïve, itinerant narrator and the very un-'tranquil' U-turner 'Hieremias Landus', both standing as fictional personae for their anonymous author, are themselves discredited as intellectually irresponsible and inconsequential. In particular, Landi, in a gesture of ironic authorial self-reference, has his Roman humanist characters extract in the end an abject apology and recantation from the main trouble-maker, 'Landus' (Landi's

---

[43] For analyses of the contents see Grendler, *Critics*, pp. 148–9.

[44] Cicero calling exile 'a refuge and harbour from punishment [by death]' (quoted by Budé in the epigraph to this section), and yet elsewhere (according to the misrepresentation out of context of Cicero's *Paradoxa Stoicorum* by the same fictional detractors) describing it as a criminal penalty — indeed, in the vein of a similarly contradictory attitude towards 'foreign travel' (*peregrinatio*): 'An non dicebat [Gaudentius] Merula, haec est inconstantia non ferenda…?…[in libro] Pro A. Caecinna exilium non supplicium, sed perfugium suppliciique portum [Cicero] vocat: in Paradoxis scelerum poenam appellat. Quinto Finibus Platonis & Pythagorae peregrinationes magnificis quibusdam verbis videtur vehementer probare: in epistola ad Caelium peregrinationem sordidam vocat, elevat & damnat' (Landi, *Cicero revocatus* (Venice, 1534), f. 5ᵛ). On Cicero's sentiments in the *Paradoxa Stoicorum* (18. 27–32), negating the reality of exile through a negation of the value and status of the *patria* itself, cf. E. Dobholfer, *Exil und Emigration: Zum Erlebnis der Heimatferne in der römischen Literatur*, Impulse der Forschung, 51 (Darmstadt, Wissenschaftliche Buchgesellschaft, 1987), pp. 42, 46, 156, 222, 246–7.

monastic *alter ego*),[45] who lamely claims that if he had initially attacked Cicero it was as a result of the wicked influence of others (f. 24[r]).

The sense of an alternative, itinerant, exiliar, or indeed, utopian, intellectual space occupied by the satirical author-outsider of *Cicero relegatus & Cicero revocatus* is reinforced by the recurring pseudonymous attributions of his subsequent works of social comment or satirical criticism: initially in the Latin *Forcianae quaestiones... Autore Philalethe Polytopiensi Cive* ['the author being Truth-lover citizen of Polytopia' (i.e. 'of Many-place(s)')] (Naples, 1535) and in the *Des. Erasmi...funus* (Basel, 1540), where the pseudonymous 'truth-loving' author is now called 'ex Utopia civis' ('citizen of Nowhere'); and later in the Italian *Commentario delle piu notabili, e mostruose cose d'Italia...da M[esser] Anonymo di Utopia, composto* ([Venice],1548) — the 'Utopian' element here being further corroborated by the fact of Landi's translation and publication in the same year (also in Venice) of Thomas More's *Utopia* (Landi alluding in his title, *La Republica...del governo dell'isola Eutopia*, to the alternative possible etymology of U(Eu)topia 'Well-place').[46]

This 'well-placed' 'polytopian'-'utopian' author of everywhere and nowhere had been actually styled as an 'exile from Italy' as early as 1535 by an unsympathetic contemporary (Joannes Angelus Odonus), when Landi was living and teaching in Lyon (and when Marot was in Ferrara).[47] Moreover, his subsequent formal introduction in 1540 into the humanist circles of Ferrara (under the ironic cognomen of 'Tranquillus') would only have strengthened for Landi this exiliar identity. For if, after the accession in 1534 of duke Ercole II, Ferrara had become notoriously a refuge for Protestant Reformers and their suspected sympathisers thanks to Renée de France, more importantly still, under Ercole II himself, Ferrara became (as we have noted) a major haven for migrant Iberian-Jewish scholars, doctors, and merchants in exile. Its initial Jewish community, dating from the late thirteenth century, had been significantly augmented by the general expulsion of the Jews from Spain in 1492 and by the further Iberian-Jewish exodus provoked by the Jews' subsequent forced 'conversion' in Portugal five years later. Then in 1538, with the new tide of emigration that resulted from the establishment of the Inquisition in Portugal in 1536, Ercole II actively invited the so-called 'New Christian' 'converts' of Jewish blood

---

[45] See Grendler, *Critics*, p. 22.

[46] See Grendler, *Critics*, pp. 28, 33, 222–5.

[47] See Grendler, *Critics*, pp. 25–6.

(who were suspected of religious duplicity and known pejoratively as 'Marranos') to settle in Ferrara's Iberian-Jewish community, and so to enrich the duchy's economic and intellectual life. This also afforded such 'Marranos' the possibility of discreetly and safely re-affirming or re-defining a now diluted or adulterated Jewish cultural and religious identity — or even of re-discovering and forging anew one that had been wellnigh lost.

Landi's presence in this quite literally exiliar space of Ferrara, with its immigrant Jewish community and religiously bi-partisan Franco-Italian court, would have coincided initially with the arrival and stay there (c. 1540–7) of the Portuguese-Jewish poet of exile Diogo Pires (Didacus Pyrrhus Lusitanus, 1517–99) and of his close relative and compatriot, the famous Jewish physician João Rodrigues de Castelo Branco (Amatus Lusitanus, 1511–1568).[48] It is also known that Landi was to enjoy there the acquaintance and even the patronage of other members of the same Portuguese Marrano circle of exiles: notably the powerful Mendes-Nasi family (to whom Diogo Pires and Amatus Lusitanus were probably related), but also their Spanish-born literary protégé, Alonso Núñez de Reinoso (born c. 1492), whose pastoral novel *Clareo y Florisea* (Venice, Giolito de Ferrari, 1552) has been interpreted by some critics as a discreet allegory of the Iberian Jews' exile and the ambiguities of their *converso* status.[49] Several of Landi's works published in Venice in that same year 1552 (mainly by Giolito as well) contain textual material bearing testimony to the mutual high regard of Landi and Núñez and further include dedications by Landi to Núñez's exiled Marrano patrons.[50]

Above all, however, it would be in the text of Landi's hugely success-ful, comically provocative *Paradossi* and their subsequent *Confutatione* (by Landi as well) that this elusive, dialogic author, parodist, and ironist would define and redefine the fluid, exiliar locus of his intellectual free-dom against a mock-display of Stoic paradox (and then counter-

---

[48] See G.H. Tucker, 'Didacus Pyrrhus Lusitanus (1517–1599), Poet of Exile', *Humanistica Lovaniensia: Journal of Neo-Latin Studies*, XLI (1992), 175–98; and idem, 'To Louvain and Antwerp, and Beyond: The Contrasting Itineraries of Diogo Pires (Didacus Pyrrhus Lusitanus, 1517–99) and João Rodrigues de Castelo Branco (Amatus Lusitanus, 1511–68)', in *The Expulsion of the Jews from Spain (1391–1492) and its Repercussions in the Low Countries*, ed. L. Dequeker and W. Verbeke, forthcoming in *Medievalia Lovaniensia*, series I, Studia.

[49] Rose, *Alonso Núñez*.

[50] See Rose, *Alonso Núñez*, pp. 50–2, 54, 56–8; Grendler, *Critics*, pp. 21–2 (n. 5), 226–7.

paradox). The subjects chosen by Landi for his initial *Paradossi* included notably the very topic of exile itself, which afforded him the exquisite possibility of humorously and ironically aping the stoicising paradoxes (or 'counter-teachings' against common opinion) of a Cicero, a Plutarch, or an Alcyonius on exile, but now in the guise of paradoxical encomium (after the fashion of Erasmus' *Praise of Folly*). Through that heavily ironic, serio-comic form Landi manages to discredit the reality of exile in the very act of praising its benefits, so satirising the shameless parasitism and hypocrisy of actual exiles.[51] Thus, once more, the elusive author Landi is seen (in his *Paradossi*) to make use of, yet also to take ironic distance from, the standard negative–positive polarities of the exile debate — just as he is also seen to distance himself satirically (as an intellectual exile himself) from the false posturing of his so-called fellow 'exiles'. Moreover, this intellectual elusiveness is only further compounded by the fact that Landi's often re-printed Italian *Paradossi* (Lyon, 1543, 1550; Venice, 1544, 1545, 1563; Bergamo, 1594 [expurgated]; Vicenza/Padua, 1602), and their antithetical sequel, the *Confutatione del libro de' Paradossi* (Venice, 1544/5, 1563), create between them a playful criss-crossing of bluff and double bluff, of ironically absurd 'counter-teaching' and mock-serious counter-'counter-teaching'.[52]

It is also interesting to note that when Landi in his *Paradossi* comes to offer equivocal praise of exile, he comically echoes, and implicitly subverts, Plutarch's metaphoric description (after Plato) of the exiled soul as a wind-and-wave-proof, island-dwelling 'oyster in a shell', by citing the Cynic Diogenes' opposing use of the mollusc image as a rebuke to those who find his exile shameful and are reluctant or incapable of leaving home: 'donde non sapendosi mai partire paiommi in tutto simili alle conchilie, che stanno del continuo appiccate alle pietruzze' (*Paradossi*, f. 31^{r–v} [1563 edition]). Landi's ironic parallel with the contrasting passage from Plutarch would be made even clearer in Charles Estienne's

---

51 cf. Tucker, 'Exile Exiled', p. 103.

52 For details of the editions of Charles Estienne's later, equally successful, French version of just the former — the *Paradoxes* (Paris, 1553, 1554, 1557, 1561 and 1638; Poitiers, 1553; Lyon, 1554, 1555, 1561, 1576, 1603; Rouen, 1583) — see Grendler, *Critics*, pp. 222–39. Significantly, Estienne even negates pre-emptively the serious heterodox value of Landi's 'counter-teachings' by proclaiming in his translator's preface 'Au Lecteur' (and initially in the very title as well) that they are but a thesaurus of forensic declamation exercises for the young (thus in fact dispensing with the need for a French version of Landi's mock-earnest 'confutatory' antidote to the *Paradossi*); cf. Saulnier, 'Proverbe et paradoxe', p. 95.

French version: 'en ce ressemblant aux oystres, qui iamais ne veulent sortir de leur escaille, & sont continuellement attachees contre les pierres & rochers' (*Paradoxes*, p. 72 [1554 edition]). [53] Moreover, in Landi's subsequent, mock-earnest 'confutation' of this, the author's common-sensical, anti-paradoxical *alter ego* launches his counter-argument on the topic of exile with a reference to an authority actually cited in the same Plutarchan passage: Empedocles' view of exile as a divine punishment ('...ciò che dello sbandito, dice Empedocle. VASSENE lo sbandito vagabondo agitato dalle divine leggi, & da giustissimi decreti persegui-tato...') — Landi further elaborating in juridic vein upon the exile's lot as a form of relegation to a remote island (*Confutatione* f. 11ʳ). Naturally also, Landi's now piously orthodox 'confutation' is equally ready to resurrect the familiar image of a dutiful Ulysses preferring the limits of home and the human condition to the infinite vistas of immortality and exile: 'Rifiutò Vlisse per disio di riveder la patria l'immortalità promessa da Calypso' (*Confutatione* f. 11ᵛ) — without an ounce of the witty scep-ticism about Ulysses (no less traditional) that we saw (with Gérard Defaux) in Marot's evocation of the same commonplace ('Ulixes sage, au moins estimé tel').[54]

The question remains, however, as to whether exile is really and quite simply shown by Landi to be an evil, either obliquely, through the irony of comic, encomiastic 'paradox', or directly, through the seemingly straightforward 'confutation' of a 'paradox' whose message has been taken all too literally. Even in the former case of the *paradosso* proper (entitled 'Meglio è vivere mandato in esiglio, che nella patria longamente dimorare'), it might not be so much the steady value of home and civic responsibility that is ultimately promoted (in implicit opposition to the sham-value of parasitical exile), as a nobler conception of exile itself, whose image has been shamefully tarnished for Landi by its cynical modern Italian exponents. Likewise, in the case of the subsequent *confu-tatione* itself it might also be argued that the indignant authorial persona is seen there to labour the orthodox point of view both absurdly and redun-dantly — as a kind of parody of the putative reactions of less perceptive readers of the ironic *Paradossi*. Furthermore, if the following advisory message of the preface 'Au lecteur' in Charles Estienne's later French version were taken at face value, and applied to the untranslated *Confutatione* as well as to the *Paradossi/Paradoxes*, one might even conclude that the *Confutatione* could also really be understood, similarly,

---

[53] See above, n. 45.
[54] See above, n. 14.

to suggest the opposite of what it purports to show (so in fact promoting the value of exile):

> Tout ainsi, Lecteur, que les choses contraires rapportées l'une a l'autre, donnent meilleure cognoissance de leur force & vertu: Aussi la verité d'un propos se trouue beaucoup plus clere, quand les raisons contraires & opposites luy sont de bien pres approchées.[55]

Even the reassuring editorial advice given here by Charles Estienne as a kind of apologetic guarantee is ambivalent; the comparison ('Tout ainsi...') which apparently forms the premise for the assertion ('Aussi...') that a counter-teaching only reinforces the apparent truth of the teaching it opposes (heterodoxy thus serving in the end as a foil to set off orthodoxy), in fact suggests much more dangerously the equal mutual reinforcement of such opposites, which thus derive their value and force from each other identically and indifferently. Unwittingly, per - haps, Estienne has indicated here Landi's true paradoxical strategy, which is to have it both ways, so suggesting a more modern, more fluid conception of paradoxical truth than mere static 'counter-teaching'[56] — so suggesting in fact an oscillatory intellectual movement akin to that 'movement of rebound from stasis towards a barely conceivable limit and back again', called 'antiperistasis', which Terence Cave has recently noted and analysed in Henri Estienne's characterisation of pyrrhonism (and in the thought of Montaigne, amongst others).[57] Thus in the end for the ambivalent Landi, truly paradoxically: if man is unfortunately confined and limited like an oyster, it is both at home and in exile; the

---

[55] C. Estienne, 'Au lecteur salut', in Landi, *Paradoxes*, translated by C. Estienne [1554] , p. 3.

[56] See Saulnier, 'Proverbe et paradoxe', p. 91.

[57] See T. Cave, 'Imagining Scepticism in the Sixteenth Century', *Journal of the Institute of Romance Studies*, I (1992), 193–205 (pp. 199–205). I am grateful to Professor Cave for having drawn my attention to the parallel with Charles Estienne's above quoted definition of paradox that is afforded by Henri Estienne's application of the term 'antiperistasis' to pyrrhonism in the dedicatory epistle prefacing his Latin translation of Sextus Empiricus' *Hypotyposes* (Paris, 1562). Cave's own further observations on the 'ironies, disclaimers, self-parody, and paradox' of Henri Estienne's epistle, comparable to 'the presentation of works like the *Praise of Folly* and *Utopia*' (art. cit., p. 199), and on 'imagining scepticism' as 'a kind of folly, inviting ironic praise' and comparable to 'imagining' the 'no-place' of 'Utopia' (art. cit., p. 194) likewise suggest strong parallels with the elusive intellectual self-positioning and self-representation of the poly(u)topian Landi.

modern exile's parasitical life abroad is merely a travesty of the life of obligation he is supposed to lead at home; both home and exile can nevertheless be true sources of freedom (and so on).

In this last respect, it may again be significant that where Landi's Italian title for his ironic 'paradox' on exile had comically suggested the parasitical exile's perception (transparently flawed) of the tediousness of dwelling at home ('nella patria longamente dimorare'), Charles Estienne's highly interpretative French version of this title would set up rather a much more abstract (yet still ironically false) opposition between exile and freedom itself ('Pour l'exil, Declamation IX. Qu'il vault mieulx estre banny, qu'en liberté' (*Paradoxes* [1554], pp. 71–7)). In fact, if in the end Landi's paradoxical and ironic texts suggest anything, it is per- haps that to be truly (not parasitically) in exile is to be truly free and so truly at home also — thus contradicting rather the commonly held op- position between exile and home itself.

For no-one could this have been truer than for the chameleon-like author of the *Paradossi* and their *Confutatione*, whose own oscillatory life of writing in the itinerant *patria* of exile itself, between France and Italy, in the close of the age of François Ier — in the cultivation of an alternative, expatriate, cosmopolitan cultural identity — mirrored exist- entially his authorial stance of intellectual freedom and fluid detachment from the fixed polarities of home and exile in an alternative kind of 'para- doxical', dialogic, 'antiperistatic' space (or rather, trajectory). The sug- gestion is of an alternative, ever shifting, vantage point of critical free- dom, peculiar to the itinerant writer and thinker, enabling him continually to re-assess his own culture and to relativise the very perceptions of the world and habits of thought that he has inherited from it.

* * *

As Jean Céard has pointed out about 'Voyages et voyageurs à la Renaissance', the intellectual flexibility and breadth derived from such a nomadic existence and shifting viewpoint would be qualities stressed later by Benedictus Arias Montanus in the admonitory preface to his translation into Latin (published in 1575) of the Hebrew *Itinerary* of the twelfth-century Spanish Jew Benjamin of Tudela.[58] What Céard terms Arias Montanus' 'apologie du voyage' runs thus:

---

[58] J. Céard, 'Voyages et voyageurs à la Renaissance', in *Voyager à la Renaissance: Actes du colloque de Tours 30 juin–13 juillet 1983. Sous la direction de Jean Céard et Jean-Claude Margolin. Centre d'Études Supérieures de la Renaissance,*

On aurait peine à dire à quel point sont différents ceux qui ne se sont formés que par la pratique d'une vie privée et ceux qui ont acquis savoir et instruction en voyageant.[59]

If in the wake of the paradoxical Ortensio Landi this holds true for his itinerant, literary successors in France and Italy — notably, Joachim Du Bellay and Michel de Montaigne — we have seen that this may also apply to Landi's contemporary Clément Marot, to the paradoxes of his existential and literary cultivation of exile in Ferrara and Venice, in the age of François Ier, in the age of Renée de France.

---

edited by J. Céard and J.-C. Margolin (Paris, Éditions Maisonneuve et Larose, 1987), 595–611 (p. 599). Arias Montanus' great medieval travel account, first printed in Constantinople in 1543, also knew, significantly, a second Hebrew edition in 1556 from the printing presses of the Iberian-Jewish exile community of Ferrara, with which Landi had been acquainted. On Arias Montanus and his literary output, see, most recently, B. Pozuelo Calero, 'Poemas introductorios del licenciado Pacecho y de Benito Arias Montanus a la coena Romana de Pedro Vélez de Guevara', *Humanistica Lovaniensia: Journal of Neo-Latin Studies*, XLIII (1994), 369–84.

[59] B. Arias Montanus, ed., 'Praefatio', in *Itinerarium Beniamini Tudelensis* (Antwerp, 1575), pp. 7–12 (p. 8); translated by J. Céard. Montanus' particular stress, however, is on Spanish travellers; see Arias Montanus (ed.), 'Praefatio', p. 8, where the Latin text translated by Céard runs as follows: 'dici vix potest, quanto discrimine referat inter eos, qui solo priuatae vitae vsu, atque eos, itineribus faciendis docti instructique euasere.'

Index

Index

Morel, Jean de 102

Cambridge French Colloquia

The following texts are also available in this series:

Ronsard in Cambridge: Proceedings of the Cambridge Ronsard Colloquium, 10–12 April 1985, edited by Philip Ford and Gillian Jondorf, price £7·50

Montaigne in Cambridge: Proceedings of the Cambridge Montaigne Colloquium, 7–9 April 1988, edited by Philip Ford and Gillian Jondorf, price £7·50

Intellectual Life in Renaissance Lyon: Proceedings of the Cambridge Lyon Colloquium, 14–16 April 1991, edited by Philip Ford and Gillian Jondorf, price £15·00

Syntax and the Literary System: New Approaches to the Interface between Literature and Linguistics, edited by Wendy Ayres-Bennett and Patrick O'Donovan, price £15·00